Shelter provision and employment generation

Shelter provision and employment generation

United Nations Centre for Human Settlements (Habitat)   Nairobi

International Labour Office   Geneva

UNCHS (Habitat)/ILO
Shelter provision and employment generation
Nairobi, United Nations Centre for Human Settlements (Habitat);
Geneva, International Labour Office, 1995

/Housing/, /Employment creation/, /Labour intensive/, /Residential construction/, /Urban area/,
/Developing country/. 02.06.2
ISBN 92-2-108523-6

HS/339/94 E

ILO Cataloguing in Publication Data

Printed in Switzerland   IDE

Preface

This publication is a collaborative effort of two United Nations agencies, the United Nations Centre for Human Settlements (Habitat) and the International Labour Office, joining their policy research and technical cooperation experiences to illustrate the dynamic linkages between shelter and employment. Shelter provision brings together issues that are at the heart of the 1995 World Summit for Social Development: poverty reduction, employment generation and social integration. It is for this reason that this publication is not only a key input of both agencies into the Social Summit, but more importantly will help put into practice the many recommendations in the fields of poverty alleviation and employment generation that are expected to come out of the Summit.

Shelter is much broader than housing. Investments in shelter not only improve and expand the available stock of housing units, but furthermore improve both the working and living environment. The shelter strategies analysed here can help reduce poverty while at the same time generating new employment opportunities for the poorest population groups. However, in addition to expanding the quantity of employment opportunities, shelter provision can also improve the quality of employment, particularly for those working in the urban informal sector, where the home and the workplace are often combined.

This publication follows up on a recommendation made by the fourteenth session of the Commission on Human Settlements calling upon UNCHS (Habitat) and the ILO to intensify cooperation in coordinating their research and operational activities on employment-generation and labour-intensive programmes. It also links UNCHS (Habitat)'s goals for adequate shelter for all with the ILO's goal of promoting full employment and improved working conditions.

The main objective of the Global Strategy for Shelter to the Year 2000 (the GSS) — as adopted by the General Assembly of the United Nations in December 1988 — is to facilitate adequate shelter for all. UNCHS (Habitat) recognizes that despite decades of direct government intervention, the urban poor in most developing countries lack access to the minimum acceptable standards of urban housing and services. Therefore it calls on Governments to leave the actual production of housing units to the private sector and to community efforts, and to provide legal, financial and institutional support to this process instead. This principle of enabling shelter strategies has since been adopted by many Governments. It is intended that this publication help them put these strategies into practice.

The International Labour Organization's body of international labour standards, including Convention No. 122 on policies for full, productive and freely chosen employment, underpins its mandate in the field of employment promotion and poverty alleviation linked to the social protection of workers. The ILO's tripartite constituency, combining workers' and employers' representatives with those of Governments, in effect complements the public-private partnership and principles of community participation which are espoused in the GSS. In addition to the guiding principles of its international labour standards, the publication also draws upon the ILO's experience and operational programmes in employment-intensive investment policies and the urban informal sector.

The main premise of this joint publication is that investments in shelter are productive investments, rather than consumption expenditure. Investments in shelter generate income, and increase the labour productivity of the occupants. This has one major implication for development policies: it implies that shelter provision is not only a goal but, more importantly, it is a tool of development policy. Any investments in housing, infrastructure or services have effects on the national income that go far beyond the direct investment itself. Shelter provision triggers additional investments — and employment — in building-materials production, transport and marketing. This additional employment in turn leads to higher demand for a variety of local goods and services — mainly by semi-skilled and unskilled workers with little propensity for buying imported goods — and thus increased employment in the production of such goods as well.

In addition, low-cost housing and basic infrastructure and services such as drainage, access roads and solid-waste management generate more jobs per unit of investment than high-cost housing and primary infrastructure since they are more suitable to labour-intensive methods. The involvement of small-scale informal construction enterprises — and indeed local communities — in the execution of housing and infrastructure projects should therefore be supported, as they use more unskilled labour, fewer imports and less hard currency than their large-scale, formal-sector counterparts. There is thus an urgent need to facilitate the activities of the informal sector in shelter provision, which includes increasing its productivity and its ability to adhere to acceptable health, safety and labour standards.

The interagency collaboration which this publication represents is just one facet of the rapidly growing partnership between the United Nations Centre for Human Settlements (Habitat) and the International Labour Office. Other elements of this collaboration include the umbrella Urban Poverty Partnership Programme which, through a series of hands-on demonstration activities in collaboration with low-income communities, will help put many of this book's findings into practice. The Urban Poverty Partnership's "Seeing is Believing" approach usefully complements the findings of this publication. Likewise, the ILO within its mandate is supporting UNCHS (Habitat) as it prepares for the second United Nations Conference on Human Settlements (Habitat II) in 1996, with a view to turning cities of despair, faced with growing unemployment and homelessness, into cities of hope.

We gratefully acknowledge the contribution of Mr. A. Graham Tipple in the preparation of the report on which this publication in based.

Dr. Wally N'Dow	**Mrs. Mary Chinery-Hesse**
Assistant-Secretary-General,	Deputy Director-General,
United Nations Centre for Human Settlements (Habitat)	Technical Cooperation and
and	Field Programmes Sector,
Secretary-General, United Nations Conference on	International Labour Office
Human Settlements (Habitat II)	

Contents

List of tables

List of plates

List of acronyms

AHF	African Housing Fund
CBO	Community-based organization
CDC	Community Development Council
DFR	Department of Feeder Roads (Ghana)
GDP	Gross domestic product
GFCF	Gross fixed capital formation
GNP	Gross national product
GSS	Global Strategy for Shelter to the Year 2000
HBE	Home-based enterprise
ILO	International Labour Organization
IYSH	International Year of Shelter for the Homeless
KMA	Kumasi Metropolitan Authority (Ghana)
NGO	Non-governmental organization
NHDA	National Housing Development Authority (Sri Lanka)
PPP	Purchasing power parities
RAJUK	The Capital Development Authority, *Rajdhani Unnuyan Kartripakkha* (Bangladesh)
SSE	Small-scale enterprise
UNCDF	United Nations Capital Development Fund
UNCED	United Nations Conference on Environment and Development
UNCHS (Habitat)	United Nations Centre for Human Settlements (Habitat)
UNDP	United Nations Development Programme
UNIDO	United Nations Industrial Development Organization
UNV	United Nations Volunteers
WHO	World Health Organization

Executive summary

I. Introduction

1. The population of the world is becoming increasingly urban. Current population growth rates pose particular problems for the shelter-delivery system in the cities of developing countries. Annual investment in housing tends to constitute between 2 and 8 per cent of GDP and from 10 to 30 per cent of GFCF. Trends in the global economy, exacerbated by policies adopted in response to them, have resulted in a significant decline in shelter investments. The fraction of GNP invested in housing has actually been reduced during the last decade.

2. Housing consumption is low not because of lack of an effective demand but because of failures in the system of supply. In response to this, provider-based solutions have been replaced in many countries, and in the policies supported by international agencies, by support-based approaches. Beginning with quite substantial intervention in the physical processes, mainly through large projects, these approaches have been giving way to enabling strategies in which small-scale enterprises (SSEs) and individual householders play a leading role.

3. The informal sector provides more than half the income-earning opportunities in many third-world cities. Its role in poverty alleviation and its considerable contribution to national incomes are both widely recognized. The characteristics of informal-sector enterprises that are of most relevance to this publication are the small scale of their operations, their family ownership, and their labour-intensive and adapted technology. Such enterprises can often offer the best value for money. However, at its worst, employment in the informal sector can be exploitative with poor contractual relationships, unhealthy working conditions and low payment.

4. The informal sector provides a very large share of the new housing stock in developing countries, both in terms of numbers and value. This is a response to the inability of the formal market to satisfy effective demand. The deeply hostile attitude of many government officials to the informal sector must change. That is a prerequisite for tackling the problems in the informal sector and for implementing the enabling process which is the subject of this publication and which is the context of much recent UNCHS (Habitat) and ILO activity.

5. Widespread unemployment and underemployment, and some 1,400 million people in poverty provide an opportunity for employment generation through shelter provision.

6. Both the Global Strategy for Shelter to the Year 2000 (GSS) and Agenda 21 of UNCED encourage governments to adopt housing policies that are realistic, comprehensive in their application, and gradual and flexible enough to respond to change. They acknowledge and seek to utilize the potential for economic development contained in the housing process and recommend that governments take a positive attitude towards the informal sector, enabling and

encouraging it instead of ignoring or harassing it. The GSS seeks to shift the emphasis of policy away from the provision of a few fine houses, towards encouraging all actors involved in the housing process to make supply as efficient as possible.

7.   Agenda 21 calls for improved human settlements management and a sustainable construction industry, emphasising the connection between employment opportunities to relieve poverty and housing provision to improve living conditions. Both documents support the philosophy that, if policies affecting the shelter sector are favourable, the sector contributes to economic development, and the gains to economic development are translated into sectoral improvements. If, however, the policies work against general economic development, the links will fail and both sectoral and overall objectives will suffer.

II.   Human settlements development and employment generation

8.   While they are difficult to prove, there are impressionistic links between improvements in housing and increased productivity, health, and other measures of well-being.   Income multipliers from construction activity are likely to be approximately double the value of the housing supplied. It is evident that these multipliers are particularly high for lower-cost housing and for housing constructed in depressed economies.

9.   Construction (including infrastructure) accounts for between 40 and 70 per cent of GFCF in developing countries.   About half of the demand for construction can conservatively be estimated as directly shelter-related.   The productivity of shelter arises in part from its being investment in an asset which yields a flow of services over time.

10.   Housing markets in developing countries tend to function poorly. This is because of bottlenecks in supply markets in materials, land, labour, and finance and poor regulatory frameworks, usually unadapted to local conditions.   A well-functioning housing-supply system, unaffected by distortions such as subsidies and price or import controls, has positive macro-economic impacts and would be consistent with current structural adjustment imperatives.   Construction activities tend to redistribute income to lower-paid workers as they are predominant in the construction industry.   Housing construction tends to be a low user of imported goods, therefore its balance of payments' ramifications are not seriously negative.

11.   It is plain that the poor have been left out of many housing efforts in the past.   Even support-based policies have been more expensive than the working poor (and even a majority among the lower income group) can afford.   New policies must respond to the gross poverty of many residents and provide for rental accommodation as well as owner-occupation.   A primary concern in housing demand should be to maximize income-earning opportunities and to minimize transport costs.

12. In order to differentiate between works which benefit directly and exclusively a local community and those of broader public interest, a distinction can be made between "major" and "minor" works. This publication argues that while many major works are capable of local participation including the use of community contracts, such local participation should not lead to substandard remuneration nor employment conditions. At the same time while minor works usually involve some form of community contribution, this should come about as a result of negotiations with local authorities; and unpaid labour should not be used systematically.

13. The choices of technology made in the past have seen labour-intensity or the need for maintenance as problems to be avoided, using equipment-based solutions. However, examples of successful use of labour-intensive technologies and labour recruited within local communities have shown that public authorities' traditional service tasks can be contracted out to smaller and labour-based contractors. This would be increasingly effective if the advantages which large-scale contractors have been given through tax concessions, import privileges, etc., are withdrawn. On their part, authorities must become reliable in carrying out their (reduced) tasks and retrain personnel so that they can enable services to be provided rather than to provide them directly.

III.   Employment potential in the process of housing provision

14. High-cost housing construction generates fewer jobs per unit of expenditure than low-cost housing, and formal-sector construction methods are less labour-intensive than informal. For each unit of expenditure in informal-sector housing, a fifth more jobs can be created than in those produced formally. At the same time, as many as six times as many (lower standard) dwellings can be built for the same investment. There is, therefore, a strong argument in favour of involving small-scale informal construction enterprises in the execution of housing projects as they use more unskilled labour, fewer imports and less hard currency than their large-scale, formal-sector counterparts. Despite these advantages and its considerable output, the informal sector has been neglected or harassed in favour of an inefficient formal sector.

15. The construction of housing is particularly effective in providing work to low-income workers. However, there is a need for an adequate and continuous supply of skilled workers, whose availability can be very influential on the efficiency of housing supply.

16. Despite the intention in sites-and-services schemes that occupants should use mainly their own labour in constructing housing, most have used at least a proportion of paid labour through local SSEs and individual artisans. The renovation of housing in upgrading programmes is ideally suited to small-scale contractors using minimal equipment.

17. In the past, in sites-and-services and upgrading schemes, attention has been paid to the householder's interface with the house which he or she was expected to build or renovate by self-help. As many chose to use contractors anyway, and as the latter can be more efficient, it is proposed that attention should be switched to two complementary interfaces: between the householder and the contractor (with model contracts, advice on payment, and the settlement of disputes), and between the contractor and the house (with access to materials, credit against staged payments, insurance, site management etc.). Building regulations should be altered to allow more affordable technologies.

18. Traditional technologies often require maintenance on an annual basis but require only locally available materials and commonly held skills. More industrialized technologies present problems when maintenance is required. However, many maintenance tasks are ideally suited to SSEs.

IV. Employment generation in infrastructure and services delivery, maintenance and improvement

19. As authorities are increasingly unable to provide services to all the people, the need to involve communities not only in crisis management but also in planning and provision of services is becoming widely recognized. Community involvement in servicing can provide positive inputs to social cohesion in addition to the care which is taken of infrastructure for which the community is responsible.

20. The labour-based approach to road building is well tested through ILO initiatives. Two thousand work-days can be created in building one kilometre of five-metre-wide earth road. While some road-building tasks on major roads require heavy equipment, work on minor, gravel-enforced roads can be carried out with an appropriate mix of trained labourers and light equipment. In addition, wherever simple methods can be used, they can have significant poverty alleviation effects, particularly in ensuring that money is disbursed locally and to the poorest workers. Even heavily trafficked roads have been successfully built in this way in Bangladesh. The training of supervisory staff is seen to be axiomatic to successful labour-intensive public works construction programmes.

21. There are many tasks in laying water pipes, drains and sewers which can be done by labour-based methods but which are often done with heavy equipment. Community-based water-supply schemes are relatively common, particularly in rural areas. In urban areas, privatization or community control of water delivery, excreta removal, and garbage disposal are becoming commonplace.

22. By handing over a service at a point distant from individual houses, responsibility for quite extensive networks and the revenue accruing from the services they offer can be handed over to a community or an entrepreneur. Within such a context, it is quite feasible for a servicing agency to hand over servicing responsibilities at any chosen threshold.

23. City authorities spend 30 to 50 per cent of their budgets on solid-waste management but few manage to keep up with the demand. There are considerable opportunities for labour-intensive composting and recycling operations which would provide employment and profit for many people while making good uses of existing resources and clearing the streets of garbage. The existing informal-sector rag-picking and scavenging operations require improvement to protect the operators and provide markets for recyclable materials.

24. While it may be assumed that the construction of transport infrastructure is necessarily an equipment-intensive operation, the building of railways has historically been done by labour-based methods. In addition, public transport based on smaller buses, taxis and rickshaws has traditionally been cheaper, arguably more efficient, and a provider of more employment per trip than large municipal transport operations.

V. Appraisal of employment-generation potential and constraints through backward linkages

25. Demand created in other sectors (for materials, equipment, and their carriage) by the construction of housing is approximately half the value of the housing, and greater in the human settlements sector than in most others. These backward linkages are inversely related to the cost of the housing and are greater for labour-intensive building operations than for those using capital equipment. In addition, self-help housing and upgrading activities are particularly effective for backward linkage generation.

26. This century has seen a move towards high-technology, low labour-intensity building-materials production. Small-scale, relatively labour-intensive building-materials technologies are generally associated with larger multiplier effects than large-scale, capital-intensive technologies because they tend to use locally manufactured machinery and local fuel, and are marketed and transported by SSEs. Most currently-used imported materials can be replaced by a local equivalent, which in turn can be produced in small-scale, labour-based plants. The difference in employment generation between large plants and small, and between equipment-based and labour-based can be very great (twenty-fold in the case of brickmaking). Despite several decades of research into adapting and improving upon local technologies, earth-based and labour-intensive technologies are often seen to be the poor relation of higher-technology, imported solutions. The use of labour-intensive technologies in ILO pilot and demonstration projects (particularly the Million Houses Programme in Sri Lanka) has produced encouraging results.

VI. The potential of various actors

27. The promotion of urban development should be a holistic process, involving all actors in the activities in which they are most effective and each sector in an integrated way.

28. The role of individuals varies from taking paid work generated by major works in local neighbourhoods, singly or through community groups, to acting as

developers, or as development consultants, creating partnerships between local authorities and community groups. Training and empowering are necessary for the successful fulfilment of these roles.

29. Communities have shown their ability to take on contracts for local infrastructure work. It is recommended that community-based organizations (CBOs) are formed to represent people, to implement projects, to act as legal entities representing their communities, to raise and disburse money on behalf of the neighbourhoods, and negotiate for services, contracts etc. with public authorities. Whilst in the past community initiatives in servicing relied on unpaid labour, this is not ideal. Under the distinction between major and minor works, all but the most local tasks should involve paid labour.

30. Local-government and other public-sector bodies are urged to adopt a more supportive role towards the informal sector, SSEs, and labour-based technologies either in their own direct works or when contracting to the private sector. If shelter and infrastructure are to keep up with demand, partnerships between public authorities and the private sector must become part of local-government culture.

31. Small-scale contractors are central to the implementation of policies to increase employment potential in the shelter sector. If they are to be assisted by the public sector to take a more central role, they must be more cooperative with regulating bodies in order to benefit from the change of attitude which public authorities are urged to make by this publication. Large-scale contractors are encouraged to make better use of labour-based technologies; and thus to behave more like small-scale contractors in technology choices.

VII. Forward linkages: Shelter as a workplace

32. Forward linkages, where housing provides an intermediate input to some other economic activity, are difficult to calculate but evidently quite significant, particularly concerning economic activities carried out within dwellings and their immediate surroundings. The use of home as a workplace is relatively common in developing countries.

33. Informal-sector activities carried out in the home range from retailing of food to giving injections, from manufacturing cigarettes to keeping livestock. The activities involve a wide range of skills and resources, and may use small or considerable parts of the living quarters, despite the small space available for all activities. The ability to use space for both living and working is a major attraction of home-based economic activities.

34. The great majority of active home-based enterprises are retail outlets. The type of activity differs between types of neighbourhood: petty retailing and cooked food preparation tend to be common in very poor neighbourhoods; areas with good communications tend to have light manufacturing and a variety of

services (especially medical and dental). The assumption that SSEs based in houses are likely to expand into the formal industries of tomorrow, however, is rather debatable.

35. Although "clever money" has tended to give rental accommodation a wide berth in recent years, low-income households show a continuing propensity to make space for renting alongside their own accommodation needs. Although it returns less money per unit of space than other enterprises, it is popular as it involves little commitment of time. This small-scale rentier activity can be crucial to housing supply on the supply side, yet, many governments are still openly hostile to private landlords and many countries have stringent rent control.

36. Efforts to improve housing conditions are likely to disrupt income-generating activities if they involve relocation, even though they may recover after several years. Improvements in services in existing areas have positive and negative benefits which are difficult to quantify and vary between uses and areas. More empirical work would allow assessments to be made with greater certainty.

VIII. A review of the consolidated experience with employment generation and poverty alleviation in poor countries

37. Significant contributions have been made recently to the equipping of communities to carry out urban works and services in partnership with the public sector and to negotiate successfully with service agencies. The ILO has been involved in promoting self-employment as well as SSEs and, therefore, SSEs and the informal sector for several years. Its interventions have been targeted at eliminating inefficiencies in the labour market and at improving the efficiency of the enterprises. In addition, there has been a complementary focus on governments' attitudes towards, and abilities to deal with, informal-sector enterprises. In collaboration with UNDP, the World Bank, and national governments, the ILO has proved the validity of labour-intensive public works, such as rural road building and have assisted governments in integrating employment-intensive approaches into infrastructure investment strategies.

38. The UNCHS (Habitat)/DANIDA Training Programme for Community Participation has made great progress with the communities and public sector personnel in Bolivia, Sri Lanka and Zambia. In Sri Lanka, the community contracts method of service provision has proved itself both in the quality of services provided and in its community development potential. It is worth testing in many other locations.

39. The UNDP/ILO Employment Generation in Urban Works Programme has successfully begun local tests on many of the strategies for increasing labour-based interventions contained in this publication. It has found that labour-based public works can compete with equipment-based approaches in cost and quality (though time taken may be longer), and that they are self-selecting in their labour force towards the poor.

40. The UNCHS (Habitat)/World Bank/UNDP Urban Management Programme has recognized the need for a multi-sectoral approach to urban development and for encouraging sustainability in improved urban conditions, including the ability to pay for services provided. Urban environment and poverty alleviation are two of the five strands of the programme.

41. The UNCHS (Habitat)/ILO/UNV/UNDP Programme on Improvement of Living Conditions and Expanding Employment Opportunities in Urban Low-income Communities (now known as Urban Poverty Partnership) focuses on urban poverty alleviation in three related ways. It looks at the issues from the perspective of the poor, it encourages the identification and eradication of institutional barriers to poverty alleviation, and it spotlights governments' roles in facilitating and enabling the private sector and community groups. The programme elements are intended to support community initiatives in environmental improvements and in urban services provision and to support small- and medium-scale enterprises involved in labour-based urban works and services.

42. UNDP has proposed a series of micro-capital grants to SSEs to increase their viability and effectiveness. Alongside this, the UNV programme is able to place specialists to assist in channelling these grants and ensuring that they are efficiently used. Other bodies, especially NGOs, have also had successful experiences with community-based and labour-intensive urban works and encouraging SSEs in low income neighbourhoods.

IX. Scope for support to employment generation in shelter, infrastructure and services provision

43. There is considerable scope for local authorities to use labour-intensive methods in their development and maintenance functions. However, there is a need for a change of political culture, away from a hierarchical rule from above towards democratization and empowerment of people and their communities. This will require new skills, moving away from technical functions to managerial and enabling functions.

44. While, in the recent past, housing policies have concentrated on helping households to develop their own housing, there are efficiency gains to be made by addressing the relationship between contractors and the housing process. Thus, instead of addressing the interface between the householder and the house, attention should be focused on the contractor/house and the householder/contractor interfaces. The contractor/house interface should be lubricated by ensuring that the inputs to housing supply are in place and available to small-scale contractors. The householder/contractor interface requires informing potential householders about contracting and empowering them to demand good value for money.

45. Clearly, while the informal sector is disadvantaged, the cheapest housing available is less efficiently provided than it need be. Legal, institutional and financial measures are required to integrate the informal sector into the

mainstream of the economy without removing its competitiveness. Land supply and the regulations governing buildings are important fields for government action to ease the supply of housing by the informal sector. Some forms of training, finance, servicing and involvement in government contracts should be offered to SSEs.

46. Legislation affecting SSEs should aim to maximize their efficiency while progressively addressing labour standards issues to prevent exploitation and improve health and safety. Home-based enterprises should be recognized as important contributors to the poorest households' economies and to the country as a whole. The best policy for current home-based enterprises is tolerance and non-intervention while allowing them to be eligible for small business loans, training assistance etc. It is proposed, however, that loans for small businesses should be permitted for the extension of the home for business use.

47. Where public-sector agencies carry out development work, they should be encouraged to use, and engage contractors who use, labour-intensive methods. International donors should take a lead here, considering employment and poverty alleviation through the implementation phase as a serious component in measuring project success. However, great care must be taken not to exploit low-cost labour and to include training for any suitable members of the workforce as a project component.

48. Assistance targeted at SSEs and implementation of labour-based infrastructure works are likely to benefit the poor as they will largely involve the poorest workers. Assistance should also be given to the construction of rental housing through the private sector, especially as rental rooms adjoining owner-occupier houses.

49. Improvement of infrastructure through handing the service over to community groups or private operators at the neighbourhood level provides potential not only for better services than can be provided by over-stretched local authorities but also for employment and enterprise. The current knowledge about appropriate building materials and technologies for low-cost housing and services requires dissemination to encourage their use and increase their social acceptability.

50. The capacity of the poor to improve their community organizations can be enhanced through training in technical matters and in organization.

X.   Proposals for assisting employment generation in shelter and infrastructure provision

51. Proposals for specific project measures financed and technically assisted by the international donor community are as follows:

- attention should be given to improving the housing supply by ensuring that the supply markets are operating efficiently and assisting small-scale contractors in increasing their efficiency through training, especially in labour-intensive techniques;

- pilot projects aimed at determining costs, timing and phasing, skills and equipment requirements, and likely pitfalls in implementing large programmes are the recommended way forward for funding agencies;
- however, pilot projects should then feed into large-scale investment policies and programmes and these links needs to be planned from the start;
- employment generation should be included as a main criterion in programme design;
- mixed uses in the form of home-based enterprises should be promoted initially in pilot projects to allow some assessment of their costs and benefits in a newly-built environment.

52. Future research should concentrate on:

- analysis of costs and benefits of labour-based approaches to urban works and services;
- the implications of home-based economic activities on residential environments and income generation;
- the implications of community control of local services, especially through the application of the "ultimate level" concept (i.e. the place at which a service is metered and responsibility is handed over to a private individual or some other legal entity — see chapter IV);
- a healthy housing supply system;
- the effectiveness of alternative dissemination paths for research on building materials and technologies;
- alternative financial institutions for the working poor.

53. Clearly, the public sector, NGOs and international donors have an important role as enablers and encouragers in the process of maximising employment opportunities in the provision of housing and infrastructure in the coming decades. The future priorities of local and national Governments — and of international development cooperation — must be to actively support and advocate poverty reduction strategies based on labour-intensive shelter delivery and using local resources, linking the goals of shelter for all and employment for all as a common strategy for poverty reduction.

I.   Introduction

Work banishes those three great evils, boredom, vice and poverty

Voltaire, *Candide*

The world's urban population has increased from 737 million (29.2 per cent of the total) in 1950 to 2,603 million (45.2 per cent of the total) in 1995. By the year 2005 — and for the first time in the history of humanity — more than half of the world's population, some 3,350 million people, will be living in urban areas. The majority of this growth will occur in developing countries (some 660 million, compared with 87 million in industrialized countries) (United Nations, 1993). The expected population growth of urban areas during the next decade alone will thus be higher than the total urban population in 1950. This growth represents an unprecedented demand for housing in urban areas. More than 100 million new housing units are required in the world's urban areas during the next decade to cater for population growth alone.[1]

Moreover, urban population growth is expected to continue. By the year 2025, 61.2 per cent (some 5,187 million) of the world's population will live in cities and towns (compared with 45.2 per cent in 1995). The challenge to house such numbers of people is only increased by their location. As much as 86 per cent of the global population growth during the next three decades will occur in the urban areas of developing countries.[2] Within the next 30 years it is expected that the population of urban areas in developing countries will increase from about 1,680 million in 1995 to a staggering 4,010 million in 2025 (United Nations, 1993).

Global economic trends during the past two decades[3] have had a particularly strong impact on the shelter sector. Worldwide, there was a reduction in the longstanding historical level of housing investments. Between the mid-1970s and the early 1980s the fraction of GNP invested in housing fell by 11–24 per cent.

In many countries, it has been the policies adopted in response to macro-economic trends rather than the trends themselves that have resulted in significant declines in shelter investment and have contributed to a worsening of housing and

---

1.   If all currently inadequate housing units in urban areas (more than 100 million) were to be replaced during the next decade and a conservative annual depreciation of the housing stock is taken into the account (2 per cent per year), the housing requirement in urban areas during the next decade would be at least 30 million new units per year.

2.   A further 9 per cent of the growth will occur in the urban areas of the industrialized countries. During the same period, the rural population of developing countries is expected to increase with 223 million "only", from 2,835 million to 3,059 million.

3.   Including the high inflation rates of the 1970s, high and volatile interest rates and declining terms of trade, increasing indebtedness and stagnating incomes in many developing countries.

infrastructure conditions. Among these policies have been the maintenance of overvalued exchange rates, imposition of import restrictions and tariffs on shelter-sector inputs, public investment cutbacks and reallocations, and policies of directed credit toward tradable goods and supposedly "productive" industries. The impact of these policies reaches far beyond the impact on the shelter sector *per se*. Not only is the direct and indirect value of output of the sector lost, but distortions which are included in the rest of the economy impose a high economic cost on the sector. This can be manifested as productivity losses, reduced saving and capital formation, disruptions in labour markets, and increased inflationary pressures (UNCHS, 1990).

Housing is a major sector in any economy with the value of the housing stock normally exceeding GDP (*Urban Edge*, 1988a). In terms of annual flows, investment in housing typically comprises from 2 to 8 per cent of GDP and from 10 to 30 per cent of GFCF (Buckley and Mayo, 1988; *Urban Edge*, 1988a). Each of these ratios has historically risen with economic development. In particular, as economic development proceeds, the fraction of household income that must be devoted to food expenditures drops sharply, and one of the first areas in which households tend to increase their spending is on housing and related services. Each year, developing countries invest US$100-150 billion in housing and urban infrastructure. Since total external assistance in terms of loans and grants is only about US$4 billion, the local input remains by far the largest component (World Bank and others, 1991).

It is estimated that at least 300 million urban residents live in absolute poverty (UNDP, 1994), 600 million live in life- and health-threatening houses and neighbourhoods (WHO, 1992), and the urban poor form a substantial and growing share of those 800 million people in the developing world who suffer from chronic hunger. Several authors, however, have estimated far greater numbers living in poverty (e.g. Ravallion and others, 1991 — see section I.F below).

In the Global Report on Human Settlements (UNCHS, 1987), it was estimated that half the urban population of developing countries — some 600 million people — lived in very poor housing. The concept of "adequate shelter" was adopted by UNCHS (Habitat) in the programme for the International Year of Shelter for the Homeless (IYSH) as a means of measuring housing performance. Adequate shelter means more than a roof over one's head: it means adequate privacy, space, security, lighting and ventilation, basic infrastructure and location with regard to work and basic facilities — all at a reasonable cost (UNCHS, 1990).

Inadequate housing can be manifested in many forms which may appear individually or in combination, and may be regarded locally as a problem or may not be. Crowding, or inadequacy of space either in terms of area or in the number of separate rooms, is a common sign of inadequate housing. In China about 5.7 million urban inhabitants (5.8 per cent of the total urban population) occupy less than 2 m² floor area per capita (Yingfan, 1987). It has been estimated that 17 per cent of the world's housing stock is made up of one-roomed shelters, but this hides those larger units which are occupied by many households, each with one room, as is common in West Africa (Peil and Sada, 1984) and the *vecindades* and other inner-city tenements of Latin America. In Bombay, about 67 per cent of the households live in single-room housing units, with an average density of 4.9 persons per room (UNCHS, 1994b — citing NBO, 1992).

The extreme form of space inadequacy is the complete absence of a shelter. In India, where the gross shortage of housing is predicted to be 41 million by 2001 (Sundaram, 1990),[4] many households live on the pavements of the large cities. However, as Jagannathan and Halder (1987) report, this is often a deliberate rational decision, by which the expenditure on housing is reduced to zero. In the case of workers on the margins of economic life[5] (in India at least 10 per cent of the population), this lack of demand for shelter is related to issues of affordability and access to income earning opportunities.

As frequent as inadequacy of space, and probably more dangerous, is the lack of services available to large numbers of people in urban housing. The lack of a clean water supply or a means of safe disposal of human, domestic, clinical, and industrial waste contributes to morbidity and mortality on a massive scale.

In a recent report on housing needs in developing countries, Struyk (1990) estimated that 45 million additional dwellings are needed each year but are, unfortunately, not forthcoming in sufficient quantities. The housing shortage besetting so many countries is not a result of lack of effective demand. Rather, consumption is low because price is high (*vis-à-vis* wages if not world prices) due to failures in the system of supply (World Bank, 1980). These are often direct results of macro-economic policies and governments' non-housing budgets claiming an ever-increasing share of a reducing pool of finance during a period of world-wide economic austerity (Buckley and Mayo, 1988; *Urban Edge*, 1988a).

It is undoubtedly true that, in general, the poor are inadequately housed, and that the poorer a country is, the less adequate are the housing conditions, at least for the low-income groups. However, there are so many variables (traditional building methods, legality of low-cost technologies in urban areas, availability of land, proportion of income spent just on food etc.) that such a generalization can only be the most crude of guides. Contrasting cases exemplify the shortcomings of the generalization.

In many countries, it is virtually impossible to predict who will occupy particular types of housing. In Lagos, Marris (1962) has shown that the physical outlook of city neighbourhoods does not necessarily reflect the abundance or

---

4. This figure is rather uncertain. Using normative criteria for the housing shortage, the Birla Institute of Scientific Research estimated the housing shortage to be 126.4 million in 1981. Census data from 1981 indicated a shortage of less than half a million units (see UNCHS, 1994b).

5. Marginal occupations include domestic servants, beggars and ragpickers.

shortage of money, wealth or capital. The wealthy are just as likely to live alongside their poor kinfolk and neighbours as they are to move away to suburbs.

The presence in squatter areas of a larger upper-income group than expected (Keare and Parris, 1982) suggests that squatter housing is not necessarily synonymous with low income, and that inadequate shelter may not be solely due to constraints imposed by absolute poverty. In fact, squatter developments themselves can be said to be a manifestation of the existence of at least some capital, wealth (Okpala, 1989) and opportunities for income mobilization.

It has been recognized for several years that urban areas contribute significantly to national development (Harris, 1989, for example). In that context, it is prudent to exert great efforts to improve the productivity of all sectors of the urban economy. Such problems as infrastructure deficiencies, ineffective or overbearing regulatory systems, and inadequate financial services for urban development, all limit the efficiency of development and productivity of enterprises of all sizes. The role of government as enabler is particularly important in the process of increasing the productivity of the range of urban enterprises and to ensure their contribution to macro-economic performance.

A. Provider-based and support-based strategies

Public expenditures in the shelter sector often represent a significant share of total public investment. Therefore, shelter is an important component of overall economic policy. Experiences during the 1970s and 1980s have convinced international agencies that direct action by government (or other large institution, e.g., a large employer) to build houses (also known as a provider-based solution) is not the answer to the housing supply issues of most countries, especially for low-income households (see Rodell and Skinner, 1983, for example).

Though the houses constructed represented a considerable financial and organizational effort, they have been very limited in numbers compared with urban populations. In addition, they tend to be of high quality and relatively expensive. In the 1980s, only a tiny percentage of urban residents could afford typical State-built houses without subsidy. Shortages lead to rationing which tends to favour the politically powerful, civil servants, and those with middle incomes who can afford the rents. Thus, there is inequity, inefficiency in reaching target populations, and redistribution of assets, for which all have paid, towards the relatively well-off.

Provider-based solutions have been overtaken by events[6] to such an extent that they have been recognized to be inefficient and beyond the capacity of governments or local authorities (UNCHS, 1989b; 1991a). In response, governments have been abandoning provider-based solutions and turning instead to

---

6. Including increasing rates of urban growth, increasing house cost to income ratios, and fiscal austerity leading to subsidy withdrawal.

the enabling or support-based approach, which has also been firmly established at the heart of United Nations policy on housing, notably in the Global Strategy for Shelter to the Year 2000 (GSS).

In their infancy, support-based approaches involved a change from building a complete house, with all its infrastructure provided, to building less and less, and expecting the future residents to add the remaining components. At the most provider-based end of the support projects, the authorities would provide an outer shell on a serviced plot or a core house which would be extendable. As the expense of such provision surpassed the ability of governments and target groups to pay, the support structures were reduced to only a "wet-core" (toilet, bathroom and kitchen) or to a serviced plot in the classic sites-and-services schemes (Rodell, 1983). Projects to support self-help activity in housing, though much publicized, have produced relatively little of the urban housing stock in developing countries — probably between 5 and 10 per cent (UNCHS, 1989b). For those who benefited, such schemes have involved significant improvements in housing conditions, but for almost all of the rest, housing has been built and financed with no help from the public sector, sometimes in the teeth of official harassment, in the informal sector.

In the past, there has been much debate about the support-based approach involved in the promotion of self-help housing through sites-and-services schemes, and other projects which relied on (or exploited, depending on political outlook) the efforts of low-income potential occupants. On one side, Turner and his followers focused on the ability of people to shape their own environment, achieve ownership at low price, and produce houses for the poor at a rate and variety which was impossible in centrally-controlled systems (Turner and Fichter, 1972; Turner, 1976). On the other side, the Marxist school led by Burgess criticized self-help as merely a ploy to relieve governments and capitalists of their responsibility to provide social goods to their people (Burgess, 1982; 1985).

More recently, it has been realised that relatively small projects,[7] with unproved replicability, inaccurate targeting, and poor cost-recovery performance were not making a significant impact on the housing supply for poor households (UNCHS, 1991a). In the 1980s, fiscal austerity, bankrupt State agencies, and the need to adjust the structure of economies in developing countries, provided both the necessity of and the context for a reappraisal of housing policies within macro-economic structures (Woodfield, 1989, and see chapter II).

At the same time, constraints to ownership have been increasing in most developing cities, largely due to bottlenecks in the supply systems. For example, access to land for the poor is becoming more difficult as land prices are rising in real terms in many Latin American (Gilbert, 1983) and other cities. Land invasions

---

7. Small in the context of need: a project of even 10,000 plots may seem large but is tiny in comparison with the total number of households needing or demanding improved housing.

by squatters, which were important in Latin America but have never been so in much of sub-Saharan Africa (Okpala, 1989), have become less widespread because of land scarcity within city limits, and illegal purchases of land are becoming more commonplace (Doebele, 1977; Payne, 1989). The result is that the proportion of households which can afford to become homeowners diminishes (Hansen and Williams, 1987; UNCHS, 1989c).[8]

This phase of support-based provision saw government as a major actor in the supply of land, services, some materials, some easy-term finance, and some technical assistance, but only in specific locations; everywhere else the supply process was ignored except for periodic harassment.[9] This project-oriented phase isolated most supply[10] into the informal sector. Individuals have either had the influence and cunning to survive unaided or have banded together, exercising community strengths to maintain their position against an often hostile formal sector.

B.   The move to enabling strategies

Recently, support-based strategies have moved to their least visible but most challenging, and potentially most influential mode to date; the enabling strategy. Enabling strategies seek to improve the functioning of markets which supply the five major components in the housing process; land, finance, the skills of the labour force, infrastructure, and building materials; and to provide an appropriate regulatory framework (Malpezzi, 1990; World Bank, 1993). While governments that support enabling strategies are not directly building houses, they cannot be conceived of as having an easier role. The enabling role calls for strong and coherent government action, including intervention in land, housing and financial markets when they fail to respond to the needs and latent demands of the low-income majority (UNCHS, 1991b).

The general principles for successful enabling strategies have been identified but the outcomes are always uncertain because different environments lead to variable effects of the policies. Many governments have already responded to the call for enabling strategies made in the GSS (see section I.G.1 below) by eschewing the role of producer and taking up that of facilitator. There has been a general recognition of the importance of encouraging individual and community participation in the shelter process but much less on the knottier issues of land allocation and finance as they affect the poor.

---

8.   Contrarily, Gilbert (1993) found that households who were too poor to rent housing in Caracas and Mexico City were being forced to build shacks and become owners in poor-quality peripheral settlements.

9.   For example, the Zambian context outside the Lusaka Project as described by Kasongo and Tipple (1990).

10. That is, the supply outside the relatively small projects.

As UNCHS (1991b) recognizes, political support is essential for successful enabling strategies. Where democratization and citizen participation and control are part of the political vocabulary, enabling strategies are more likely to be adopted and implemented. The perfect society for enabling shelter policies would be "efficient, liberal, open, pluralist, literate, economically successful and egalitarian" (McAuslan, 1985, p. 66). Although such a society does not exist, some countries have been democratizing so that the principles required for successful enabling strategies have been placed on the normal political map. Thailand is a case in point, as is India where the huge resources of people and materials, in combination with the political will, have allowed successful enablement.

It has become evident that success in innovations is dependent on social, cultural and other conditions which cannot be replicated from one place to another. Land-sharing, which has been successful in Bangkok because it is culturally appropriate there (UNCHS, 1985a; 1991b), may be completely impossible in another part of the world (West Africa, for example). While secure land tenure may be axiomatic for housing improvement in one city, it may be unnecessary in another (Baross, 1983).

The issue of finance is often introduced with the assumption that the poor need favourable interest rates, a condition which inevitably creates rationing of money. However, it is evident that they can afford to pay market interest rates, indeed market rates would be a major improvement for many who already borrow money through private moneylenders who may charge anything up to 10 per cent per day.[11] The problem confronting potential borrowers among the poor is that, because funds are limited, banks and lending institutions prefer the wealthy and influential whose loans are large enough to be worthwhile administering. Enabling policies require loans to be flexible, locally administered, and easy to negotiate through a company (probably a secondary lender) which is prepared to lend small amounts and regards a good past record in small loans as establishing entitlement to larger ones in the future.

Within the enabling approach, there is a tension between liberalization and intervention (UNCHS, 1991b). A liberalized market may provide a lively supply of housing goods but it may easily be overtaken by speculation, concentration of ownership into a few hands, and problems of access for the poorest in society. Though Dowall (1989) shows that Bangkok's highly liberal market operates very efficiently in housing provision, Niyom and others (1990) claim that conditions for the urban poor give grave concern. The GSS recommends that some interventions are required to keep land speculation in check and help the poorest groups. These include upgrading, resettlement where upgrading is impossible, and provision of services to areas of high concentrations of tenants. Because the poor are so

---

11. This type of loan is targeted at a trader who borrows to buy the day's stock and settles the debt in the afternoon.

numerous, these activities will need to be widespread and substantial and run alongside the enabling environment created for those who can help themselves.

Although we know comparatively little about the shelter-supply process, it is obvious that, in many countries, individual households are the main provider of houses. The decision to build; collection of finance and materials; hiring and firing of skilled, semi-skilled, and unskilled labour; and the other tasks in building a house are all done on an ad hoc basis. The building process has mainly been in the hands of small-scale enterprises (SSEs), often single artisans in walling, roofing and servicing trades, being brought together by the individual owner. This informal activity has, as we have seen above, provided large shares of all new housing in developing countries over the last 20 years. Housing agencies and large-scale developers, who have such an important role in developed countries, currently play a relatively small part in housing supply, although there is potential for both to build houses for sale and, thus, avoid the problems of stocks of low-rental housing which have dogged large-scale suppliers in the past.

C.   The informal sector

Accumulating evidence from developing countries shows that an increasing proportion of employment and output is originating from what is known as "the informal sector" (Sethuraman, 1981; Maldonado and others, 1987). This sector accounts for half or more of the urban employment in many developing countries and perhaps a third or more of what is produced in urban areas, though this varies substantially between countries. It is this sector in which more and more poor and new job seekers are finding opportunities to earn an income and many of these income-earning activities originate in and/or continue to operate from residential premises (see chapter VII). The sector's role in poverty alleviation in the third world is now widely recognized (ILO, 1990).

Besides providing employment and incomes to the poor, the informal sector has been a major source of human resource development since it serves as a training ground for millions and enables them to acquire productive skills at low cost and without any public expenditure. Despite low incomes, many workers have mobilized considerable savings both in cash and in kind to develop their businesses. Since all the capital investment in this sector is financed through participants' own savings, there is no burden on the public sector. The sector does not receive any public subsidy (unlike many public-sector enterprises) and yet has expanded. It has therefore passed the market test of viability and it generates goods and services of value to the society. In many branches of economic activity the informal sector coexists with the formal sector and competes successfully; in other areas the two are complementary with the informal sector distributing goods and services produced in the formal sector or providing inputs and services through sub-contracting (ILO, 1990).

It would be appropriate at this point to introduce and discuss the characteristics of the informal sector as it has an important role in most of the following discussion. There is far from universal acceptance of what constitutes the informal sector and what distinguishes it from the formal sector's activities (ILO, 1991). The tendency is to describe the formal-informal relationship as a dichotomy, whereas it may be a continuum. Indeed, it is often described in terms of its dichotomous relationship with the formal sector rather than directly, and to do this writers have offered several distinguishing features. It is possible to recognize typical informal activity but less so to recognize the point of division. In addition, a single individual or activity may move in and out of the informal sector in the course of a single process or at different times of the day.

What might be called the classic view of the differences between the formal and informal sectors is presented in table 1. The table tends to address employment rather than housing but most of the characteristics, insofar as they are useful, would seem to apply to both activities. The most important, from the point of view of this publication, are the scale of operation, the ownership, and the type of technology. These typify the SSEs which are regarded as synonymous with the informal sector by the ILO (ILO, 1991) and upon which much ILO effort has been concentrated.

The ILO's focus on SSEs, particularly in construction, has been explained as follows (ILO, 1987b):

• They are powerful generators of income and employment, often with less capital investment per job created than larger enterprises, but they face difficulties which are different from those of bigger firms. This is particularly the case with small-scale contractors, whose problems deserve separate consideration and action.

• They are often the only type of enterprise willing and able to take on small construction projects. Moreover, potentially they can offer the best value for money to clients on such small, disparate and often geographically dispersed

Table 1. Comparison of the formal and informal sectors

	Formal sector	Informal sector
Ease of access	Difficult to enter	Easy to enter
Main origin of resources	External	Indigenous
Scale of operations	Large	Small
Ownership	Corporate	Family
Technology	Capital-intensive and often imported	Labour-intensive and adapted
Skills	Formally acquired, often expatriate	Acquired outside the formal education system
Market	Protected through tariffs, quotas and trade licenses	Unregulated and competitive

Source: Meier, 1976, p. 214.

schemes as schools, rural health centres, village water supplies, low-cost roads, and similar projects which can be key components in national development programmes.

- There will be some small-scale contractors whose business will grow by undertaking successively larger projects, even if such success stories will be relatively rare. The more soundly based the small-scale sector can be made, the better will be the prospects for the development of medium and large-scale national firms to replace firms with expatriate origins which currently dominate large modern projects in many countries.

1.   Employment

According to Harberger (1971), the basic distinction between the two sectors turns on the idea that employment in the formal sector is protected in some sense. Workers within the formal sector are generally protected against exploitation, dangerous machinery or hazardous substances, and unfair employment practices by the regulatory bodies of ministries of labour guided by the ILO's conventions and recommendations. Those in the informal sector are, however, largely hidden from official control and may be exploited (especially children, women and apprentices), operate in hazardous conditions, have no limits on hours of work, and are not liable to receive pensions or other employment benefits. Employment in the informal sector is often characterized by variable hours of work over a period of time. This is because a substantial part of total employment is on a daily or hourly basis; and self-employment is very common (Mazumdar, 1976).

As Bose (1990) points out, the self-employed are very often only "disguised wage-workers" or "dependent workers." There are many manufacturing firms, wholesalers and insurance companies which retail through commission sellers, vendors who receive an agreed sum as their commission for each sale, and who only sell the products of one firm or of a few related firms. There are also the artisans who work in rented premises and buy their equipment with a loan, and taxi drivers or rickshaw pullers who operate someone else's vehicle keeping what they can earn over and above a fixed rental and running costs (Bromley and Gerry, 1979). It may be said that it is indeed the very absence of the attributes of genuine self-employment which lies at the root of the unfavourable conditions under which the self-employed in the informal sector carry out their productive activities (Bose, 1990).

The nature of contractual relations is taken by Bose (1990) to be the crux of the difference between the informal and formal sectors, not only for employees but also for self-employed workers. Bose argues that informal-sector entrepreneurs suffer from poor contractual relationships with society, in comparison to their registered, formal-sector peers. Most of them are not eligible for credit through formal lenders, their access to raw materials may be baulked by legislation or non-market supply mechanisms such as rationing, and, as will be seen later, they are usually ineligible for government contracts.

There is no doubt that there is a large percentage of low-income earners in the informal sector but there is also evidence that earnings in the informal sector are significantly lower than in the formal sector because wage rates are lower, because there is a significant degree of underemployment, and because many of the participants are young and female, both groups being poorly paid in comparison with adult men in developing countries. Mazumdar (1976) found that, for a single group across both sectors (workers aged 35–49 with incomplete primary education), informal-sector earnings are only 55 per cent of those in the formal sector for males, and 47 per cent for females.

Poorer conditions of work, evident in the informal sector, are likely to be found in their extreme form where work is done in the home, either by self-employed artisans and retailers, or through wage labour working within an employer's home. Not only are wages uncontrolled but also physical conditions such as lighting, ventilation, safety, hours of work, and other matters of concern to employment regulators are more difficult to control in the informal sector than in the formal, and in the home than in a factory or other recognized work place. As the most invisible form of employment, this is probably the most difficult to regulate and the most open to abuse. However, as will be seen in chapter VII, many people find worthwhile and profitable employment in the home and regard the option of outside employment to be the poorer one.

The informal sector's lack of regulatory hurdles is said to benefit both the self-employed and their employees. Owing to its ease of entry[12] and the lack of long contractual relationships, the informal sector can be expected to act as a buffer between employment and unemployment. Some job-seekers who are unable to find regular employment in the formal sector may, for short or long periods, participate in the informal sector rather than be wholly unemployed. The lack of regulation allows employers to take on these workers more readily than if long-term commitments were involved.

Many of the workers in the informal sector will be the "secondary workers," i.e., those who are not the main earners in the household. As would be expected, therefore, a disproportionately larger proportion of females as well as those outside the prime working age group (say under 25 and above 50) will be found in informal-sector employment, if they are employed at all. Similarly, migrants are probably disproportionately represented in the informal sector (Mazumdar, 1976). In addition, it is not uncommon to find that a formal-sector worker also has a secondary job in the informal sector.

---

12. This is in contrast to starting up in the formal sector. De Soto (1986) showed that it took 289 days to complete the formalities to start up a formal-sector enterprise in Lima, Peru, and its cost could be about US$1,000 (not counting bribes).

Table 2. Some empirical estimates of the scale of informal-sector employment in selected cities

Area	Date	Criterion of employment	Number employed	
			Total	Informal sector (percentages)
Bombay (India)	1961	Employment reported to DET[a]	1,687,000	55
Jakarta (Indonesia)	1971	Registered establishment	1 million[b]	50[b]
Belo Horizonte (Brazil)	1970	Social security payment	n.a.	69
Lima (Peru)	1970	Size of establishment	619,000	53
8 cities (Peru)	1970	Size of establishment	n.a.	62

a. The employment reported by DET (Directorate of Employment and Training) pertains to all public-sector employees and those in private sector establishments with more than 25 workers.
b. The figures are just over 1 million and 50 per cent respectively.

Source: Mazumdar, 1976, p. 659.

In collecting data on the scale of employment in the informal sector, problems of definition have been compounded by the invisibility of much of the work to official databases. Table 2 indicates the scale of the sector by some estimates and the criteria used to identify the informal sector.

2.   Housing

The production and occupation of housing in the informal sector is not a result of householder perversity, a need to break out of conformity or an iconoclastic stand for individuality. It is a rational response to the shortage of effective housing supply within the formal, controlled sector. It is likely, therefore, that if formal supply were efficient, informal-sector housing would become a thing of the past. In the long term, indeed, the ending of informal-sector development should be a result of effective enabling strategies and the extent to which the sector is losing ground could be used as a test of the success of a government's commitment to enablement. Yet, so far it seems that an ever-increasing share of housing in developing countries is provided through informal-sector activities.

Hardoy and Satterthwaite (1981) define informal-sector activity in housing according to the house being constructed by informal-sector operators, whether it meets official standards or not. Payne (1989) identifies several sub-markets which together form the informal housing sector. These are characterised by being spontaneous, unplanned or unregulated and include both self-help housing and squatter settlements. Their share of current housing production in many developing countries is very large — 86 per cent in the Philippines, 82 per cent in Brazil, and 77 per cent in Venezuela (Payne, 1989). The sub-markets within the informal sector have, however, some important variations. While much of the literature in the 1970s concentrated on squatter settlements through non-commercialized, community-controlled initiatives, more recent studies (which Payne, 1989, reviews) have shown the rise of a system by which land is purchased from its legal rural owners and then subdivided into house-lots which are sold on, illegally, for whatever the market will bear. The houses built thereon may or may not conform to the building regulations and may or may not be built by informal sector contractors.

The informal sector may be very large in proportion to the housing market as a whole.

In Kenya, for example, the construction of traditional dwellings in 1976 contributed almost 60 per cent of gross fixed capital formation [for housing], while the informal construction sector contributed around 30 per cent to the gross domestic product generated by construction between 1969 and 1978. In Côte d'Ivoire, it has been estimated that informal construction activity accounted for 30 per cent of the value added by the construction sector, for 39 per cent of the intermediate consumption of materials and services, and for 35 per cent of the total value of the output of the construction sector (UNCHS, 1987, p. 76).

In Indonesia, it was responsible for at least 85 per cent of all urban — and 99 per cent of all rural — housing production in 1990 (UNCHS, 1994c).[13]

There has been a tendency in the past among writers and theorists to glamorize the informal sector as containing enterprising people in settlements which are automatically improving in some kind of Darwinian evolutionary process. This view is difficult to support empirically and is far from the reality for many of the poorest urban residents who must now rent tiny rooms in ramshackle structures owned by squatter landlords. On the other hand, there are many settlements in which Turner's (1976) "bridgeheaders" have become "consolidators" and established considerable dwellings far better than they could afford in the formal sector.

In contrast to their academic peers, city officials responsible for housing tend to nurse a deep hostility towards squatters and any developer who uses informal-sector routes to development. A change in attitude is a necessary prerequisite for a realistic attempt to introduce enabling strategies. This is usually easier said than done. For example, while Nigeria makes favourable responses to enabling strategies, it also demolishes the Maroko settlement in Lagos (UNCHS, 1994e); similarly, the Indonesian Government endorses the GSS (see section I.G.1) while

---

13. The recent series of four UNCHS (Habitat) publications on national trends in housing-production practices, provides an overview of the roles and responsibilities of the actors in the housing-production process in India, Indonesia, Mexico and Nigeria (UNCHS, 1994b; 1994c; 1994d; 1994e). The publications provide national as well as city-level data. An overview of the particular problems faced by the poorest population groups in the same four countries are outlined in a separate publication (UNCHS, 1994a).

embarking on a programme involving the demolition of *kampungs* in central Jakarta (UNCHS, 1991b; 1994c).

The lack of homogeneity in informal-sector housing causes not only complications in definition but also the need for a variety of responses from national and local governments. While some areas need only land-ownership regularization to assimilate them into the city, other areas may be so poorly built or badly sited that little improvement is possible without major upheaval of the people and their activities. It would be inappropriate to remove such areas by force, especially as their residents may be too poor to obtain better conditions in the market. Thus, they require to be either left well alone, with all the social consequences of having people occupying very poor and completely unserviced housing, or substantially assisted at public expense.

An increasingly common phenomenon, that of informal extensions to formal housing, creates an extremely complex mix of formality and informality within many old government housing areas. These so called "transformations" occur when small government-built dwellings are extended by their occupants, against planning, building and tenancy regulations, in order to provide more room for the household, improved levels of services within the dwelling, rooms for renting, or space for economic activity (Tipple, 1991; 1992b). In such cases, part of a building is in the formal sector and part in the informal. While the effect may be chaotic, there are no grounds for believing that the formal is well-built and in sound condition while the informal is not; quite the reverse in some cases. Neither can it be assumed that lack of legality means anarchy; in some cases, as in many squatter settlements, the physical appearance of the settlement is the result of complex negotiations between neighbours (Dasgupta, 1990).

The informal sector in housing, like its employment counterpart, may benefit from the lack of regulation which enables cheaper construction technologies to be used. However, it also suffers from its illegality in that formal finance cannot be raised for construction or improvement, and few services will be extended to informal housing areas while they remain beyond the legal pale. Furthermore, this illegality, combined with rigorous enforcement of zoning and building regulations, results in enormous hardship for those unable to comply with them and obliges the informal sector to operate at great distances from work-places and potential markets for products and services from home-based activities (ILO, 1991). However, as the sector contributes a larger share of urban areas every year, the need to recognize the validity of its contribution and to normalize informal areas with respect to servicing, finance, taxation and other urban duties and privileges becomes more urgent. At the same time, the arguments against doing so command less of the moral high ground and become increasingly untenable.

D. Employment, underemployment and unemployment

Employed people are defined by the ILO as those who, during a specified brief period (one week or one day) have worked, had a job but did not work, or were self-employed. Productive employment is that which contributes to the production of goods and services, for the market and outside the market, for consumption or fixed capital formation. The periods chosen for determining a person's employment can vary with particular circumstances. The 1984 Census in Ghana used one day's work in the previous week as the minimum qualification for being employed (Ghana, Government of, 1987).

Gilbert and Gugler (1981) define underemployment as the underutilization of labour. They maintain that it takes three distinct forms. Probably the most common form of underemployment in developing countries is the State when workers are so numerous that at all times a substantial number are less than fully employed. In this case, a reduction in the number of workers would not lead to an aggregate loss of output. The most numerous example of these in developing countries are street vendors, many of whom have a stable output to known customers and still only eke a living. These are said to constitute invisible unemployment by the ILO (1987a). The second common form of under-employment is related to fluctuations in economic activities during the day (e.g., at markets), over the week or month (e.g., in recreational services), or seasonally. These fluctuations result in idleness for the self-employed and laying off of the wage earners. The third type is hidden underemployment in which a solidarity group continue to employ people rather than discharging them even when there is insufficient work to keep them fully occupied. Family enterprises or work groups based on churches and other religious and philanthropic organizations would support hidden underemployment. The communist principle of full employment falls into this category.

Underemployed persons are defined by the ILO as those who have worked less than the normal duration (visible underemployment), or those whose skills have been underutilized (disguised underemployment), or whose productivity is inadequate (potential underemployment) (Hussmanns and others, 1990). The underemployed can also be defined as those who work fewer hours than they would like (World Bank, 1980).

It is also possible to define underemployment in terms of income. Sabot (1979) defined underemployment among urban Tanzanians as those jobs for which the earnings were less than the average rural wage. By this criterion, 10 per cent of urban workers were underemployed, in addition to the 10 per cent unemployed.

A definition of unemployment is extremely problematic in developing countries. Some would limit the unemployed to those who are actively seeking employment (World Bank, 1980). The ILO definition embraces those who are without work but available for and actively seeking work (Hussmanns and others, 1990; Mayer, 1991). Others would include those who are available for work but have become so discouraged that they have given up looking. The ILO criteria for those seeking work includes those —

> taking steps to indicate availability for work (by registering or any other overt means) [but] may be relaxed in non-industrialised countries where self-employment predominates, in order to include persons discouraged from seeking work, especially women (Mayer, 1991, p. 348).

Perversely, the unemployed are not necessarily numbered among the poor. Glewwe and Van der Gaag (1990) found that the unemployed[14] in Côte d'Ivoire are hardly more likely to be among the poor than those in employment. Depending on which of their eight definitions of poverty was used, unemployment varied from a low of 9.4 per cent (using floor area per capita as the measure of poverty) to a high of 16.3 (using adjusted per capita consumption — see definition in section I.F below), compared with 13.4 per cent unemployed in the population as a whole. Being unemployed usually signifies being provided for by someone else; perhaps waiting for the right job which can be a rewarding strategy for the better educated who may not find a job to which they aspire if they take one of lower status (Gilbert and Gugler, 1981).

Under Article 1 of the Employment Policy Convention, 1964 (No. 122), member States agree to pursue a policy designed to promote full, productive and freely chosen employment. This policy should aim at ensuring that there is work for all who are available for and seeking work; that such work is as productive as possible; and that there is freedom of choice and the fullest possible opportunity to qualify with and use skills. This policy should take account of the level of economic development and the mutual relationships between employment and other economic and social objectives.

Under the spirit of the Employment Policy Convention, 1964 (No. 122), it is not sufficient merely to promote economic growth and assume that employment will follow; there is no automatic link between economic growth and the reduction of unemployment (Mayer, 1991). In addition, the Convention is not only concerned with work carried out in employment in the formal sector, it is also concerned with other ways of earning a living including self-employment and with work in the informal sector.

The active population is defined to include all persons above a specified age who fulfill the requirements for inclusion among the employed or unemployed (Hussmanns and others, 1990; Mayer, 1991). The labour force is defined as comprising all employed and unemployed persons, including those seeking work for the first time; it covers employers, persons working on their own account, salaried employees, wage earners, unpaid family workers, members of producers' cooperatives, and members of the armed forces (Plant, 1983). Estimates put the

---

14. Unemployed is defined in this case as those reporting that they did not work for any employer or themselves.

labour force of the world at 2,546 million in 2000, 750 million more than in 1980. However, percentage increases in Africa (67 per cent) and Latin America (77 per cent) between 1980 and 2000, show the imperative of job creation in developing countries (Plant, 1983).

E.   Living conditions

Just as housing or shelter are defined as more than just the structure in which people live, so living conditions encompass more than just the conditions in the house.   UNCHS (Habitat) (1987, p. 5) prefers the term "settlement conditions" because it extends —

> to all those components of the physical environment with which an individual or a community comes into contact and which are used on a regular basis for the whole range of human activities — the individual dwelling and its related services, the dwelling's immediate surroundings, community facilities, transportation and communications network, and so on.

While 40 years ago it might have been thought that building quality was the key to good living conditions, there is now a serious body of literature (Harpham and others, 1988, for example) detailing the horrors which face many millions of people every morning when they wake from a mosquito-disturbed sleep.   Their

Plate 1. Many urban residents continue to live under such poor conditions (Bangkok, Thailand)

night may have been spent on a mat in a room with four, six, or up to ten others, with inadequate ventilation (either because windows are too small or because they have been boarded up to prevent burglary as poor preys on poor), and an earthen floor which allows dampness to rise. Their morning ablutions will comprise either a wash from tepid and cloudy water in a tin or a queue to use the only bathroom in a tenement house shared by 50 or 100 people. The toilet queue is too long, so a visit to the rubbish dump to defecate in the morning mist, or to the Augean public latrine where privacy is marginally better, is in order. The working clothes are rescued from their place over a string extended above the bed and the man sets off on the routine of queuing for crowded transport to his place of employment many miles away, often without breaking his fast.

His wife is left to feed the children on last night's left-overs or some rice porridge cooked in cloudy water over a charcoal stove on the floor by the door, then to do the household chores and fetch water, before she clears a small space and begins the daily business of preparing food for city workers, or laundering clothes, or smoking fish, or sewing up garments for a manufacturer to export to Europe. At dusk she cooks the day's meal, squatting on the floor before the round of washing her children from a soapy bowl in the space outside the room. On wet days, the whole household is caked in mud, on dry days, the dust blows into the food and water, carrying cysts and parasites to plague them. The earth on which they tread harbours parasites, eager to enter a human host through bare feet, the dusty air they breathe brings hepatitis A and meningitis, the fumes within it come from the sulphuric acid plant at the copper mine or the chemical works down the hill, adding coughs to malarial fever. Their water is a breeding ground for mosquito larvae, salmonella, shigella, and *E. coli*, sometimes in as high a density as found in the human intestine (Gracey and others, 1976) waiting to strike the children down with malaria or diarrhoea. Their neighbours on the steep slopes suffer added danger from land-slips in the heavy rain; down by the river, flooding is regular and brings added dangers from sewage and other pollutants. Such, and similar, are the living conditions of poor people in the cities and towns of developing countries.

F.   Poverty

> *It is...a well established fact that the poor derive most of their incomes from labour, the only income-generating asset at their disposal.... But since provision of shelter is itself an activity calling for substantial labour input, one wonders if it is not possible to promote both housing and employment goals simultaneously through a common strategy*

Sethuraman, 1991, p. 300

The definition of poverty has inspired much discussion. As Szal (1977) points out, a standard of comparison is a *sine qua non* of identifying who are the poor. Economic measures fall basically into three categories:

- Absolute measures of poverty, which usually specify an amount of money that an individual or a family must receive to obtain a minimum standard of living;
- Relative measures of poverty. These are based upon percentages, e.g., a percentage of the total population or of total income;[15]
- Absolute/relative measures of poverty which combine absolute measurement with a relative standard.

The non-economic aspects of poverty involve basic human needs such as self-fulfilment, participation in society, clean air and a healthy environment, security, and freedom of movement. Drewnowski (1974) attempted to measure non-economic needs by constructing a type of "quality of life" index with each component weighted. From this could be calculated the proportion of the population below the prescribed levels of need satisfaction.[16]

The use of income distribution in developing countries has merits but data are often unreliable. Anand (1977) set a poverty line for Malaysia as one half the national per capita income or M$25. Some countries have used the level of officially set minimum wages as the standard of poverty but they should be looked upon as a policy instrument to reduce poverty rather than as the method of setting the poverty standard.

Glewwe and Van der Gaag (1990), working with the rich variety of data available in the Côte d'Ivoire Living Standards Survey, argue for the use of per capita consumption. However, this ignores possible economies available to larger households (e.g., in housing). To allow for these, allowance can be made for the smaller per capita demands placed on a household's budget by additional members (especially children who may be counted as a fraction of an adult) in an estimate of household equivalence (Sawyer, 1975). Using this against an estimate of the cost of a minimum level of welfare (which is a value judgement based on societal norms), a measure of poverty referred to by Glewwe and Van der Gaag (1990) as the "adjusted per capita consumption" can be determined.

Other measures which can be used in defining poverty, in addition to those which use income and consumption, include the fraction of the household's budget used for food (the food ratio), calorie intake of members of the household, medical data based on body measurement against age in children or physical tests, or measures of how far a household fulfils levels of consumption which may be regarded (subjectively) as basic needs, for example in education or housing space available. In deciding which, Glewwe and Van der Gaag (1990) recommend that any definition of poverty used to decide policy should correspond with the specific

---

15. These imply that the problem of poverty cannot be solved: statistically, there will always be the specified percentage at the bottom of the distribution of income.

16. The difficulties involved — the relationship of weights, subjectivity etc. — are self-evident, yet Drewnowski's work can be regarded as a valuable first step toward a social welfare index.

policy under consideration. Thus, in the context of employment and housing, poverty definitions based on consumption, such as the "adjusted per capita consumption" would be suitable.

Ravallion and others (1991) have attempted to quantify absolute poverty in a worldwide context. They argue that one can pick the cost of a bundle of goods which is reasonably well recognized as constituting an absolute minimum by international standards.[17] In this context, one can think of the poverty line as having an "absolute" component which is constant across all countries, and a "relative" component, which is specific to each country.[18] They suggest the assessment of a "typical" poverty line amongst the poorest countries. In addition, in converting local poverty lines to a common currency, Summers and Heston (1988) suggest the use of purchasing power parity (PPP) which adjusts local costs through official exchange rates to, in their case, 1985 United States dollars.

From Ravallion and others (1991), it is possible to estimate that, though there is a clear tendency for the local poverty line to increase with mean consumption, a range of $23–31 per person per month (at PPP) represents the bounds of poverty, with the lower amount as defining "extreme absolute poverty", or "food poverty." They calculate that about one in three people in the developing countries could be regarded as in poverty, while one in five could be categorized as in extreme poverty. The combined population size of the countries covered is 3442 million, so the estimated total number of poor people is 1137 million, of which 645 million live in food poverty. Yet, despite the staggering number of poor people, Ravallion and others (1991) suggest that, with less than 0.5 per cent of world consumption, perfectly targeted without distortion, one could guarantee that everyone in the world could reach at least India's poverty line.

Comparative studies of poverty are fraught with difficulties, owing to the relative nature of the concept and problems in data comparability, among others. A recent UNCHS (Habitat) publication makes a point of using several terms when analysing, debating and working on poverty (UNCHS, 1994a). The scale of poverty can be divided into "starvation poverty" or food poverty, (narrow/broad) subsistence poverty, and relative deprivation of either a social coping or social

---

17. In calculating the value of a basic basket of goods, Szal (1977) argues that it should not be limited to food alone. He would include such things as shelter, water provision and fuel, and even some non-basic necessities such as furniture. This is in line with the "basic needs" approach which was adopted by the World Employment Conference of the International Labour Organization (ILO, 1976) and, modified by criticisms of its subjectivity, still holds its place in ILO policy.

18. The absolute poverty line may be the *lowest* poverty line observed in any country. However, the answer may be distorted by particular circumstances and measurement errors. It will also be influenced by inter-country differences in non-income factors; a country with good public services benefiting the poor, or a relatively low-cost climate, will naturally have a lower income poverty line.

participation type. When talking about poverty as limited access to social participation, it becomes easy to confuse the concept with inequality and with different life-styles in the same society. There are thus good reasons for not using the term "poverty" regarding this latter category. The "poor" comprise those who cannot obtain an adequate diet plus those who are in basic-needs poverty in a narrow sense (shelter and clothing). The lower-income group includes only those in basic-needs poverty in a broad sense and excludes the poor. This group of people has a sufficient material consumption to allow them an active and fairly secure life concerning food, water, shelter and clothing. They do, however, have an income below what is typically necessary for complete social coping and participation in a society's normal events and activities. When referring to both the poor and the lower-income group, the term "low-income groups" is applied. The "working poor" are those among the poor who have the ability to respond positively to, for instance, a shelter project. The term does not necessarily mean that individuals are employed, but rather that they are employable. The remainder of the poor are the "destitute", those living in utter destitution who only in very favourable circumstances will be able to achieve an improved life. They are often handicapped in some way, or are either very young or old. For the purpose of the present discussion it is not necessary to operationalize the above concepts for quantitative analyses. They are used as broad and descriptive concepts indicating levels of needs satisfaction of both a material and psychological kind.

The focus of this publication is the "working poor." It should, however, be noted that the distinction between the "poor" and the "lower-income" group has become somewhat blurred in many cities of developing countries. The GSS (UNCHS, 1990) acknowledges that enabling shelter strategies have little to offer the destitutes, and that they might have to be assisted directly through programmes shaped by principles other than affordability and cost recovery (i.e., by some kind of social benefit — possibly some kind of subsidy). Yet, the impact of enabling shelter strategies for the working poor and the lower-income group may be indirectly beneficial to the destitutes because they enable scarce public resources to be targeted at those that are unable to help themselves.

G.   Recent international policy responses

1.   The GSS

In response to the 600 million people lacking a shelter unit fit for habitation and the IYSH, the United Nations adopted the GSS at its forty-third session in December, 1988. Through its provisions, it is intended that "... all countries [should] have coherent, effective and functional national shelter strategies well before the year 2000" (UNCHS, 1990, p. 6). It advocates that shelter policies should:

- be realistic at the stage of development in a particular country;

- show awareness of the correct choice of priorities and actions to prevent the deterioration of the housing situation and the emergence of new problems;
- be comprehensive in their appreciation of the various aspects of the shelter issue;
- involve gradual, step-by-step setting and implementation of goals in accordance with the actual possibilities;
- be flexible, adjusting action in response to changes in circumstances and requirements.

The GSS recognizes that there are critical differences between countries which make it necessary to adjust the implementation of the Strategy to the local needs in each. In countries where the majority, or at least the urban majority, is poorly housed and where public resources are insufficient to house everyone adequately, resources will need to be distributed broadly and the people will largely need to house themselves. It is clear that any appropriate national shelter strategy will need to take account of differences in the balance of government and private participation, the strength and characteristics of the informal sector, and the health of the input markets, to ensure that innovations are not incongruent with existing conditions.

In the context of this publication, it is significant that the GSS calls attention to an increasing realization around the world that shelter and development are mutually supportive and interdependent, that "people, habitat, and development are part of an indivisible whole" (UNCHS, 1987, p. 6).

The GSS recognizes and hopes to utilize the increase in demand which follows economic development and enables it to be translated directly into a favourable investment climate for shelter. The shelter sector should then be able to bid successfully for resources in the competitive arena of economic development. The GSS therefore calls on policy-makers to become aware that housing and infrastructure investments are productive investments from both the economic and social points of view and an important source of income and employment.

Recognizing the broad economic and demographic trends which, though outside the shelter sector, shape its outcomes, the GSS calls on policy-makers to take account of population growth and urbanization so that societies can benefit from these changes rather than being penalized by them. As a corollary, however, if these demands are not met, the costs to society will grow. To this end, GSS adopts a positive attitude towards the informal sector in housing, recommending support and encouragement so that those who build in this sector can make the best use of their resources rather than having them inhibited by government "tolerance" or discouragement.

2. Agenda 21

In Agenda 21 of the United Nations Conference on Environment and Development, which was convened at Rio de Janeiro in 1992 (UNCED, 1992), it is recognized that high priority in development should be given to the shelter and employment needs of the poor, the unemployed, and the growing number of people without any source of income; the no-income group. Chapter 7 of Agenda 21 addresses the promotion of human settlements development, recognizing the extremely good value that agencies like UNDP have found technical cooperation expenditure on human settlements to be.[19]

In pursuing adequate shelter for all, improving human settlements management, and promoting sustainable construction-industry activities, Agenda 21 proposes that —

> All countries should, as appropriate, support the shelter efforts of the urban and rural poor, the unemployed and the no-income group by adopting and/or adapting existing codes and regulations, to facilitate their access to land, finance and low-cost building materials and by actively promoting the regularisation and upgrading of informal settlements and urban slums as an expedient measure and pragmatic solution to the urban shelter deficit (section 7.9).

Agenda 21 calls for government agencies and non-governmental organizations (NGOs) to cooperate in a wide range of activities to reduce urban poverty, *inter alia*:

- generating employment for the urban poor through the provision, improvement and maintenance of urban infrastructure and services;
- raising awareness of the means, approaches and benefits of the provision of environmental infrastructure facilities, especially among indigenous people, women, low-income groups and the poor;
- developing a cadre of professionals with adequate skills in integrated infrastructural service planning and maintenance of resource-efficient, environmentally sound and socially acceptable systems;
- supporting economic activities in the informal sector, such as repairs, recycling, services and small commerce;
- strengthening the institutional capacity of local authorities and administrators in working in partnership with local communities and the private sector in the provision of adequate infrastructure services;
- adopting appropriate legal and regulatory instruments, including cross-subsidy arrangements, to extend the benefits of adequate and affordable environmental infrastructure to unserved population groups, especially the poor.

---

19. Every dollar of UNDP technical cooperation expenditure on human settlements in 1988 generated a follow-up investment of $122, the highest of all UNDP sectors of assistance (UNCED, 1992, section 7.2 — citing UNDP).

Furthermore, Agenda 21 proposes active promotion of sustainable construction-industry activities recognizing that they are vital to the achievement of development goals.[20] Thus it proposes that all countries should:

- establish and strengthen the indigenous building-materials industry, based, as much as possible, on inputs of locally available natural resources;
- expand technical support and incentive schemes for increasing the capabilities and economic viability of small-scale and informal enterprises which make use of local materials and traditional construction techniques;
- promote the use of labour-intensive construction and maintenance technologies which generate employment in the construction sector for the underemployed labour force found in most large cities, while at the same time promoting the development of skills in the construction sector;
- develop policies and practices to reach the informal sector and self-help house builders by adopting measures to increase the affordability of building materials on the part of the urban and rural poor, through, *inter alia*, credit schemes and bulk procurement of building materials for sale to small-scale builders and communities.

It is recognized that human resource development and capacity-building is essential for upgrading the capabilities of the small entrepreneur and the operatives and supervisors in the construction and building-materials industries. Local authorities are called upon to play a pioneering role in promoting the increased use of environmentally sound building materials and construction technologies, e.g., by pursuing an innovative procurement policy.

H.   The significance of enabling shelter strategies

The GSS and Agenda 21 reiterate the UNCHS (Habitat) philosophy: that if policies affecting the shelter sector are favourable, the sector contributes considerably to economic development, and the gains of economic development are translated into sectoral improvements. If, however, the policies work against general economic development, the links will fail and both sectoral and overall objectives will suffer.

The opposite of enabling strategies can be seen in the highly interventionist housing systems operated in China and, in past times, in Hungary. In the former case, Lalkaka (1984) shows how what the Chinese Government regarded as "non-productive" construction, especially housing, took a very small share of investment in China over the period 1954 to 1978. Although housing would be expected to take at least 15 per cent of GFCF even in poor countries like India, in China it was between 4 and 6 per cent up to 1975 rising to 11 per cent only after 1979. The

---

20. However, it also recognizes that they can also be a major source of environmental damage through depletion of the natural-resource base, degradation of fragile eco-zones, chemical pollution and the use of building materials harmful to human health.

situation in past times in Hungary is described by Szelenyi (1983) as a "strangely self-defeating article of faith": because housing was seen as a basic need, it was removed from market processes. It seemed to follow, therefore, that housing was not a useful economic commodity but merely a consumption good. Thus, when the horse-trading between industrial spending (say) and housing investment was carried out, housing was starved of capital while industry received plenty. Thus, the workers, who toiled in vast cathedrals of factories, heard politically beneficial lectures in vast assembly halls, and were administered from expensive offices, went home to inadequate housing. The housing was regarded as outside of the production process (simply as a consumption good) because it was part of the workers' daily consumption. Peattie (1987) uses the above story to advocate that those who have authority for improving the quality and quantity of housing and infrastructure should have a seat at the table of macro-economic planners. She argues that there is as much sense in counting housing as part of production as in so counting the factory structures because they, also, are used and enjoyed as part of the daily consumption of their workers. The same argument, that production comes before "living well" and that factories, therefore, are more important than housing, is reiterated and condemned as the heart of the Chinese housing problem by Lalkaka (1984).

Over the last two decades, the prevailing housing policies in developing countries have been aimed at individual house-ownership for every poor household. It has been assumed that each target household constructs its own house. The narrow focus on sites-and-services and settlement-upgrading schemes as the cornerstone of housing strategies has diverted attention from the central issue of establishing sustainable shelter-delivery systems which can operate at the required national scale. The GSS calls for a scaling-up of housing programmes to encourage output for all consumers by all possible means of production.

Well chosen shelter sector policies at the national level, followed by effective implementation by a broad group of actors at national and subnational levels, have the potential for not only addressing short-run economic problems but also laying the foundation for a productive permanent link between the shelter sector and the macro-economy. The intention is that a multiplicity of actors shall be involved; at all levels of government, and in NGOs and community-based organizations (CBOs) to increase production of housing and to improve existing housing. The emphasis must be on the production of quantities of housing which meet basic needs — land, basic shelter and minimal services — and the gradual improvement of existing shelter for the majority, rather than on the production of new high-quality housing for the few. Further emphasis is placed on the necessity of involving people, in their communities, in the shelter process.

As UNCHS (Habitat) (1991d) points out, while participation has been practised in the past, it was often as a means to other ends (for example, cost recovery) rather than as an end in itself — to empower people in increasing control over their lives. However, this will involve governments becoming aware of the limitations of their previously pursued shelter strategies and the effects of other policies on the shelter sector. Key strategic improvements will be needed in shelter delivery.

In general, it has been found that economic development improves housing conditions, space and access to infrastructure. On average, even the poorest members of society benefit from economic growth and well-functioning markets. Sometimes, however, the shelter and access to infrastructure conditions of many of the people, especially the poorest, remain very poor, despite general gains in living standards. To deal with this problem, subsidies have been applied in a variety of forms. It is likely that there will always be a group, perhaps those in absolute poverty, who can only afford the most meagre of shelter provision if it is heavily subsidized (even to the point of being free). However, the volume and size of subsidies, and their targets, need to be carefully appraised against the scale of the need and available financial resources.

The dichotomy between those who regard the role of governments as that of an enabler and those who regard government provision of housing as a correct use of public money is recognized in the GSS as well as in Agenda 21. Both documents call for public and private sectors to cooperate to ensure that housing is produced in the most efficient possible way. Whereas virtually all housing in developing countries is produced by the private sector (formal and informal), governments tend to impose explicit or implicit obstacles through financial restrictions and counter-productive codes and regulations. Both the GSS and Agenda 21 propose that governments review existing legislation and regulations and their impact on shelter production and improvement, and remove those which clearly appear to be pointless and unenforceable. At the same time, governments should deploy their own resources in strategic areas, for example, in the provision of trunk infrastructure, in the development of land, in the regulation of construction and in the promotion of a variety of housing-finance institutions.

Shelter is affected by the macro-economy; the availability and price of finance, trade policies affecting raw materials, etc. In its proposals for reorganizing the shelter sector, the GSS maintains that shelter strategies should be released from their largely parochial past orientation which allowed policies to be chosen which paid no attention to the real cost of housing units to the economy as a whole. At the same time, the GSS recognizes that policies adopted as a response to macro-economic trends have had an adverse effect on the viability of shelter delivery. Rising rates of inflation in the 1970s, high and volatile interest rates, declining terms of trade, and stagnating economies, have driven investment away from housing into more "productive" sectors.[21] In the decade following 1975,

---

21. At the same time, some policies impacting directly on shelter have further reduced the profitability of housing as a prudent investment. Paramount among these has been rent control which, although successful in minimizing the price of housing, has frequently benefited the tenant far less than it has cost landlords, and has contributed, in no small way, to a reduction in housing

there was a downward shift in the percentage of GNP spent on housing (these values fell by between 11 and 24 per cent) compared with the historical trends. The GSS imputes as much of the blame to policies responding to declining economies as to the decline itself.

Enabling shelter strategies imply a shift from a government's direct construction effort, which is often only a fraction of the scale needed to fulfill its own targets let alone the need, to the encouragement of individuals, SSEs, and large contractors in their endeavours in shelter sector construction. As the construction industry in developing countries is relatively undeveloped, and the housing construction sub-sector is dominated by SSEs, a shift to enabling strategies will almost inevitably increase the role of the informal sector.

As will be shown later in this publication, informal-sector operations, dominated by SSEs, tend to be more employment-intensive than those operated in the formal sector. In addition, there tends to be a larger proportion of unskilled workers as the materials and technology involve simpler tasks, closer to the techniques with which the low income worker will have grown up. Thus, more people will work to provide the same quantity of output. As the Employment Policy Convention, 1964 (No. 122), encourages all governments to promote full employment, and as it can be demonstrated that labour-intensive production can be as price-efficient as capital-intensive production, it can be argued that the increase in employment itself is sufficient reason to increase investment in housing through the enabling process.

The enabling strategy implies that, rather than competing with private and household producers, governments should, instead, restrict their role in the production of housing to the needs of specific vulnerable groups who are not provided for by any other sector. This is an effective use of scarce resources and brings immediate shelter benefits to the very poor (UNCHS, 1991b, p. 37). Among these, women are over-represented.

I.   Women in shelter-related activities

Unlike men, women have a major reproductive role as well as a role in production and in the wider community. However, shelter policy has usually focused on women's reproductive role ignoring their contribution to the production and improvements of housing, to income-generation and enterprise development, and to community organization and action. Both the GSS and Agenda 21 recognize the important place of women in the shelter process; both in their particular needs and in their potential participation in development. It is recognized that gender discrimination, severe poverty, lack of education and training, and their double and

---

starts, especially for rental occupation (Malpezzi and others, 1990; Malpezzi and Ball, 1991; UNCHS, 1991b; Urban Edge, 1988b).

triple burden as household workers and workers in the formal and informal sectors, conspire to prevent women from fulfilling their potential in the shelter process. Removing these constraints is important not only because equity in distribution of development benefits is a fundamental principle but also because increasing numbers of households, especially poor households, are either solely or largely supported by women.

The implications for women in shelter-related activities are concrete and identifiable. Women have distinctive shelter and other needs which follow from the "triple role" outlined above (Moser and Peake, 1987). Their economic role is tied more closely than that of men to their reproductive role because women cannot travel so far or so often to work, this being precluded by childcare responsibilities. Resettlement therefore affects women to a greater extent than men. Moser and Peake (1987) exemplify this with the example of relocation of squatters in Delhi during 1975–1977, when female employment fell by 27 per cent and male employment by only 5 per cent as a result of the move.

The GSS recommends the necessity that women's participation in shelter and infrastructure management as contributors and beneficiaries should be enhanced to an equal status to that of men. It recognizes that women's demands for shelter goods and services should be assessed and that their participation in the design and implementation of shelter will increase. Given the subordinate position of women worldwide and the difficulty of reversing centuries of discrimination and inequality, it is not surprising that little progress has been made overall in promoting the strategic needs of women. There has, however, been some progress in the fields of access to land, finance and tenure security, in representation and participation in policy- and decision-making, and in the legal arena (UNCHS, 1991b). In many cases, the most successful organizations have been those which have initiated their activities around practical gender needs (such as health and service-provision), but which have utilized these concerns as a means to reach strategic gender needs identified by women in particular socio-economic contexts (Moser, 1989).

II. Human settlements development and employment generation

A. Direct impacts of housing developments

Housing is the leading component of urbanization, it is more numerous, more extensive, and usually represents more investment than any other single use. Housing can be seen simply as a consumption good but among the first in recent times to point to the production aspects of habitat improvements were Klaassen and Burns (1963) who formalized their approach into two assumptions:

• housing is an investment good capable of generating income and influencing the productivity of the occupants at their work; and

• housing is therefore not only a goal of development policy (as it is in the traditional view) but also a tool of this policy (Klaassen and others, 1987).

Burns and Grebler's (1977) seminal work attempted to support the hypotheses that shelter improvement raises productivity at work, lowers absenteeism from work, raises the level of health, increases the productivity of education, and lowers the incidence of social deviation. Yet, their findings were not conclusive:

...in no single case did better housing make matters worse for the rehoused populations studied. On the other hand, there are remarkably few cases where location in new housing generated unequivocally favourable results.

However, as Klaassen and others (1987) argue, the fact that there is no full proof does not mean that favourable results do not exist or are not important. Logically, they say, the relations must exist, for how can people work if their health is weak owing to bad living conditions? The problem is that the impacts, especially on productivity, are hard to quantify in practical research.[1]

In addition to the benefits which occupants garner from improved housing, others also receive benefits. Employers of people whose productive capacity rises or whose absenteeism decreases benefit, although some of the increased profit may accrue to the workers as their wage payments are raised. Governments may also benefit as improved shelter can be expected to diminish fire hazards, reducing municipal outlays for fire brigades and payments in support of victims. As the health of the population improves, less needs to be spent on hospitals, medicine and other supportive payments. The negative effects of crime and deviant behaviour and the cost of combating them will also be lower than before (Klaassen and others, 1987).

---

1. See Burns and Grebler, 1977; Klaassen and others, 1987.

The findings of that early study suggest that the benefits of successive shelter improvements are descending in magnitude. Therefore, both Wegelin (1978) and Burns and others (1970) suggest avoiding relatively expensive types of constructions and choosing "second-best" solutions. Projects which improve the worst housing conditions are likely to have the most significant benefits. In addition, such second-best solutions will be within the financial reach of most people (Klaassen and others, 1987). This is in line with Cotton and Franceys' (1991) argument about improvements to services in residential areas. They argue that, in reality, many slum dwellers exist in an environment which totally lacks drainage, sanitation, suitable access, solid-waste removal, and power supply. Their only service provision may be access to small quantities of grossly polluted water. In effect, this corresponds to a "zero baseline" service level. It is argued that any improvement in service is likely to result in some benefit to the inhabitants. By improving the level of service in an incremental fashion, to give several relatively small benefits in health, safety, social well-being and convenience over a period of time, affordable improvements in quality of life can be gained without the major, and unaffordable, step to conventional service standards.

B.   Income multipliers

Housing can make underutilized labour productive at low cost (Raj and Mitra, 1990). Moreover, in the current economic climate, shelter sector investments are attractive because their typically low import requirements imply that incremental investments generate a higher domestic multiplier than do investments that are import sensitive (UNCHS, 1990, section 46). If $1,000 is invested in housing, the national income of a country will be affected in some way. This is measured as a multiplier which can be defined as a ratio of the change in national income to the initial change in the sectoral investment. While there is a direct increase of $1,000, that will be added to by indirect increases as consumption expenditure is generated as a result of the $1,000 spent. In the case of housing, the builders will earn money which they will spend on food and other products produced in the country. Insofar as this produces chains of consumption within the country, so the consumption multiplier effect will increase. In discussions on multipliers, the direct increments to income and employment are referred to as first round effects. The spending generated by these fall through subsequent rounds owing to a propensity to spend money on imports, to pay tax, and to save.

In addition to the consumption multiplier effect, there are considerable indirect multiplier effects through the creation of investment in other sectors generated by the demand in the construction sector for their products. The builders buy raw materials for the building and hire transport to move them; the occupants of the houses buy furnishings and fittings, and pay for maintenance, all of which creates paid employment and the use of materials. These linkage effects are discussed in later chapters and are not included in the discussion here for the sake of clarity.

As Klaassen and others (1987) maintain, governments which wish to increase employment, especially among the poorer sections of the population by means of shelter investments, probably do best by investing in those that are directed to the poor. Such a policy will generate much employment but the potential benefits can only be maximized if shelter and non-shelter policies are substantially changed. The direction of these changes will be referred to later in this publication.

If a shelter investment involves capital-intensive technology and the workers spend their income on imported goods, or taxes, or do not spend but save, the multiplier is likely to be close to 1. If the technology is labour-intensive, and the workers consume only local produce, do not save, nor pay tax, leakage in that round would be lower and the multiplier would probably be much higher than 2. As lower-income workers tend to have lower marginal propensities to import, pay tax, or save than higher-income workers, multipliers would be greater *ceteris paribus* for investments involving low-income labour. As we shall see in chapter V below, informal-sector housing construction tends to involve local materials and local, low-wage labour and so has potential for very high income multipliers.

However, this is not the end of the story. If growth rates for the housing sector can be accelerated under conditions of economic stagnation (which undoubtedly exist in many developing countries), the multipliers (especially from backward linkages — see below) may play a more important developmental role than the notional multiplier of about 2 would suggest. First, the increases in housing and infrastructural investment is likely to trigger an increase in investment in building-materials manufacture — both in new plant and increasingly efficient operations as orders for materials increase in scale and regularity — transport, and marketing. Secondly, the first and second round increases in individual incomes would largely be obtained by semi-skilled and unskilled labourers who have little propensity for buying imported goods.[2]

Grimes (1976) estimates, on evidence from Colombian Government research, that the income multiplier for low-cost housing construction is about 2. In other words, for every unit of currency spent directly on house construction, an additional unit of currency is added to demand in the economy. Similar results can be gained in India, Mexico and Pakistan. This is supported by Moavenzadeh (1987) who predicts developing country multipliers of less than the United States of America where it is estimated at 2.35. The World Bank (1993) uses Grimes (1976) to predict a total income multiplier of 3.

---

2. As Woodfield (1989) points out, the elasticity of demand for imported goods (i.e., the relationship between any increase in income and the amount which would be spent on imported goods) is low among low-income workers. In addition, they have borne the brunt of fiscal adjustment exercises and would benefit greatly from increased employment opportunities in a revived shelter production sector.

Grimes (1976) further estimates that about seven additional jobs are created for every US$10,000 spent on housing construction — higher than for manufacturing and close to that of the economy as a whole. In the Republic of Korea, the income multiplier was also two but fourteen jobs were created for every US$10,000. As much of the labour used in construction is low income, unskilled or semi-skilled, much of the employment benefit affects the lowest echelons in society.

C. Macro level issues in housing development

World Bank estimates show that construction and infrastructure generally constitute between 40 and 70 per cent of GFCF in developing countries (Moavenzadeh and Hagopian, 1983; Moavenzadeh, 1987). The value of the GFCF in construction may, however, be quite low. Edmonds and Miles (1984) found that, in countries with GNP per capita below US$500, annual GFCF on construction was only US$19.5 per head. A typical developing country will spend about 70 per cent of its annual budget on construction and infrastructure. About 40 per cent of international loan funds are spent on construction and infrastructure.

In 1979, value added in construction averaged only 4.6 per cent of GDP in countries with incomes of less than $500 head, as against 7.8 per cent in countries with incomes above $2,000 a head. The implication is that as economies grow, construction output will grow at a faster rate. Analysis of time series data from a number of fast growing economies confirmed this conclusion. It also showed that the increase in construction activity is particularly marked in middle-income economies (Wells, 1985; Spence and others, 1993)

The establishment of a close relationship between construction activity and economic growth has shown how pivotal construction can be in the process of growth and development. It has also led to some debate as to whether investment in construction is the cause, or merely the effect of economic growth. While further research is clearly needed in this area, common sense leads to the conclusion that construction activity is both growth-initiating and growth-induced. It is growth-initiating in that infrastructure, factories, hotels, offices, housing etc. are prerequisites for further growth and additional wealth is created in the actual construction process. It is growth-induced in that income generated in that economic growth facilitates expenditure on construction facilities that satisfy consumer demands for shelter, places of work, education, health and other services (Spence and others, 1993).

Within the demand for construction, 35 to 40 per cent is for residential stock, 22 to 27 per cent for non-residential buildings, and 35 to 38 per cent for infrastructure (Moavenzadeh and Hagopian, 1983). Thus, if at least part of the last is assigned to residential areas about half of the demand for construction can conservatively be assumed to be shelter-related. Moreover as Moavenzadeh and Hagopian (1983) show, the share of residential construction demand varies with a country's level of development represented by per capita income. From the 53 countries they surveyed, at US$200 per capita (in 1978 prices), residential development had a share of about 28 per cent, while at $2,000 per capita, the share was nearly 40 per cent. At the same time, the infrastructure share fades from 50 to 30 per cent.

The macro-economy of a country affects the construction of housing through inflation rates, interest rates, taxes and subsidies, which obviously affect people's willingness to invest in housing. However, the connections running from the macro-economy to the housing sector tell only part of the story because the performance of the housing sector also has important implications for broad economic performance.

At the most obvious level, Burns and Ferguson (1987) argues that an adequately housed labour force is a necessary condition for economic development. However, it has not been established how much housing there must be in order to make some other investment actually pay off. They make no claim that shelter and settlement programmes have special qualities that promote economic progress, but only that they accommodate it. Housing development is usually assigned a low priority among competing programmes because of its presumed poor performance according to internal rates of return, capital-output ratios, cost-benefit analyses, and the like. However, Burns and Ferguson (1987) report that a compilation of rates of return on World Bank urbanization projects in 22 developing countries shows favourable outcomes. Returns, defined as increased rental or capital values of improved plots, were estimated for sites-and-services and upgrading projects. Although no global generalizations can be made from these, within-country comparisons showed that the projects fared well relative to industrial and commercial investments. The median rate of return was roughly 17–18 per cent for sites-and-services and marginally higher for upgrading projects.[3]

As the World Bank (1993) explains, the housing sector is connected to the broader economy through a number of different circuits — the real, fiscal and financial sides of the economy. "Real" effects of the housing sector include those associated with investment, output, employment and prices. Financial effects are those associated with the financing of housing and related residential infrastructure through financial intermediaries. Fiscal effects are associated with the taxation and subsidization of housing.

Some of these linkages are direct and easily measurable, particularly those associated with real-side linkages, which have been well researched. Linkages through the fiscal and financial sides of the economy, however, are less well documented. As direct spending on the housing sector averages only about 2 per cent of government spending in developing countries (a tiny fraction of the

---

3. When positive externalities are added the figure will be even higher.

resources flowing into the sector) governments' "off the books" policies tend to matter more rather than their "on the books" policies (World Bank, 1993).

The close relationship between construction activity and economic growth establishes construction in what Spence (1993) calls the pivotal role in the process of growth and development in which construction activity is both growth-initiating and growth-induced, as already discussed. Additional wealth is created in the actual process of construction itself.

The macro-economic effects of shelter policies are often misunderstood by housing specialists and macro-economists alike so it is useful to turn to a recent paper by Malpezzi (1990) for a review. Different shelter policies have very different macro-economic effects. Examples of policies with harmful macro-economic effects are those involving heavy subsidies and direct government production of housing services. Good policies (from the macro-economic viewpoint) are those which improve the supply of the key inputs to housing (a skilled labour force, a sound and functioning regulatory framework, and the efficient supply of building materials, land and finance at prices people can afford) and ensure their efficient use (Malpezzi, 1990).

The productivity of the shelter and infrastructure investments arise at least in part from being investment in an asset which yields a flow of services over time. To label such investment as "consumption," as is quite common, is incorrect. As the World Bank (1993, p. 101) points out,

> normative thinking about the role of the housing sector in the economy has, among many economists, been coloured by a perception that housing investment should rank low as an investment priority because it has a high capital-output ratio compared with other investments. For example, housing output, measured in terms of annual house rent, is typically less than 10 per cent of house value or construction cost. Such thinking, however, represents a misunderstanding of even the most elementary project investment analysis, which suggests that investment priorities be determined on the basis of the present discounted values of outputs in relation to project costs or on comparative rates of return for otherwise similar investments. The durability, adaptability, and relatively low maintenance requirements of housing make it an investment with long and stable flows of housing services (rents). As such, it is often a highly attractive investment compared to other alternatives with lower capital-output ratios, whose outputs may quickly become obsolete or unprofitable to produce.

In many developing countries, the housing market functions poorly because of problems in the markets in materials, land etc., and a poor regulatory framework. It is insufficient just to build more houses by direct intervention and public-sector spending. Instead, the required response is public action (including, but not limited to, some expenditure) to improve the functioning of land and finance markets, to provide infrastructure, and to provide a regulatory framework appropriate to local conditions (not least, affordability).

The fact that housing can be considered a social sector does not mean that it is "non-productive." Housing investment produces a flow of housing services which can, in turn, be considered an intermediate input into the production of other goods and services. In the consideration of housing as an investment with macro-economic benefits, Malpezzi (1990) requests that special treatment should not be considered. Rather, a "level playing field" is required; we should avoid special pleading, but insist that shelter investment should be considered on its true economic merits. Housing policies which are internally sound from an economic point of view will be efficient from the macro-economic point of view also. Conversely, sound macro-economic policies are a precondition for the health of the shelter sector.

1. Housing in structural adjustment programmes

In recent years, many governments have embarked on structural adjustment programmes in which housing policies have been a part, though some economists would have argued that structural adjustment and housing improvements are inconsistent. Typically, structural adjustment focuses more on overall targets for reducing consumption (including government expenditure) and less on how it is to be reduced. Governments can choose to cut elsewhere but housing has often been an easy target, with investment being cut or stifled as an ill-conceived part of structural adjustment.

The key to structural adjustment is expansion of the traded goods sector (that is, goods which are exported and goods which substitute for imports). This requires, among other things, that relative prices for such goods, and for foreign exchange, reflect their real source cost. Housing is a non-traded good and structural adjustment may seem to imply that expansion of the traded goods sector must entail contraction in the non-traded (housing) sector. However, if resources are not fully and efficiently employed, there may be scope to expand the traded goods sector without contracting the non-traded sector. In addition, and perhaps most importantly, housing and its associated infrastructure are *sine qua non* for the production of any other goods, tradable or not. They can properly be viewed as intermediate inputs to the production of tradables (and non-tradables).

Shelter policies which include such distortions as subsidies (i.e., are "bad" at the micro-level) may have undesirable macro effects. Heavily subsidized housing finance has contributed to increasing general interest rates, fuelling inflation, and increasing budget deficits in Argentina and Turkey (Buckley and Mayo, 1989); to the extent of one fifth of the inflation rate in Colombia (Ljung and Farvacque, 1988). Some housing programmes are consistent with structural adjustment (those which improve financial intermediation, for example), while others are not (simple housing allowances). In general, projects which improve the efficiency of input markets (in land, finance, materials, skills and labour; and move towards appropriate regulatory frameworks) are consistent with structural adjustment. In fact, they may be required for successful adjustment (Woodfield, 1989; Malpezzi, 1990).

2.   Effects on balance of payments

If expenditure is switched from one sector to another, the effect on the balance of payments reflects whether the shift is from a higher import-using sector to a lower, or vice versa. In addition, if demand for shelter is increased, insofar as that demand is satisfied by imports, the balance of payments will be adversely affected. In general, housing is quite a low user of imported materials although this varies greatly between countries. Moavenzadeh and Hagopian (1983) report variations in the import content of building materials from as little as 5–10 per cent in some countries to 60 per cent or higher in others. As materials constitute about half the value of construction inputs, variations in materials have considerable foreign-exchange implications; minimizing imports can have major positive effects on the balance of payments.

Grimes (1976) reported that only 6 to 10 per cent of every dollar spent on housing in Mexico and the Republic of Korea was devoted to purchasing imported materials. This percentage is higher in smaller developing countries, and averages

Plate 2. Minimum labour and maximum foreign-exchange inputs: high-technology, heavy-panel prefabrication of flats (15th of May City, Egypt)

about 20 per cent (Woodfield, 1989). The share has been growing in recent years as more countries adopt high-technology, Western habits of building, despite their unsuitability for their people. However, more countries have established industries to make materials, such as cement, locally. There is considerable scope for encouraging the substitution of imported materials by local ones in many countries. This will not only reduce the direct import costs but also reduce the energy (usually a high foreign-exchange user) needed to produce the materials. Only for high-income housing are imports substantial.

The change in net imports accruing from an increase in shelter-sector demand depends, therefore, on the import content of the housing built and its relationship to the import content of what would have been consumed in the absence of the new housing. As long as the housing built is not of the more expensive kind, there will probably be a lowering of the overall imports. In addition, the cheaper the housing units are, the more likely they are to consume very few imports. From a long-term perspective, therefore, the production of housing — especially low-income units — does not present a problem for a country's balance of payments (Chatterjee, 1981).

3.   Effects on income

As the demand for housing stimulates the demand for labour in the construction and building-materials industries, its effect on income production in the economy can be very marked. In micro-economic terms, housing is a significant component of household consumption and savings. In developing countries expenditure on housing, on the average, accounts for between one seventh and one fifth of all consumer expenditures. In addition, for the majority of households, this investment is one of the primary objectives for savings. As the house is regarded by many as the most important hedge against inflation on which they can protect what little wealth they have, the housing sector is a major factor in income both for citizens and for the countries themselves (Chatterjee, 1981). Furthermore, as the construction industry is a significant source of employment for unskilled urban migrants, the effect of increasing that employment is generally redistributionary — helping the poorer household more than the richer.

Efforts to reduce construction costs can stimulate demand for low-income housing by enabling the poorest households to participate. What is perhaps more important, however, is that by increasing the participation of the working poor in urban areas in the production of construction materials it is possible to improve the incomes of households and hence the effective demand for housing and related services (Sethuraman, 1985). In addition, the positive effect exerted by the provision of shelter space on residents' ability to get work, either by being close to employment opportunities or by having space in the house and a ready market for their services in the neighbourhood, cannot be underestimated, particularly for the second and third earners whose incomes may raise the household out of poverty (Chatterjee, 1981).

4.   Effects on prices

An increase in shelter investment will produce an increased demand for inputs. Experience in developing countries has shown that the supply markets may be incapable of responding quickly to increased demand, leading to increases in prices.

In Colombia in the late 1960s, the Government encouraged private housing demand as a means of both increasing employment and accelerating economic growth.   This policy quickly revealed inadequate capacity in local industries supplying the construction sector and it collapsed in the face of rapidly rising prices and an increasing import bill (ILO, 1987a).   In Sri Lanka, the setting of ambitious output targets for the construction sector in 1977 led to rising prices and a substantial increase in imports of materials, equipment and labour.   Construction costs rose in the range of 40 to 60 per cent each year in the 1980s, and the foreign-exchange costs of construction programmes were pushed up to between 50 and 80 per cent of the total, and the programme was seriously curtailed (ILO, 1987a).

Thus, it seems that attempts to expand construction output from the very low levels now prevailing in many of the poorest countries may come up against serious constraints on the supply side of the construction industry.   Detailed investigations of the conditions of supply in the construction sector carried out in a large number of low-income countries reveal a number of problems, as follows:

•   In many countries the local contracting industry is poorly developed. Local contractors, where they exist, generally carry out only the smallest projects. Thus, governments are forced to rely upon foreign contractors for the implementation of their construction programmes.

•   There is a very heavy dependence on imported building materials and components, plant and equipment.   In some African countries as much as 60 per cent of materials may be imported.

•   Locally produced building materials and components are frequently overpriced, of poor and variable quality and subject to long delays in delivery owing to the inadequacy of the transport system, monopoly, hoarding and lack of essential inputs.

•   There may be severe local shortages of all kinds of skilled labour, particularly of craftspeople, technicians and supervisors; such skills have to be imported, frequently at high cost, from the developed world.

These conditions represent the underdevelopment of the indigenous construction, building-materials and components industries, as well as the transport sector and the industries supplying construction tools, plant and equipment.   When attempts are made to accelerate construction programmes, acute shortages of key inputs may develop and severe inflation is probable unless due attention is paid to the alleviation of supply deficiencies and/or there are adequate reserves of foreign exchange to fill the gap (ILO, 1987a).

Increases in wages consequent on increasing demand for labour will depend greatly on the elasticity of supply. Where there are many unemployed or underemployed unskilled workers, labour prices (wages) for unskilled construction jobs (the majority in low-technology building) are unlikely to rise very much. Increases in demand are unlikely, therefore, to induce wage rises and fuel inflation. Increased investment in more expensive housing, however, is likely to have a contrary effect. As skilled labour is more important in the more expensive housing, and its supply is usually scarce, an increase in high-cost house building is likely to have inflationary effects (Klaassen and others, 1987).

The inflationary effect of increased housing demand can be minimized by increasing the proportion of local, unsophisticated materials and by encouraging larger numbers of smaller-scale producers — who would use less capital-intensive methods, more unskilled labour, and accrue lower transport costs and, thus, produce more cheaply than large, capital-intensive operations (this is discussed in detail in chapter III).

In general, effects of low-income shelter are likely to be less inflationary than those in high-income shelter. In either case, bottlenecks in the supply of building materials are likely to make the situation worse, making the comments in chapter V all the more pertinent.

5.   Effects on the poorest population groups

The women of the third world are the poorest of the poor, but their work can make the difference between poverty and hope...

Barber Conable, President of the World Bank

It is useful to make a distinction between the working poor, who with an enabling environment would be able to make a living, house themselves, and have some level of services for which they could pay, and those who, through old age, infirmity, disability, and other disadvantages, can only have a rewarding life through being helped directly by the State. In a humane world, the latter would be eligible for assistance to maintain themselves with dignity; indeed, all of the major world religions regard them as deserving succour. The matters being discussed in this publication are not focused on their plight or on their needs as they must be provided for by the rest of the State as an act of humanity. Rather it is the former group to whom what follows is addressed.

The working poor include groups of very different needs. A large number are households whose head and other members work long hours at unremunerative jobs or in marginally profitable businesses. They have been joined, recently, by many workers in the lower grades of government and private formal-sector employment who have seen their incomes eroded in real terms (Asiama, 1985). It is not uncommon for negotiations for minimum wages to fix a rate of only a fraction of what a household of six needs in order to eat basic food. Other groups may be condemned to poverty despite working as hard as they can. Female-headed households, in which the woman struggles to combine child-rearing and income-earning, constitute a significant proportion of households in many urban areas in developing countries. Indeed, numerous studies have shown that female heads of households are the poorest of the urban poor. Women are sole breadwinners in 25 to 33 per cent of all households and their numbers are growing (*Urban Edge*, 1988b).

Employment opportunities for the urban poor remain severely limited, particularly in the formal sector. In the case of women, the situation is compounded by lack of access to credit, low educational levels and lack of marketable skills. This coupled with the fact that government support to the informal sector tends to be geared towards artisan-, technical- and skill-oriented activities such as motor mechanics and furniture making which are male-dominated areas does not help matters (Mirikau, 1992).

The impasse in which poor workers seem to be concerning the improvement of their income reflects on their demand for housing which depends on what households are able and willing to pay. In the past, support-based housing projects have tended to be unsuccessful in reaching the poorest groups. Even in upgrading, which is cheaper per head than sites-and-services schemes, the poor have often been ignored or pushed out. This is partly due to the problems of recognizing and meeting the needs of tenants (Edwards, 1990) who are a majority of the poor in many cities. In addition, as affordability criteria have been unrealistically high, the poor have preferred to trade their benefits and leave (UNCHS, 1991a). This upward filtering of housing (more prosperous households occupying housing intended for lower-income households) is seen by Strassmann (1977) as a failure in planning for housing.

Although, in the past, a simplistic 20 per cent of income was regarded as a reasonable norm for all income groups[4] to pay for housing, demand is now seen as a function of households' preferences for housing relative to other goods and services and their income. In terms of preferences, Linn (1983) has identified five key attributes of housing demand: access, space, security of tenure, on-site services, and shelter:

- Access to employment opportunities, community, health and education facilities, and so on, is an important element of housing demand. Household location decisions by migrants and low-income families reflect the basic trade-off between transport costs and rents (or site costs).
- Space, in terms of lot size, is a key element of demand reflecting the basic trade-off between the size of the shelter structure and other commercial or agricultural activities that can take place on the lot (Linn, 1983).[5]

---

4. A notion rejected by the United Nations (United Nations, 1978).

5. In Manila's Tondo area the mean lot size was 66 m² (Jimenez, 1983). In Nairobi (Chana, 1984) and Ismailia (Davidson, 1984), sites-and-services project lots typically exceed 100 m².

- An extremely important aspect of housing demand is security of tenure. As Turner (1967) observed, households assured security of tenure will invest substantially more in their housing than those who are unsure of their rights to the property.[6] Also, households with secure tenure can enjoy the capital gains of increases in property value, the ability to use the property as collateral, and supplementary income from renting part of the house and from using the property for commercial activities.

- Households derive direct and indirect benefits from the availability of on-site services such as water, drainage, electricity and waste disposal (Laquian, 1983a). The direct benefit is the service itself; the indirect benefit is the resultant increase in property value.

- The structure itself provides basic shelter from the elements, privacy, and, for many households, a space to rent or a place to carry out commercial activities.

Hansen and Williams (1987) point out that the demand for housing services can be broadly characterized in terms of these five elements and, within them, household preferences will vary considerably with household income, as well as other factors. In general, the poorest households are mainly interested in location and accessibility to employment opportunities (Jagannathan and Halder, 1990). Their primary concern is to maximize income-earning opportunities and minimize transport costs (including time). Since their meagre incomes allow only for food and other essentials for survival, their demand for housing space seldom extends beyond a place to sleep (Hansen and Williams, 1987).

These imperatives create and maintain a demand for cheap, centrally located, rental housing the tenants of which form a significant proportion of the poor. Policies aimed at encouraging owners to improve housing are unlikely to help them, without special attention to their needs and characteristics, as better conditions would lead to higher rents and probably drive these low-income tenants into other unimproved areas. An example of the contrary situation can be found in Khulna, Bangladesh, where tenants are reportedly prepared to pay more rent after an upgrading exercise (UNCHS, 1991b).

Some housing programmes have been successful in reaching the poorest. The Kauwi women building in *pisé de terre*[7] ("pisé" for short) and the Undugu Society's programme in Nairobi (see chapter IV) have both addressed very poor households. In India, the Housing and Urban Development Corporation (HUDCO) is obliged to reserve 5 to 15 per cent of its new plots for low-income households. In addition, new night shelters for pavement dwellers in Delhi, financed by letting

---

6. As mentioned in chapter I, however, Baross (1983) claims that legally secure tenure is less important in some cities than perceived security from removal.

7. The potential and limitations of pisé, rammed earth blocks, are discussed in chapter V.C and D.

parts of the buildings for commercial purposes, have been replicated in other urban areas with a view to complete provision for pavement dwellers by 1995 (Sundaram, 1990). Also in India, rural people assisted in the Falaknuma Project have succeeded in establishing their own housing colony. In the project, tribal families not only contributed their labour, but also took active part in brickmaking, masonry, carpentry and grill-making for windows and ventilators. Indeed, the tribal women have broken the age-old male monopoly of occupational skills based on segregation by sex. Now there are women masons, carpenters, and other skilled jobs; a few have even gained driving licences for light commercial vehicles and heavy trucks (Seshachalam and Rao, 1987).

Countries (and cities) where average income is low appear to have a greater share of their urban households unable to afford even the minimal shelter investment. In Malawi, for example, a minimally-serviced plot, which cost a total of only US$155 in the late 1970s, is beyond the reach of the majority of urban households, even before the expense of actually constructing a house thereon (Monahan, 1980).

D. The potential for labour-intensive work in shelter, infrastructure and services provision

1. The concept of major and minor works

The theme running through this and earlier UNCHS (Habitat) publications (UNCHS, 1989b, for example) is that increasing employment and income-generating opportunities should not simply be an "optional extra" but a major consideration in the development of the most suitable approach to shelter delivery. It examines, therefore, the potential for reducing costs and improving efficiency in the provision, maintenance and management of urban services while at the same time increasing employment opportunities.

In most developing countries, the informal sector is largely responsible for the provision of shelter in low-income settlements but, because very little hard data exist, it is difficult to estimate its contribution to the construction sector and to economic development. Estimates made for some countries, however, leave little doubt that the contribution is very substantial.

In their ability to take part in housing and infrastructure provision independently of, and sometimes despite harassment from, public authorities, the low-income groups may be seen as potential workforces, willing to contribute labour for no monetary reward, in the interests of some improvement in their living conditions. The Marxist critics of Turner's philosophical stance have argued that it is wrong that the poor should have to labour and contribute in other ways in order to enjoy the facilities which the better-off receive as of right. In what circumstances is it reasonable to expect people to contribute free labour and under what circumstances should they be paid a wage? These are issues which have exercised the ILO in its capacity as a promoter of improved working conditions on behalf of governments, employers and workers.

As suggested by the ILO, a clear distinction between "major works" and "minor works" is helpful in creating a sustainable approach to employment-intensive development in the urban sector. UNCHS (Habitat) concurs with this view for the shelter sector. As Lyby (1992) points out, in the urban context, major works are those which are based on wage labour and minor works are those within which a labour or cash contribution from client groups is acceptable. Two Conventions on human rights are important here, the Forced Labour Convention, 1930 (No. 29), and the Abolition of Forced Labour Convention, 1957 (No. 105), which were established in order to curtail abuse in cases in which people were forced to work for no payment in tasks for which they would normally be entitled to a wage. In the Abolition of Forced Labour Convention, 1957 (No. 105), the most important case of forced labour which is of concern here is that used "as a method of mobilising and using labour for purposes of economic development" (quoted in Mayer, 1989). The Convention sought to suppress this in any form and 111 member States of the ILO had ratified the Convention by 1992.

Some of the poorest countries tend to resort to "voluntary" unpaid labour owing to their lack of resources and as a means of increasing political commitment to the country. They argue that the self-help work is a means of paying taxes through labour rather than cash, and if the work were not done in this way, it would not be done at all. The alternatives of higher effective taxation or the repercussions of not having the drains or streets or other environmental improvements may create more hardship than contributing the labour.

However, the Forced Labour Convention, 1930 (No. 29), does stipulate that "minor communal works" can be exempted from the above definition as long as they are really both minor and communal; in other words that they are of direct benefit to those who contribute their labour. As a result of this, Lyby (1992) has defined major works and minor works as (see also table 3):

• Major works include roads, drains, sewerage, electricity etc., which belong to the public domain proper.
• Minor works comprise local stormwater drainage in flood-prone areas, small-scale paving of access streets and footpaths, on-site sanitation, community buildings, and locally-based waste-disposal systems. All these are items of direct interest to the inhabitants and tend to recur as high-rated priorities in local surveys around urban areas in developing countries (Lyby, 1992). The building of houses by self-help and mutual aid would fit into this definition of minor works if the people who build them also live in them as owners, or with a share in the equity equal to the value of their labour inputs, so-called "sweat equity."

In minor works, therefore, unpaid voluntary labour inputs are acceptable but this does not prevent participants being paid if resources allow. It should be noted, however, that the distinction between major and minor works is only concerned

Table 3. Major and minor works: types of activity

Major works	Minor works
Main infrastructure and services	Minor infrastructure and services
• main roads	• lateral drains
• storm drains	• streets/footpaths
• water supply	• on-site sanitation
• sanitation (sewerage)	• communal building improvement
• solid- and liquid-waste management	• primary collection and treatment of solid waste
• electricity supply	
Housing development	Individual house improvement
• new housing estates	
• sites-and-services	

Source: From Lyby, 1992.

with whether the workers should be paid rather than being expected to contribute labour free of charge as a community service. The major/minor works distinction does not govern who does the work and, therefore, receives the payment. Local, under- or unemployed people should be employed rather than non-local (or even foreign-paid) people. Thus, the wealth accruing from the employment would enrich the local area (i.e., have large local multiplier effects).

There has been a tendency for public works in developing countries to move the boundary between major and minor works in an upward direction; increasing the scale and "publicness" of the utilities provided. While European and North American home-owners are quite willing to control the environment within their own property boundaries, policy-makers in developing countries have accepted the need to allow individuals or groups to dig drains and lay pipes within the public land around their plots. In some squatter settlements, residents have taken the definition of minor works even further up the scale continuum by fitting settlement-wide water mains and electricity supplies (usually clandestinely connected to the city mains).

The experience of the 1970s and 1980s has shown that most cities in developing countries cannot keep up with the demand for extensions to the mains infrastructure let alone private connections. In building sufficient houses to match demand, government agencies have been totally overwhelmed. As government projects based on direct labour or large contractors rarely fulfill expectations or needs, the community-based approach may be the only realistic alternative for neighbourhood-level public works (Kombe, 1992; Lyby, 1992). The challenge of using this approach to the full includes protection of the people in the neighbourhood from the exploitation of forced "voluntary" labour, and the encouraging of payments for workers, while enabling the works to go ahead.

Major works have considerable potential for employment creation if the latter is recognized as a priority in the selection of technology, contract procedure, etc.

Table 4. Major and minor works: actors involved

Actors	Major works	Minor works
Individuals	• take paid employment • pay taxes	• contribute labour and cash • take paid employment • build/improve own house
Communities	• execute sub-contracts locally	• form development committee • decide priorities • collect local contribution • sign contracts • execute works
Small-scale contractors	• execute sub-contract	• specialist jobs
Large-scale contractors	• execute larger contracts • give out sub-contracts	• no role
Local government	• organize tendering • technical control • support contractor training	• technical support and control • issue contract to community • adapt building standards
NGOs	• limited role	• technical support • administrative support

Source: Adapted from Lyby, 1992.

These will be discussed in more detail below. It is noteworthy that employment creation through labour-based approaches to public works are currently self-targeting because of the low wages offered. People with better options to go elsewhere leave the temporary, unskilled work to those without other options, the poorest (Lyby, 1992).[8] Table 4 provides an overview of the potential roles of various actors in major and minor works.

2. The potential for employment creation in major works

There is no place in the 1990s for making work for its own sake. The paying of unemployed people to dig countless holes only to pay others to fill them in again may have seemed like a good idea once but in these days of fiscal austerity and the need to devote every effort to meaningful development, it makes no sense. The absorption of labour is not an end in itself. Thus, the increase of labour inputs to housing and shelter-based urban works programmes should be done on the understanding that they provide better productivity than other methods, when the multiplier effects have been accounted.

The GSS recognizes that the shift from implementing (or rather failing to implement) to enabling does not mean that governments abdicate their responsibilities. It will, however, pose new and largely unfamiliar demands on

---

8. This is not inevitable, higher waged employment could be created in public works.

planning, management and policy formulation tasks at both central and municipal government levels.

As a large proportion of low-income houses are developed by their owners, the self-help housing sector has great potential for income generation among small-scale contractors and for the use of locally made materials. In addition, this type of building work makes an ideal entry point into learning skills and gaining experience in the logistics of development (UNCHS, 1989b). What applies to the construction sector, here, applies also to other public works and services. If there is a choice between importing refuse skips and encouraging a local contractor to manufacture them, there should be a supposition in favour of the local alternative. If the transport system can be operated with small buses (e.g., the *matatus* in Nairobi) or with large one-person operated buses controlled by a multi-national investor, there should be encouragement for the former.

If employment generation were to be positively valued, a change of technology could increase labour requirements for direct labour operations by local authorities without increasing cost overall. However, although direct works activities provide considerable opportunities for increased income generation, it can be further argued that there are sufficient problems with them currently without adding the problems consequent on employing more workers. Local authorities in urban areas are usually so unequal to the task of keeping the services provided and maintained that added complications are unlikely to be welcome. In addition, many local authorities are such poor collectors of revenue that their direct activities are very small indeed and the potential of major proportional increases in employment are unlikely to provide much real employment. Thus, the chief means by which public authorities can support labour-intensive methods is likely to rest on their attitude towards SSEs.

UNCHS (Habitat) (1989b) has called for governments at the national level to support the role of SSEs in the construction sector (for buildings and services), reducing the advantages larger enterprises have through preferential import practices and creating a favourable regulatory, legal and research environment to boost their productivity. Similarly, local authorities are called upon to create a conducive local environment for the growth of SSEs. Bye-laws and licensing requirements should support the use of local supplies of raw materials, their contracting and selection procedures should include SSEs using labour-intensive methods as acceptable bidders for public works programmes, and there should be a deliberate policy of using local contractors and locally manufactured building materials for public buildings.

Economies of scale potentially make the provision of on-site services by the public sector more efficient than by the private sector (Linn, 1983). In the same way, in an efficiently operating construction industry, large numbers of houses should be built more efficiently by large-scale contractors than by small. Nevertheless, the real-world condition is that the large-scale housing and services delivery systems are not well developed in developing countries in general and the local authorities are inefficient. Thus, because service provision is increasing at a slower rate than the growth of housing stock (Beier and others, 1976), and there is a widespread absence of public services in low-income settlements, it is not uncommon to find on-site services such as water and sewerage provided by private land developers or, more often, by the inhabitants themselves (Hansen and Williams, 1987). This supply situation not only represents inefficiencies (because the work may not be done adequately and is unlikely to plan for more than immediate local needs where larger considerations may be appropriate) but also represents a situation where, by default, major works are being done by community labour. In this situation, the charge by Marxist scholars that the poor are being exploited to support capitalism holds much weight. If a constructive relationship is to be developed between enabling governments and cooperative people, local authorities' and government agencies' default on service supply is not a good foundation.

In parallel with this, there is a recognition that SSEs and medium-scale enterprises possess an underutilized potential for implementing infrastructure works and providing services which are beyond the level of the community effort, while simultaneously generating local employment. To assume their place and realize their potential in the new division of labour, the small enterprises need support to become more productive and take on larger contracts (Lyby and others, 1991).

SSEs have a number of strengths which include:

• They tend to use labour-intensive methods.
• They have knowledge of local conditions, work within local neighbourhoods and can offer a service based on customers' special requirements.
• They can develop from a very small scale, often in the home, and can give employment to local skilled, unskilled and unemployed labour.
• They can use a variety of local materials and a minimum of imported inputs.

Most of these strengths are shared with the community-level works which have in the past been carried out using voluntary (or coerced) unpaid labour. Within the context of major and minor works, however, the community can be encouraged to act in concert as a contractor in its own right — as a community contractor. The ramifications of this are dealt with in detail in later sections of this publication.

Table 5 summarizes the discussion which follows concerning the feasibility of transferring responsibilities traditionally held by local authorities to SSEs and community contractors.

Table 5. The scope for transfer of traditional responsibilities from public to private sector

Activity	Potential for community contract or small-scale enterprises	Potential problems or limitations
House construction	Ideal for SSEs but the scale of the problem calls also for large-scale developers who construct using SSE labour-intensive methods using local materials. Proved in Sri Lanka. Enormous cost savings possible. See below for services provision.	Very dependent on input markets being efficient. Government control over land, materials, finance etc. may need redirecting for this purpose. Labour force may need more protection.
Sites-and-services schemes	Road, drainage and sanitation works suitable for splitting into small contracts (and see below). House building ideally suited for SSEs:	As above. May benefit from very hierarchical layouts to separate intra-city infrastructure from that only serving local needs.
Upgrading of existing settlements	Generally very suitable as infrastructure can be developed gradually and sites are often cramped and scattered. Cost minimization important.	As above.
House maintenance	Ideal: small-scale, scattered.	Where high-rise and high-technology materials have been used, SSEs may not have the plant to cope.
Building-materials production	Generally very suitable.	Some social resistance to local materials.
Urban road construction and maintenance	Yes, as long as the right level of technology is used for the task.	Very heavily trafficked roads may require the quick completion possible with very high technology.
Rural road construction and maintenance	Ideal, proved in Ghana, Kenya, Lesotho.	Long distances involved may make management and control difficult.
Drainage	Yes, for digging, lining, maintenance and clearing.	Some need for large equipment for trunk drains unless large labour forces can be gathered and managed. Again a clear hierarchy could be helpful.

continues...

Table 5 (continued)

Activity	Potential for community contract or small-scale enterprises	Potential problems or limitations
Water supply	Small systems are ideal. In large systems, labouring work in digging and backfilling can be sub-contracted.	Tube wells and other high-technology systems more difficult than piped supplies.
Sanitation	Possible with centralized water-borne systems. More local systems with septic tanks, or using on-site composting with later removal are ideally suited.	Systems which involve the handling of raw faeces are very dangerous for the health of workers.
Solid-waste collection	Ideal.	Requires protection from hazardous waste (industrial and clinical) which should stay with specialized agencies.
Solid-waste disposal	Ideal for recycling, not for dumping, sanitary landfill or incineration. Limited in composting.	As above. Recycling requires a holistic approach to materials use in the economy.
Transport	Considerable potential for passengers and freight. Even some potential for building dedicated routes (e.g., Calcutta Metro, and railways generally).	Needs controls for passenger and others' safety and to ensure that uneconomic but socially necessary routes are served.

Source: UNCHS, 1993d.

III. Employment potential in the process of housing provision

A. Construction of new houses

> *...no species of skilled labour...seems more easy to learn than that of masons or bricklayers*
>
> Adam Smith, *The Wealth of Nations*

Dwellings are the leading output of the construction sector if both formal and informal building activities are counted. Formal and informal housing tend to be conceptualized as different in quality; formal housing is characterized as using more durable inputs and will last longer than informal housing. There is also a tendency to assume that formal housing should be built by formal-sector enterprises whereas this is not necessarily either the case in reality nor need it be an aim of policy. On the contrary, there is a strong argument in favour of involvement of small-scale informal construction enterprises in the execution of housing projects. They use more unskilled labour, fewer imports and less hard currency (Bhattacharjee and Nientied, 1987). This section examines the potential for increased employment in construction, in particular through the informal sector and SSEs.

The construction sector in developed countries tends to employ around 8 per cent of the economically-active population. In the least developed countries, however, the official figure is only about 3 per cent[1] (ILO, 1987a). The formal construction industry in developing countries currently tends to rely on equipment-intensive methods. On average, the proportion of the population employed in the construction sector is only one fifth of that of industrialized countries (UNCHS, 1989b). Even where labour is plentiful and inexpensive, highly capital-intensive methods have been used and represent a commitment which would be expensive to reverse.[2]

Reasons for utilizing these equipment-intensive methods include the wish to appear "modern", biases in technical education towards "sophisticated" solutions

---

1. This is undoubtedly an underestimate (as official data seldom record informal-sector or casual employment) but the figures serve to illustrate the current gap between the rich and poor countries in employment in construction.

2. In Egypt, for example, contracts were signed in 1975 linking local companies with 10 foreign industrialized building companies. The New Cities in the desert and many residential areas in the existing cities are now uniformly constructed using the high technology, prefabricated panel systems which have such a poor record in industrialized countries. Similar reliance on high-technology systems has featured in countries as far apart as Brazil and Indonesia (Hardoy and Satterthwaite, 1981).

to demonstrate the status of professionals, and (most unfortunately in the present context) a desire to avoid the problems encountered in employing large numbers of workers. Laquian (1983) explains this phenomenon in projects in Jamaica where project rules stipulated that people should be hired from the area being developed. The workers were recommended by the local political leaders and felt themselves answerable to them rather than the contractor. In addition, to share out the jobs, workers were alternated on two-week shifts. In this environment, strikes, slow-downs or stoppages are the rule rather than the exception. To escape this, the superficial simplicity and low employment of prefabrication is seductive. Contractors are output- rather than process-oriented and profit- rather than employment-maximizing.

Governments and private developers with an eye on meeting delivery deadlines within known costs (even though they may be high), favour large- and medium-sized contractors who tend to use mechanized methods and imported goods in preference to labour-intensive methods and locally made components. They are often protected from supply bottlenecks and fluctuating prices by being given import concessions and tax breaks so that their materials may be many times cheaper, and certainly more readily available, than those used by the SSEs which would compete with them.

Plate 3. Labour-intensive house construction by small-scale contractors (Kathmandu, Nepal)

In countries where labour is abundant, increased construction activity would be one sure way to increase employment. As a recent UNCHS (Habitat) (1989b) publication points out, and as a number of authors have suggested (UNIDO, 1969; Germidis, 1974), construction has the potential to be a very labour-intensive sector, particularly so when housing is concerned. An analysis of a low-cost housing project in Ghana (Ziss and Schiller, 1982), suggests that 30 per cent of the construction cost can be attributed to labour utilized directly in the construction process and an additional 11 per cent to labour utilized indirectly in the production and distribution of construction materials. A study by UNCHS (Habitat) (1982) suggests that the share of labour in total cost of construction of core housing is probably around 25 per cent.

The literature is also clear that there are considerable differences in employment potential (and whether the low-income groups benefit from the jobs) depending on whether investments are directed to housing low-income or high-income households. Low-income housing developments in the formal sector tend to be more labour-intensive than high-income housing. Strassmann's study in Mexico (1970) points out that the cheaper the conventional housing, the greater is the proportion of total construction cost that goes to labour. A more elaborate study of low-income housing in Kenya also shows that less expensive forms of housing generate more employment (Hughes, 1976). Syagga (1989) argues that, in Kenya, the labour to materials ratio is 45:55 for low-income housing whereas it is 30:70 for high-income housing.

Plate 4. Labour-intensive construction, a stone mason (Cairo, Egypt)

Employment potential in housing provision   53

In a study carried out in Sri Lanka, the employment generated by three types of house, conventional, luxury and traditional, was compared (Ganesan, 1975).[3] The employment generated in construction of the three types of houses is shown in table 6. The employment considered is the total amount generated from the house building, including on-site labour, labour in the production of building materials, in the supply of raw materials to the building materials industries, and in trade and services.[4] It can be seen that the conventional and traditional houses generate about the same amount of employment for each unit of expenditure, but the luxury house generates only half this amount. The primary reason for this difference is the higher level of services and finishes in the luxury house.

Spence and others (1993) explore the possibility of predicting the amount of employment likely to be generated in building housing for likely levels of population growth. Assumptions are made that the current average amount of living space per head of population in the urban areas of low-income countries (6 m²) would be maintained, and that the urban population is growing at 6 per cent a year (a typical figure for many urban areas in developing countries in the 1980s). Table 6 shows that traditional and conventional methods generate in the order of 0.04 to 0.1 jobs per m². These are shown to create employment for between 1.8 per cent and 3.6 per cent of the total population (maybe up to 10 per cent of the workforce) in addition to whatever employment is generated by the construction of roads and infrastructure.

These figures are very considerably higher than previous estimates in employment in construction, which suggests that for countries with a GNP per

Table 6. Employment generated by construction (Sri Lanka)

House type	Average area (m²)	Cost (Rs/m²)	Employment generated (work-years)	
			Per m²	Per Rs million expenditure
Luxury	181	475	0.133	280
Conventional	50	190	0.097	510
Traditional	37	76	0.038	500

Source: Spence and others, 1993.

3. The conventional house was made with fully permanent materials (brick walls, clay tiles on timber roof, lime and cement mortar for foundations and flooring), but had very limited servicing. The luxury house had the same material for walls, but used cement-based roofing sheets. It was fully serviced with electricity and electrical fittings, water, flush sanitation and had a high standard of finishes. The traditional house used local materials, such as clay for walls, round wood and thatch for roofing.

4. The indirect employment effects of shelter construction are dealt with in detail in following chapters.

capita of less than US$1,000, less than 1 per cent of the population may be employed directly in construction of all types and a further 1 per cent indirectly. In very-low-income countries the estimates would be half of this amount (ILO, 1987). Spence and others (1993) explain that the difference between their calculations and the ILO figures may be traced to one or both of two issues. First, they may point to a considerable amount of hidden employment in urban construction. The employment is hidden because it takes place largely unreported, much of it in local small-scale building-materials manufacture and associated services. Secondly, the assumptions of 6 m² per person, actually constructed, to the existing regulations, and using locally produced materials, may be unrealistic. Nevertheless, the figures do indicate the very significant potential for employment generation through house construction.

In the building of the standard house used in Strassmann's (1985a) study,[5] labour costs ranged from 15 per cent of the total in Sri Lanka to nearly 30 per cent in Tunisia and averaged 21.7 per cent. It took 224 workdays to build the house according to the workers, and 183 work-days according to builders. If the unit was changed so that the share of the shell in total costs fell, the share of labour costs was found to rise, but the rising proportion of skilled workers nevertheless was found to lower employment by a fourth or more compared with the standard plan.

It should be noted that these figures refer to "formal" housing meaning that the units, built within the building regulations, are served with running water supply, power etc., and thus include such facilities as kitchen, bathroom and toilet. In consequence, a wide variety of manufactured construction materials are also utilized. The study estimates that the construction of such a unit requires a total of 17.4 work-months (Sethuraman, 1985).

The more public policy favours conventionally-built apartments, single-household dwellings on their own plots, and estate development, the greater will be the use of skilled and supervisory, as against unskilled, labour, and the more capital-(and import-) intensive methods and materials will be used in the formal building sector.[6] By the same token, a shift to self-help or low-income housing will help the informal sector with its greater labour-intensity, use of indigenous techniques, unskilled labour, and small firms and operators.

Employment generation through construction not only depends on the sheer quantity of skilled labour and supervisors, but also on the ease or difficulty of training more of them. If the quantity is low and the difficulty of training is great, relatively high wages for skilled workers will be an inducement to use more

---

5. A standard house plan was developed for which cost and employment estimates were obtained in seven developing countries. The house was a small, single-storey, flat-roofed, rectangular dwelling covering an area of 24.9 m².

6. The pisé building technique (Tipple, 1993) is an exception to this in that it has been developed to be suitable for operation by large- as well as small-scale contractors.

unskilled workers or more equipment. In other words, little can be said about employment possibilities without first measuring substitution elasticities. A widespread but unreliable rule of thumb has been that on-site labour costs about half as much as materials and equals off-site costs and profits (25 per cent). If this is true at different levels of development, substitution elasticities would be unity. Then, whenever wages rise 10 per cent compared with other input prices, employment falls by 10 per cent,[7] and the labour share in costs remains unchanged. However, Strassmann (1985a) found substitution elasticities of between 0.7 and 0.9; thus, when wages rise by 10 per cent, employment falls by between 7 and 9 per cent.

Employment opportunities also vary with the type of public subsidy to housing. Studies in Colombia, Mexico and Venezuela suggest that mortgage subsidies to lower income groups (for example, with household income less than $2,000 annually in 1970) tend to create more employment than subsidies for upper-income groups (over $7,000) (Strassmann, 1976).

The construction industry is particularly important for absorbing unskilled labour; giving work to the lowest income sector in the economy. In India, the National Buildings Organization has estimated that an investment of Rs.10 million (about US$1 million) in building construction at the 1980–1981 wage rate generated 624 work-years in on-site employment (420 unskilled, 204 skilled) and 1,000 work-years in indirect employment in the building materials industry and other support sectors (Moavenzadeh, 1987). In rural areas, because of the scattered nature of developments and their concentration on improvement rather than new building (as quantitative demand is relatively small), investing in shelter induces considerable employment benefits, especially in SSEs (Klaassen and others, 1987).

In a study of housing in Eldoret, Kenya, it was observed that, on average, each low-cost housing unit directly employed 1 to 5 skilled and 4 to 10 unskilled workers (Syagga and others, 1989). Semi-permanent structures used relatively less labour, while permanent structures had 3 to 5 skilled and 4 to 10 unskilled labourers per unit. The construction period was 3 to 4 weeks for the semi-permanent and 12 to 16 weeks for permanent structures. Other jobs were created for infrastructure development as this was a site-and-service project. In summary, the construction of low-cost housing projects in Kenya can generate 32 work-weeks of employment per unit built in semi-permanent materials, and 240 work-weeks of employment on permanent buildings (Syagga, 1992).

Stretton (1979) found that there are mechanisms which increase the regularity of employment for some daily-paid labourers but this tends to be at the expense of others. In Manila in the 1970s, he found that there were a number of independent foremen who maintained a "regular" workforce whom they employed on each of

---

7. Because equipment will be substituted for labour, *ceteris paribus*, to the value of 10 per cent of labour cost.

their jobs. Most members of this permanent work-force were relatives or old friends of the foreman and usually came from the same *barrio* or district. Regular members of the workforce received training in carpentry, masonry and other associated skills, which provide them with some prospects of improvement, both in terms of wages and the type of work performed.

If a labourer is excluded from a foreman's regular workforce, he is deprived of most of the above advantages, has to cope with the instability of employment and falling real wages, and few prospects of improvement. Under these conditions it is not surprising that these labourers leave the industry after a relatively short period (around two years) and search for unskilled work in other urban industries where wages are higher[8] and employment is presumably more stable. Alternatively, the labourer may enter an urban informal-sector activity or return to his *barrio*.

Stretton (1979) found that, because of the relationship between foremen and their potential labourers, an increase in the level of employment in the construction sector in Manila resulted in the migration of labourers from the provinces specifically to work on building sites. Few of the jobs went to low-income earners already resident in the city. Hence while labourers working in the industry can be viewed as part of the urban poor, most jobs within the industry are not available to members of the urban poor in general.

Conventional building relies on masons (and their equivalents in brick and block laying) and one or at most two unskilled mates per skilled worker. As the mason's (or bricklayer's) is a skilled job, supply can only respond to upward fluctuations in demand as rapidly as the supply of masons or equivalents can be increased.

Depending on the trade and country, skilled workers generally received 70 to 130 per cent more than the unskilled, with no particular trend among countries (Strassmann, 1985a). Three unskilled workers were generally used for every two craftspeople, but this could be altered by varying the house plan and its sophistication. If there was a larger share of services (skill-intensive components) in the value of the construction, more skilled workers were required. The higher-wage countries in this comparative study were more inclined to leave the shell unplastered and unpainted, hired unskilled labour was eliminated there, while extra skilled workers were needed to install more elaborate plumbing facilities.

If programmes to increase the rate of housing supply and infrastructure are undertaken, shortages of skilled labour (as in Kenya and Nigeria) may frustrate housing goals. A group of experts convened in 1976 by UNCHS (Habitat) concluded that it is relatively easy to train skilled labour through, for example, 9 to 12 month training programmes at a government training centre (UNCHS, 1978).

---

8. While most building labourers receive the legal minimum wage, this is less than the average wage paid for unskilled labour in the Greater Manila Area.

However, the main difficulties are found in training middle-level, or project-level supervisors and technicians. In addition, the group reported a need for the training of small contractors. The importance of skilled and semi-skilled labour in all types of housing and related infrastructure construction is, therefore, a major consideration to be taken into account in designing employment-related housing programmes. Training and skill acquisition of building workers is essential to prevent rising construction prices (Chatterjee, 1981).[9]

There are exceptional technologies which break out of this standard mix of skilled and unskilled labour which is required for masonry construction of walls. In pisé construction, there are nine unskilled workers (who are, alternately, mixers, carriers and pounders of laterite) and one supervisor in every gang (all nine of

Plate 5. Housing construction using unskilled labour and local materials: the pisé building method (a tea plantation, Malawi)

9. At the same time, employment in the building industry is thought to be "precarious" (Sylos-Labini, 1964). This results from annual fluctuations in the level of output, the seasonal nature of building activity owing to climatic factors, and the variations in the size of the work force required on each building site (Stretton, 1979). However, in empirical work on Manila, Stretton (1979) found that the precariousness was less evident in reality with a majority having fairly regular work. He estimated that members of the construction workforce were employed in the industry for an average of 80 per cent of the working year during 1974–1975. The time in which this work was undertaken was a construction boom, especially for large buildings, so it may be too biased to be reliable for elsewhere.

whom can be unskilled at the point of employment). One skilled mason-equivalent can control two gangs. This is a huge increase in productivity per skilled worker over the mason-plus-mates team in conventional contracting and requires a much shorter lead-time for moving into high levels of production (Tipple and Willis, 1992b).

B.   Informal-sector construction

It has been shown that, in the formal sector, lower-cost houses tend to consume more labour per unit cost than higher-cost houses. If the lower-cost house had been built by the informal sector, however, the pattern would have been different because, even though materials are relatively inexpensive, housing in the informal sector appears to consume less labour per unit cost. Table 6 shows that traditional construction creates marginally less employment per unit of expenditure than conventional construction. This seeming anomaly is explained by the fact that the construction process in the sector is simpler than in the formal sector.

Sethuraman (1985) holds that, in informal housing (basic minimum shelters without private services), only a fifth of the total construction expenditure may accrue to labour directly engaged on site. In the informal-sector in Ghana, Ziss and Schiller (1982) estimate that housing costs only a sixth of the formal sector cost for the same floor space. In line with Syagga (1992) they report that informal housing requires less labour (only 2.9 work-months per unit) than formal housing at over 17 work-months. However, the lower unit cost meant that, in the Ghana example in the late 1970s, for an expenditure of C1,000 (US$364 at that time), informal housing generated 8.8 work-months of employment compared with only 7.4 work-months in formal-sector housing. In other words, investment in informal housing is likely to generate some 19 per cent more jobs besides contributing six times as many (lower standard) dwelling units (Sethuraman, 1985).

Korboe (1993) shows how the minimum privately built, formal-sector house (a 42 m² "bedsitter" unit) cost C60,000 (US$170) per square metre to build in 1991 (i.e., net of land and mains infrastructure) while the equivalent cost of a room in a compound with shared facilities (the standard informal-sector provision) was only C10,000 (US$28.50) per square metre.

Government direct assistance to the informal construction sector may be inappropriate as governments do not initiate the informal-sector subdivision and building activities. The role of public authorities is, however, to remove the planning and regulatory measures which hinder and harm informal housing supply and provide a policy framework which helps private- and household-sector construction, even on informal subdivisions (see chapters VI and IX).

There are examples of government attempts to initiate improvements in the efficiency and viability of informal-sector enterprises in construction. The

Colombian innovation of minimum standards (*normas mínimas*) has simplified standards in irregular settlements with the intention of stimulating developments in "pirate settlements" on illegal subdivisions (UNCHS, 1991b). It is evident, however, that these have been more profitable for the developers than for the poor and that the new regulation lengthened development times because of delays in even the simplified bureaucracy. As a result, State agencies and investment banks are being encouraged to develop their own planning norms as alternatives (Useche de Brill, 1990).

C.   Sites-and-services schemes

The concept of sites-and-services is based on two suppositions; first, that it is cheaper (or at least that financing is more easily managed) to build houses gradually, and secondly, that the house-owners will invest their own labour in the construction, so adding what has been called "sweat equity" into the value of the house. Rodell (1983) has criticized the first assumption as analogous to saying that one can reduce the cost of transport by buying only tyres. Yet, the expense of the housing completed is not the main concern here, where concentration is on the second assumption (that houseowners will contribute their own labour), which has become almost a statement of moral purpose in some projects. It is founded on the idea that surplus labour, which was assumed to exist in project areas, could be transformed into productive employment leading to additional fixed capital.

Plate 6. Labour-intensive construction by small-scale contractors and self-help in a sites-and-services scheme (Ismailia, Egypt)

As it has turned out, there has not been as much surplus labour in project sites as originally anticipated (Laquian, 1983b). In some early projects, participation in building operations by the allottees (often called mutual-aid) was required. In El Salvador, for example, one third of the participants withdrew before the mutual-aid phase was completed; they were not allowed to substitute paid (and sometimes skilled) labour for their own (which was often extremely unskilled). Reasons for not being involved directly in building work include:

- lack of skills;
- the cost of time to devote to the building is higher than the price of a labourer;[10]
- higher status is accorded to a house built by professionals;[11]
- building materials stipulated often require more skills than even a fairly handy lay-person may have;
- project managers insist on completion in too short a time to allow self-help labour.

Preliminary data from sites-and-services schemes in the Philippines suggested that paid employment generated (in number of work-days) was twice as large as unpaid. Only about a fifth of the households concerned seem to have relied on their own labour exclusively (Keare, 1983). Evidence from El Salvador and Zambia also echoes this finding (David, 1983). In Matero in Lusaka, 92 per cent of the households in the sites-and-services project used hired labour (Laquian, 1983b). These findings cast further doubt on the assumption that the opportunity cost of families' own labour was zero or near zero (Keare, 1983). This has been further reinforced by G. Hughes' (1976) work in Kenya and more generally in East Africa (Hughes, 1991). After a detailed analysis of Kenyan residential buildings, Hughes (1976) stated that —

> housing projects cannot be considered a particularly good way of generating employment for unskilled workers unless...the requisite supply of skilled labour is assured (quoted by Strassmann, 1985a, p. 395).

In fact, an evaluation of selected projects suggests that the beneficiaries neither had the "free" time nor the construction skills. Given that about half of the beneficiaries of sites-and-services projects belonged to non-target groups (i.e., the upper three quartiles), it should have been foreseen that they would choose to engage skilled labour on a wage basis (Sethuraman, 1985). What has been seen has

---

10. It is assumed that low-income people have free time in which they can build and that sites-and-services schemes can absorb under-used time. This has rarely proved the case as the household which is vigorous enough to be involved in developing a house is usually fully committed to long hours of, often low-paid, work.

11. In Lusaka, this translated itself into higher rents which could be charged for houses built by professionals or with professionally manufactured materials; either would do (Bamberger and others, 1982).

been a different type of employment from that which was, perhaps, intended. Instead of mopping up spare capacity-to-work among the project participants and their kin, tasks have been contracted to SSEs and have provided paid employment.

The contractors who work on house construction in sites-and-services schemes are virtually all small-scale. The nature of the work (small-scale, scattered, minimal cost-yardsticks, etc.) dissuades the larger firms. Laquian (1983b) reports that, despite the enthusiasm of small-scale construction enterprises to work in sites-and-service house-building, local authorities in charge of such projects have been somewhat ambivalent towards their involvement; as if it were somehow wrong. Ironically, however, in the Dandora sites-and-services scheme in Nairobi, owners using self-help construction used more hired workers than any of the other participants (8.9 on average, of whom 76 per cent were paid labourers). Where several owners banded together into a building group, an average of six workers were employed per plot (60 per cent of whom were paid). On plots on which the owner supervised the work of a small contractor, about 7.5 labourers (all paid) were used on each plot. The last, where the owner provided the materials to a labour-only contractor, was the cheapest method of construction, some of the economies occurring because the process was very quick (Laquian, 1983b).

In the sites-and-services schemes which acted as overspill areas for squatters relocated in the Lusaka squatter-upgrading project, some participants had to move on-site quickly to allow their squatter house to be demolished while others, who moved voluntarily, had no such pressure. Bamberger and others (1982) report that 85 and 92 per cent of plot holders in Lilanda and Matero, respectively, employed hired labour in building their houses. However, despite a male unemployment rate below 7 per cent for each settlement, self-help labour[12] accounted for 41 per cent of labour inputs in Lilanda (a cheaper basic sites-and-services scheme) and 27 per cent in Matero (a standard sites-and-services scheme.)[13]

The reasons for Zambian participants not expending self-help labour are interesting. According to Martin (1983):[14]

> The reason for lack of attempt by householders to build their own house was more a lack of confidence than a lack of time. The original intention was that the construction advisers…would train those who wanted to do simple bricklaying tasks: not just men, but women as well. However, (a) the pace of the resettlement programme exceeded the capacity of the staff to serve the customers, so to speak, and (b) the construction advisers themselves

---

12. Accounted for by imputing a value to unpaid labour.

13. The main differences between basic and standard sites-and-services schemes in Zambia are that the basic scheme has lower standards of roads than the standard scheme, and pit latrines instead of water-borne sanitation.

14. In communication with Bamberger and others (1982), and quoted by them.

preferred a bureaucratic role of checking standards and qualities of materials used to that of training. In other words, if we had the time to mount a simple training programme, they could have had the time to use the skills. It cannot be assumed that paid labour was always efficient: much of the time the householder spent chasing their 'contractor' could have been used in building.

Martin raises important points in the above quotation. First, because sites-and-services participants employ paid labour, it is supposed that they are buying time which they cannot spare themselves. Instead, they may be buying confidence. Secondly, staff of local authorities are currently more at home in administrative tasks rather than working as enablers (training participants in simple skills). Thirdly, as is pointed out in chapter VI, there are inefficiencies in small-scale contracting, especially when an individual householder acts on his/her own to hire a contractor for the house. The time and energy consumed chasing the contractor represent lost economies of scale which a larger speculative developer could harness.

Even in projects which promoted a culture of owner-participation in the actual building operations, many preferred to use paid artisanal assistance, or leave the job to a small contractor. In the El Salvador projects, while 27.6 per cent (by value) of the labour came through mutual-aid, the whole of the remainder was hired.[15] In terms of scale of employment, each house provided an average of 2.5 work-months mutual-aid work, 2.2 work-months for labour hired by the owner, and 1.7 work-months for labour hired by contractors; a total of 6.5 work-months labour per house (Laquian, 1983b).

D.   Upgrading of existing housing

Upgrading can be considered in two ways:

* the upgrading of infrastructure in a settlement by government or other initiative with house improvement following as an integral part of the project (this is discussed in chapter IV);
* the upgrading of the housing stock independently of any servicing plans or projects. This is distinguished from maintenance by its scale (involving major building operations) and its likelihood of including extensions and even complete rebuilding of units.

Because of its incremental nature and small scale, the renovation and extension of houses has traditionally attracted smaller-scale contractors than new housing developments. For a medium-to large-scale company, the overhead costs

---

15. 38.6 per cent were hired directly by the participants, 33 per cent by small contractors, and 0.8 per cent by cooperatives.

of doing small contracts are just too high for their profitability. Small companies and individual tradespeople, however, have thrived on the low-technology, low front-end cost environment in which renovations and extensions are carried out. Capital equipment can be limited to small-scale machinery, wheelbarrows, hand tools and, perhaps, scaffolding. Water and power are usually available on site from the existing building, security of materials and equipment are ensured because the site is occupied.

As fairly large numbers of post-Second World War government housing projects reach the end of their economic lives, the upgrading of houses within settlement upgrading is not limited to informal areas. It is becoming a major concern of hard-pressed local- and central-government housing departments. Some have "solved" the problem simply by abdicating responsibility; they have either passed ownership over to the former renters (or anyone who wanted them if the renters did not) as they stood, or they have ignored the scale of the problem by continuing with ad hoc repairs. When the renovation work is carried out, the potential for using SSEs is considerable except where high-technology and high-rise buildings have been used. The process could be treated as a very intensive version of the maintenance exercise which is dealt with below.

Upgrading of the housing stock has been observed by a small but increasing number of scholars. In a recent review of the literature on such work in government-built housing areas, Tipple (1991) demonstrated how these so called "transformations" are carried out, mainly by self-help or small-scale contractors in a very-labour-intensive fashion. In a recent study of transformation activity in multi-storey walk-up flats in Egypt, Kardash (1990) describes the contracting system for the four- or five-storey stack extensions made cooperatively by householders and implemented by small contractors. She presents a detailed study of a contractor called Bassioni who employs a carpenter, a blacksmith, and three helpers as permanent staff and hires labour on a daily basis. He obtains work through personal contacts in the area where he has lived all his life. Not only does he assist the extenders with the financing of their project through working on credit with a half down and 20 months to pay the rest, but he also assists workers to set up on their own by buying them enough timber for shuttering to lay 5 m² of concrete, again on credit with time to pay. Even though Bassioni appears to be the personification of a public spirited entrepreneur, he has to complete his work rapidly to avoid problems with the police because the extensions encroach on public land. He has served six months' imprisonment, paid £E10,000 (US$3,000) in fines, and has learned to keep some labourers standing by in case his workers are arrested while constructing an extension stack. Although he knows he is acting illegally (and has suffered for it), he believes that he should continue to help people follow the tenets of Islam and separate boys' and girls' sleeping accommodation by extending the one- and two-roomed flats.

Not all the employment created in upgrading is related to production or servicing of buildings and their contents. The presence of large numbers of hungry workers on-site can generate economic activity to feed them. Treiger and Faerstein (1987) report that, during the implementation phase of upgrading 13 residential areas in the Zonal Improvement Programme in Metropolitan Manila, a large number of *biroscas* began operating, selling refreshments. It appeared that everyone with a refrigerator sold drinks to the workers. Most of these operations were discontinued when the workers left the sites.

E. Maintenance of existing housing

Traditionally a labour-intensive task, the employment potential for maintenance is increased as the housing stock expands. However, the extent of the income multipliers is largely dependent on technology. Traditional technologies in developing countries, largely originating in subsistence agricultural communities, have minimized capital cost through accepting considerable maintenance commitments. Because of the seasonal nature of agricultural life, off-season time could be spent on maintaining housing — replacing bamboo mats as they rotted, replastering a mud wall after a heavy rainy season, rethatching a roof. The materials were readily available and cheap (or free) and time was not of the essence.

Housing technologies inherited from industrialized countries tend to use the concept of cost-in-use, adding capital and maintenance cost over an economic life. This leads municipal engineers to minimize maintenance through high capital cost. If the materials are durable, the argument goes, lifetime cost is reduced because maintenance can be minimal. In a society where labour is scarce and expensive, this is a very cogent argument. In developing countries, however, where labour (even in cities) is plentiful and relatively cheap, but capital is very scarce and expensive, the argument for reducing maintenance by dint of increasing initial quality and cost (and, thereby, increasingly substituting capital for labour) loses some of its logical appeal. However, low-maintenance materials and technology have been adopted in many developing countries despite the abundance of labour and scarcity of capital.

High-technology building methods not only, in theory, reduce the need for maintenance (by the use of very durable materials) but also reduce the ability of ordinary artisans to carry out maintenance which becomes necessary owing to unforeseen failure of components or because of damage. Housing constructed with heavy prefabricated components is particularly difficult for artisans to repair as they do not tend to use materials in conventional ways, and components that are likely to fail, especially joints and filling compounds, are not in the artisan community's sphere of competence. This is especially acute where multi-storey accommodation is constructed in this way because the problem of access to components high on the façade requires major investments in scaffolding, lifting gear, and other capital inputs beyond the scope of all but the largest (sometimes expatriate) contractors. As Angal (1991) notes, the most recently constructed flats in Algiers may be in good condition and look beautiful in the first few years of their life, but the Danish technology with which they are constructed will be difficult to maintain and is likely to fall into disrepair along with the earlier projects built using French and other foreign systems. The potential for maintenance using local labour, and, therefore, the scale of income multipliers, is minimal.

Whatever technologies have been adopted by governments in their direct provision exercises, the informal sector provides a large proportion of housing in developing countries and maintenance of this stock will continue to provide substantial, and increasing, employment opportunities for SSEs. In line with technologies used in construction, maintenance of informal-sector housing tends to involve straightforward masonry, woodworking, roofing, plumbing and electrical skills. Little machinery is required, jobs are usually small and rarely require credit for more than a few days. Such activities automatically fall to SSEs, often single artisans, and contacts tend to be word-of-mouth and based on local knowledge. Local multipliers are likely, therefore, to be at least equal to, if not greater than, those for new building work.

There is a large stock of government-built housing, built on the "high capital cost, low maintenance" principle which is approaching, or has passed, its design lifespan. Substantial portions of this is passing into private hands at highly discounted prices through the sale of government housing to its occupants. Thus, maintenance automatically passes from government direct labour to SSEs. It may be appropriate to redirect maintenance of all government housing built in conventional materials to SSEs based, initially, on current employees' being encouraged to become independent contractors with some guarantees of initial contracts and some training in business management.

F.   Encouraging SSEs in shelter provision

It can be argued that the scale of the housing supply problem is so great that all sizes of contractor are needed. At this stage, it will be necessary to make a brief examination of the issue of firm size and effectiveness in the house building industry, especially related to using labour-based techniques.

Given income levels in developing countries, the vast majority of dwellings will be small ones, hence Strassmann's (1985a) minimal units make a good starting point for studying the viability of labour-based small firms in shelter provision. He found that small firms producing a single unit generate most employment, but without special assistance their costs were 52 per cent above those of a medium-sized firm producing at a low volume. The medium-sized firms have the lowest share of labour costs, use the fewest workdays per unit, and have the lowest costs for this type of work. They therefore create more jobs and units for a given expenditure than do large firms. While Strassmann's (1985a) findings cannot be generalized without caveat. It appears that the most cost-effective way of building, given existing company structures, is through medium-sized firms with a volume of around 100. However, small firms could reach that level of efficiency with practical forms of assistance.

On their part, SSEs cannot compete with the larger concerns because of lack of knowledge of the "tricks of the trade" — how to programme work, control and predict cost, and meet deadlines. Furthermore, they rarely have the opportunity to bid from contracts as they are not on the list of qualifying contractors. They tend to be under-capitalized, cannot obtain credit, cannot survive delays in payments for work done, and have no insurance. They are thus both ideally suited for and largely confined to the self-help and low-income sector.

Despite its contribution to general development and the specific provision of affordable shelter for low-income groups, the informal construction sector enjoys few of the benefits of the formal sector. The disbenefits to the sector find expression in the low quality of products and services, higher than necessary costs of production, and, in some cases, patterns of economic activity which have few positive effects on other sectors of the economy (UNCHS, 1987).

It has been demonstrated that low-income housing is more labour-intensive than other types of housing. The employment of labour is not, of course, an end in itself. If it were, the existing overstaffed State housing agencies would be exemplars of good practice.[16] However, as long as the labour is not simply idle, it follows that low-income housing can be an important source of employment opportunities.

There are a few good examples of local authorities giving building contracts to SSEs. The Tunisian Government housing agency, Société Nationale Immobilière de la Tunisie (SNIT), constructed about 1,400 of Strassmann's (1985a) housing units during 1980 at Tunis, Monastir, Mahdia, Gabes and other locations, supported by a US$5 million loan under the Housing Investment Guarantee programme of USAID. Later SNIT resumed financing somewhat larger expandable dwellings with a floor space of 35–45 m² for cities, and the original 24.9 m² type was limited to rural areas.

In this programme, SNIT gave contracts only to small and medium-sized builders with an annual capacity for constructing at least 20 of the 24.9 m² dwellings but not more than 145 units. SNIT helped small contractors by suggesting work plans with schedules for hiring workers and ordering materials.

---

16. For example, the National Housing Authority of Thailand employed 2,000 people and produced 640 units (159 work-weeks per unit) in 1988, and 2,500 units (41 work-weeks per unit) in 1990 (Boonyabancha, 1990). In Chile, employment in the Housing Ministry stood at 30,000 at a time when it produced fewer than 20,000 housing units annually. After a series of reforms, employment in the Ministry was reduced to 3,000 while production rose to 80,000 units (World Bank, 1993). Such stories of inefficiency could be told in country after country; the office worker with too little to do and the labourer with no materials to move are not results of successful labour-intensive programmes.

They assisted with the layout of the site and sent technicians to interpret blueprints and specifications. Material suppliers were pressured to give better price and credit terms to the small builders. If unforeseen problems or expenses delayed construction, SNIT often did not charge the penalties specified in the contract but gave cash advances so that work might continue. As a result of using the small and medium-sized builders, costs were probably lower and employment was certainly higher (Strassmann, 1985a).

If labour-intensive methods are to be adopted, the bias towards large companies and large single contracts needs to be overcome. There is no encouragement for SSEs quite as effective as involving them in the implementation of contracts for central or local governments. It surpasses all the tinkering with details which may be suggested by well-meaning policy-makers and, for their part, confronts the SSEs with the need to put their operations on to an efficient footing.

Policy-makers' determination to plan for self-help labour in sites-and-service and upgrading schemes can be changed to accept and allow for SSEs to be the lead actors in the building process. Assistance to participants should be directed towards helping ease the relationship between individuals and contractors rather than between the individuals and the building process. Support in the past has taken the form of help with setting out or manuals on how to lay blocks, fasten roofs down, fit window and door frames etc., that is, at the householder's interface with the house itself. In future, in acceptance of the reluctance of householders to expend their own labour and to assist SSEs to participate, assistance should be directed towards two interfaces as follows (this is discussed further in chapter IX):

• between the householder and the contractor, in the form of model contracts, advice on pricing, methods of payment and the settlement of disputes;
• between the contractor and the house, in the form of access to materials, credit against staged payments by the householder, insurance, site management and other potential sources of increased efficiency and economy.

IV. Employment generation in infrastructure and services delivery, maintenance and improvement

The provision and maintenance of infrastructure offers considerable potential for increasing employment opportunities particularly for unskilled labour through labour-based and local resource-based approaches. First, they require substantially less capital and foreign exchange than the equipment-intensive technology typical of conventional investment programmes. Secondly, they can produce a rapid and much needed increase in the volume of employment, either in the urban areas where open unemployment is a serious problem, or in the rural areas where there is both seasonal and permanent underemployment and a chronic labour surplus. In addition, through the provision of employment and the creation of improved infrastructure, they can be a means of redistributing income in favour of the most needy sections of the population (the rural and urban poor) and areas which have hitherto been neglected in the development process. For all of these reasons, labour-intensive public works have occupied an important place in the employment policies of certain developing countries — notably Asian countries such as China, India, Indonesia and Pakistan — for the past 20 or 30 years. The Government of Cameroon, too, as early as 1960, earmarked 32 per cent of total investment (public and private) for the development of labour-intensive schemes (ILO, 1987a).

In the past, the provision of mains infrastructure to and within housing areas has been regarded as the task of central and local government whose land (roadways and service reserves) is used for their passage and who can have both the broad view of regional or city-wide infrastructural requirements and the resources to tackle large-scale and widely distributed capital and maintenance works. In recent years, however, urban services have been the subject of considerable discussion in terms of the public sector's ability to provide and manage them efficiently (UNCHS, 1989b). As it becomes increasingly hard to keep the potable water flowing, dispose of sullage water, solid waste and stormwater, and keep the traffic moving, the need to involve communities not only in crisis maintenance but also in planning and provision is being widely recognized. This is not only born out of a movement towards democratization of decision-making, but also from sheer necessity as fiscal austerity prevents formerly routine local-authority tasks, especially in the context of unprecedented growth in demand for services.

Agenda 21 calls upon governments to accelerate efforts to reduce urban poverty through a number of actions, including generating employment for the urban poor (particularly women) through the provision, improvement and maintenance of urban infrastructure and services; and through strengthening the institutional capacity of local authorities and administrators for the integrated provision of adequate infrastructure services in partnership with local communities and the private sector (UNCED, 1992).

In the past, the direct labour of occupants of housing areas has largely been limited to what Lyby (1992) categorizes as minor works, which involve a certain element of self-help. More recently, however, with the introduction of community contracts and other methods of employing local people in public works in exchange for a wage, the scale of task for which it is reasonable to use local initiative has increased. It depends, however, on the political will of government bodies to subcontract.

Discussions on the potential advantages of alternative infrastructure provision approaches have centred on their comparative advantages in terms of costs and improved management. In few of the debates has increasing the use of labour-intensive methods to expand employment opportunities been given as much consideration as questions of efficiency and cost recovery. In fact, efficiency in provision and management is usually associated with reducing rather than increasing the labour force.

The connection between reduction in the capital cost of the provision of urban services and the maintenance of these services can be taken a step further by looking at the potential for services to be extended, managed and maintained using labour-intensive methods at the neighbourhood level. To do this it is important to think through the separation of each service into what can be undertaken by the public sector and what might be undertaken by the private or community sectors (UNCHS, 1994f). In this discussion, there appears to be no automatic gain in employment to be made simply by transferring the functions of the local authority or government to a large private agency whose use of capital-intensive methods might be close to that of the original authority. The argument is more concerned with moving operations down the scale of enterprises to those which tend to use labour-intensive methods; switching parts of major works to SSEs and to community contracts.

Briscoe and de Ferranti (1988) suggest the following five conditions necessary for success in community-based projects:

- the communities must be involved in all stages of the project, not simply as unpaid labour;
- the roles and responsibilities of community and government agency must be clearly defined at the outset and both parties must be prepared to fulfill their obligations;
- the facilitator agency must act as a supporter of the community, not as the owner or manager of the programme;
- the contact between the community and the facilitator agency should be through staff whose primary skills are in organising and motivating communities rather than in technical matters;
- government agencies need to fulfill their limited but vital tasks of motivation, facilitation, training and technical assistance.

It is important that, in the transfer of public works contracts to community contractors, very clear guidelines are laid down such as those used in the Sri Lanka community contracts (UNCHS, 1994f). In these, the division of responsibility between the National Housing Development Authority and the legal entity (the Community Development Council) representing the community contractors is clearly laid out. It is clear, therefore, who is responsible for materials, labour and standards, when the work should be completed, and what training and assistance is to be provided. Without this clear-cut approach, i.e., treating the community contractors as if they were ordinary contractors (except for clearly defined assistance), it is doubtful whether relations between the authority and the community could be maintained at a satisfactory level for continued mutual trust.

In the maintenance of infrastructure, and the payment for the service flow, greater participation of communities and SSEs may be possible through the use of Cotton and Franceys' (1991) concept of the "ultimate level": the place at which a service is metered and responsibility is handed over to a private individual or some other legal entity. To do this is simply to apply enabling principles to services as well as houses. The following is suggested as a context within which employment can be generated in infrastructure and service delivery, maintenance and improvement.

It would be quite feasible for local authorities and communities (represented by CBOs or by individuals whom they license to operate a commercial distribution and maintenance system) to negotiate an "ultimate level" of servicing anywhere between a single plot and the whole of the settlement. At this point, a charge would be levied (which would be lower the more remote is the "ultimate level" from a house-level service) and the community (through its representatives above) would be responsible for paying for that level of service. The person or group who take over the service at that point can then provide a higher level of provision on a commercial (or any other) basis either as the local market demands or as the community decide to have. Maintenance and other activities with income multipliers, and any profits made, would be locally enjoyed. Responsibility for maintenance and pricing of services would rest close to home. Among the many advantages of this system would be a clear division of responsibility and a locally enforceable payment system. The level of service can be decided by the community but it is likely to be better value for money than that provided by the central authority as local reputation is at stake. In addition, the suppliers of mains services (local authorities and service agencies) are likely to receive more revenue as their billing procedures would be simpler for fewer (and larger) consumers.[1]

The technical requirements for such a service are different from those for one in which "ultimate levels" are single consumers. For example, in water

---

1. It is, of course, possible to negotiate discounts to take account of this and further reduce the price of the service while maintaining the profitability of the utility corporation.

supply, sewerage or drainage, a branched main system would be simpler to divide up into areas than a ring main system, but either are suitable as long as the ultimate level forms the stem of a finite sub-system. However, normal levels of ingenuity should be able to overcome any problems which may arise on existing systems and the design of suitable new systems would be very straightforward.

A.   Roads

Experience has demonstrated that labour-based road construction and maintenance can be not only cost-effective, but also result in comparable technical quality. The ILO has been promoting these technologies through the development of modern management methods, the introduction of suitable hand tools and light equipment and the modification of institutional systems and procedures.

As a rough generalization, when wages are US$3 to 4 per day or below, labour-based methods are competitive with equipment based. The construction of 5 metre wide earth roads in rural areas can generate 2,000 work-days work per kilometre using labour-based methods. This is an increase from about 300 work-days generated by doing the work through equipment-based methods.

In the District Roads Programme in Botswana, all construction and maintenance operations are carried out by labour-based methods. Haulage is by donkey carts which were specifically designed for the programme, locally manufactured and owned by the District Councils. The donkeys are hired from local people. The only sophisticated equipment used are the four wheel drive utility vehicles which are essential for senior supervision and wage payments. Roughly 80 per cent of the cost was accounted for by wages with obvious social and economic benefits to the local rural population (McCutcheon, 1988).

The programme has shown the following:

•   In areas with very low population densities (1–5 persons/km²), the supply, reliability and productivity of labour were more than adequate for the development of highly labour-intensive methods of construction.

•   It was possible to develop a standard of construction which was low-cost, technically sound, maintainable by simple means, and of adequate strength to allow all weather passage of two wheel drive pick-ups.

•   Gangleaders with very little formal education but having received adequate practical training were able to produce high quality results with gangs of up to 25 labourers.

•   Most haulage of locally available surfacing materials could be carried out using simple carts; in this case drawn by donkeys.

•   The nature of the work meant that, during training, as much attention must be paid to labour management capabilities as to technical competence.

•   The labour-based methods and organizational structure developed were suitable for replication by the Central District Council of Botswana.

An ILO-supported US$50 million programme of labour-based road building in Kenya produced 8,120 kilometres of good quality gravel roads over an eight year period with 14,000 people employed at its peak, of whom 3,000 were semi-permanent maintenance contract workers. Wages and other labour costs constituted 59 per cent of the total costs (von Braun and others, 1991). In addition, 50 to 60 per cent of the investment costs went into the rural area as wages of local people.

In Ghana in the 1980s, the rural (feeder) roads had suffered deterioration until many were impassable for much of the year to two wheel-drive vehicles. Large amounts of Ghana's precious cocoa crop had been "locked up" in the villages in the past for want of a passable access road.

The Department of Feeder Roads (DFR) of the Ministry of Roads and Highways collaborated with the ILO using UNDP funds for technical assistance and a World Bank credit for capital investments. The DFR experimented by mobilizing small, locally based contractors and an underemployed labour force.

A pilot project was launched in the forest area around Sefwi Wiawso in Western Region; a particularly wet region bordering Côte d'Ivoire, which produces 100,000 tonnes of cocoa annually. A Contractors' Training Programme was set up by the ILO to teach contractors, trainee supervisors and DFR staff in a 23 week course. They learned labour-based construction techniques, work programming, site organization, setting tasks, reporting and control, incentive bonus schemes, work measurement, quality control, labour management, costing and estimating, work and labour records, and mechanical maintenance. The equipment selected was purposely light, with tractors and trailers instead of trucks and simple hand-operated vibrating rollers.

Following their training, each contractor was awarded a 5 km trial contract for assessment purposes, with ILO and DFR staff to advise and supervise; equipment was hired to them but otherwise normal contract conditions were in force. The successful contractors were awarded contract of 25 km of road rehabilitation. Within the project framework they were then given the opportunity to raise a loan through a local bank and took control of a set of equipment.

By 1993 the project had produced 26 contractors capable of handling 520 km of road per year. They are achieving high standards of road works with up to 50 per cent reduction in foreign exchange cost and significantly reduced local cost (US$14,000 per km as against US$16,000 per km for equipment-based roads). Cash and employment opportunities have been injected into the rural economy, a major achievement in poverty alleviation. The project output during the period from April 1987 to December 1993 included the 26 trained and fully equipped contractors, 45 trained contractors without equipment, trained supervisors, and trained DFR engineers, 1,190 km of road, and 2,740 culverts. At a daily wage of US$1, on average 3,500 jobs were created. The ILO has written training materials and has a number of successful training and demonstration schemes completed.

In comparison to the size of the labour force in a country, labour-based road construction and maintenance do not create large numbers of permanent jobs[2]. However, the total volume of work available to the poor is increased considerably through labour-intensive methods. It is for this reason that labour-intensive methods result in an increased total volume of sustainable employment. Also the technology, if implemented properly, does save money, allows what little money is available to be utilised in an efficient manner, and ensures that as large a proportion as possible of the capital spent on infrastructure reaches down into the low-income groups living in the area served. In addition, it creates spin-offs in terms of increased employment in maintenance of the services (see below), though not necessarily for the same people as did the construction. It is, thus, a poverty alleviation measure as well as work generation programme.

Similarly, the maintenance of urban services can also generate a stream of employment opportunities depending on the technology used in its provision and that used in the maintenance task. The concept of cost-in-use, refers to the continuing cost of a service (capital plus maintenance plus vehicle operating costs) rather than just the initial provision. In simple terms, the argument is that the choice of construction standards in road building should be determined by adopting the least cost solution of construction costs, maintenance costs and vehicle operating costs over a national economic lifetime. For highly trafficked roads the latter far outweighs the former two and therefore high construction standards should be adopted. For low-traffic roads an appropriate balance between construction and maintenance costs has to be found.

Earth roads will have relatively higher routine maintenance costs than gravel or tarmac roads and may create more long-term jobs. In the case of high standard tarmac roads, construction costs will be high but less jobs will be created for maintenance. Also repair can be carried out using sophisticated heavy equipment or the job can be done using more labour-intensive methods. While there is no substitute for equipment in some parts of roads construction, the important issue is whether the piece of equipment is necessary and appropriate for the job. The judicious use of appropriate equipment can augment the efficiency of labour-based methods.

The simple tasks of pothole filing in gravel roads can demonstrate the potential for employment generation. Experience in the United Republic of Tanzania has shown that using labourers instead of a machine loader to load the gravel used can produce 30 per cent savings in costs if all resources are being used efficiently. If the system is less efficient, an idle machine can be many times more

---

2. Two of the most important constraints are the lack of small contractors familiar with labour-based techniques in infrastructure works (as opposed to house construction, where many are active in the production of sand-cement blocks, etc.) and the lack of suitable and enabling practices in the government to encourage small contractors to become involved in infrastructure works (Lyby, 1991).

expensive than a group of workers who are kept idle. In addition, the machine cost has a high foreign exchange component and, therefore, poor income multiplier effects while the labourers' pay would be spent mainly on local produce, saving valuable foreign exchange (Lyby and others, 1991).

Urban roads tend to have more complicated design, with services underneath. Also traffic loads tend to be heavier and there may be a problem in closing a heavily used road for any longer than the quickest technology demands. However, in some locations, especially in the dense inner core of old cities, the use of labour-based methods is the only effective solution as sites may be too confined for heavy machinery. This is especially relevant in upgrading projects where sites are often cramped and the people who will use the services are already on site, may seeking remunerative work close at hand. In addition, there are many urban locations where traffic levels are very light and may consist mainly of light-weight vehicles, motorised rickshaws, donkey carts, etc., and construction using simple machinery and labour-intensive methods can be very effective.

An ILO/UNDP pilot scheme in Namuwongo, a recently upgraded informal settlement in Kampala, has shown the viability of hand-laid paving as an alternative to machine-laid bituminous surfacing. To surface the market parking yard, people from the settlement were hired and equipped with simple hand tools (hammers, chisels). Stone paving slabs turned out to be comparatively expensive (UShs 22,800/m²) but their production was found to be the most labour intensive, with

Plate 7. Labour-intensive road construction, brick paving of roads (Dhaka, Bangladesh)

labour cost being 73 per cent of the total cost, and requiring almost no input of foreign exchange. Concrete paving blocks produced on locally made machines were found to be the cheapest alternative and strong enough to carry loads equivalent to a 7-ton truck. The cost of labour varied between 22 and 30 per cent of the production cost for the paving blocks, whereas labour accounted for more than 40 per cent of the total cost.

In Dhaka, Bangladesh, RAJUK (the Capital Development Authority) has considerable experience in labour intensive roads construction in which organization through gang-leaders is an important feature. Large contracts provide opportunities for comparison of labour and equipment-based technologies. A recent new road scheme, in which the large contractor has 50 per cent of the road and two smaller contractors have the other 50 per cent between them, has demonstrated that the larger contractor uses rather more equipment, builds more quickly, and has less trouble controlling quality because there are more supervisory staff. On the other hand, the smaller contractors do the job more cheaply. Neighbourhood roads in Dhaka are often surfaced in burnt brick which gives a highly durable, labour-based paving utilising locally produced materials. Heavier duty roads are often constructed using brick paving which is covered with asphalt.[3]

B. Operation and maintenance of water supplies, drains and sewerage

Much of the above is equally applicable to drainage, water supply and sanitation. Major sewage works may require the use of heavy equipment to lay the large main sewers leading to the outfall. The smaller sections of work, however (smaller sewers leading to the main sewer) could be constructed using labour-based methods, depending on the designs adopted. This is especially relevant in digging trenches and backfilling where mechanical diggers would normally be used.

In the Soweto experience (City of Soweto, 1992), alternative design approaches allow labour-based solutions where they would otherwise be impossible. A good example is the substitution of large-diameter (900 mm) spun concrete stormwater pipes (too large for manhandling) with a box conduit (a rectangular section, masonry-lined trench), 1.2 m x 0.85 m, capped with reinforced-concrete planks. The function is the same but sophisticated technology reliant on heavy lifting equipment is replaced by labour-based blockwork and in-situ cement.

Drains can also be subject to trade-offs, not only between different linings, but also between lined drains and those which are unlined. The building of the drains can be labour-intensive by using manual digging and laying of linings, and by selecting the lining materials for its labour content. Lyby and others (1992) found that masonry lining would out-perform precast-concrete slabs, unreinforced

---

3. Source: Emdadul Islam, Executive Engineer, RAJUK.

concrete, plastered brick, and prefabricated-concrete linings in a squatter settlement in Kampala. However, similar comparisons would probably yield different results in other locations.

In terms of maintenance, cement- and masonry-lined drains tend to be forgotten and can easily be left blocked and useless. Earth drains, however, also require maintenance. They are often covered with grass and other soil-stabilizing vegetation which must be cut and cleared regularly, thus generating a healthy source of unskilled (though perhaps seasonal) work.

In water supply, direct labour operations can also turn away from equipment-oriented systems of ditch digging, both in installation and in repairs. One project in Tamil Nadu in India was recommended to install water-pipes above the surface, to facilitate location and repair of leaking pipes without using heavy equipment (Kirke, 1991). The provision of water to low-income areas as far as standpipes can create income and ensure payment for the water used at the same time. This can be achieved by awarding a franchise to a local individual to sell water by the bucket in exchange for care and maintenance. While it has been shown that households who pay for water by the bucket pay more than those who receive it directly through a tap, this is not intrinsic in the system. It is rather a result of pricing policy, which usually undercharges for the full cost of water production and distribution (UNCHS, 1989b). As the same document points out, "middlemen" can provide a house-to-house delivery service at little cost to users while saving their time walking to and waiting in line at a free public tap. This system would also allow tenants to be independent of their landlord for water-supply costs.

There is potential for individual or consortia of SSEs, and community contracts under the overall control of a major contractor (probably the municipal or regional authority) acting as a facilitator of these smaller tasks, rather than as executor. In the Soweto experience, a programme of laying some 65 km of secondary mains and replumbing 56,000 plots can be broken up into labour-based small-scale contracts (City of Soweto, 1992).

While the advantages of using machinery for the quick execution of works in congested areas of the city centre has to be recognized, work in cramped side streets allows different techniques to show their advantages. The difficulty in manoeuvring large machines and the resulting disruption to traffic and businesses would indicate that pipes in side streets could be more successfully laid using labour-intensive methods. There are also plenty of opportunities for labour-based methods in the laying of the smaller distribution lines, as is widely practised at present (Lyby and others, 1991).

There are many examples of successful community-based water-supply and -distribution systems. Piped rural water-supply programmes in Nepal (Joshi, 1992) and Malawi (Msukwa and Kandole, 1981) being cases in point. There are also successful examples of community-agency partnerships in the construction of drainage networks (see the Sri Lankan experience discussed in chapter VIII).

While water-borne sanitation systems allow few opportunities for increasing labour-intensity, apart from lower technology practices in installation and maintenance, other systems can be acceptable from a hygiene standpoint and provide considerable opportunity for employing labourers. The digging of pit latrines, especially the ventilated indirect pit (VIP) in all its variations, e.g., KVIPs in Kumasi (Christie and Harris, 1992) and the *Phungalutho* in South Africa (Louw and Holiday, 1992), can be very effective in providing income for direct labour as well as SSEs.

Sanitation can also be organized by community groups. In India, an NGO called Sulabh International has facilitated the construction of more than 500,000 double-pit water-seal latrines in low-income settlements (Sulabh International, n.d.). The Orangi Pilot Project in Pakistan has a successful community-organized sanitation system provided at affordable cost. The settlement was organized according to lanes, the residents of which were responsible for their part of the network. Despite little central control there are few technical problems and each lane's section fits very well into the network (UNCHS, 1991b). The project's technical staff gave technical advice and assistance only; the finance came through ordinary commercial channels. By the end of 1988, almost 35,000 houses had been connected to the network (Hasan, 1990).

The privatization of water delivery, excreta removal, and garbage disposal have been experimented with and have been found to provide efficiency gains. Whittington and others (1990) show how, while private water vendors deliver twice as much water in Onitsha, Nigeria, as the public sector, they collect 24 times as much revenue in the dry season and 10 times as much in the wet season. However, the customers of the same private vendors pay over twice the cost of operating and maintaining a piped water system per year. In the absence of city-wide infrastructure, the sale of water by commercial vendors (or through community-elected representatives) can provide a useful service. As revenue collection is very difficult in publicly-operated systems, some local commercial intermediary may be an ideal solution and studies have found that they tend not to make large profits even though their charges are quite high (WASH, 1988).[4]

Many large-scale water systems that have been built with external finance lie unusable through lack of commitment to maintenance. There is thus a need to link provision, ownership and maintenance to the people who benefit from services and pay the bills (Barrett and Shahidullah, 1992). Bassir (1991) and Joshi (1992) point out that there is evidence from developing countries that rural water-supply schemes developed by the community stand the greatest chance of being maintained in working condition. Implicit in this are community decisions about, and ownership

---

4. It is more likely that the profits are dominated by the owners of private taps who sell the water to the vendors (Cotton and Franceys, 1991).

of, the means of producing the water. Thus, the choice of technology rests with those who will operate and maintain it.

At city level, there are obviously levels of provision about which decisions must be taken at a high level and paid for out of central funding. However, mains water supply seems to offer some scope for exercising a change of control at the neighbourhood boundary; a local "ultimate level" as it is called by Cotton and Franceys (1991).

In the few basic servicing schemes which were carried out in Zambia it was intended that services should be provided to groups of 25 houses (a party section in those days) with pipework etc. large enough to cope with increasing demand. The water standpipe or the stub of a road entering the group could then be extended to serve individual houses at the owners' initiative and specifications. This approach avoids the danger of over-specification by the professionals of service standards in a context where conventional standards are too high and do not reflect the needs and priorities of the beneficiary community (Bahl and Lin, 1987) or are too expensive for them.

The comments and experiences relevant to water supply are also relevant for drainage of rainwater and sullage, and for sewerage if it is used. A group of households or a community development committee can be responsible for construction and maintenance and be paid for the work, or receive discounts on bills, or both. Within a neighbourhood, it can be argued that drains leading from small groups of houses, and those within the groups, would fall within the minor works category and qualify as appropriate for unpaid, community labour. For trunk services, community contracts appear to have many advantages and few disadvantages, not only for construction but also operation and maintenance.[5] Engineering problems encountered are unlikely to be beyond the capacity of SSEs or community contractors except where land is steep or particularly liable to flooding. However, revenue collection must be done by a separate grouping as otherwise there will be seen to be a conflict between those representing the community and those policing it.

One important difference between water supply and drainage is that, in the latter, the delivery point or ultimate level receives liquids from the community rather than providing them. In this case, cutting off supply is unlikely to be a viable option for the public authority. Thus, there are few practical sanctions which can be applied in case of default on payments for drainage services. By charging the cost of drainage to that of water supply, where a piped supply is in existence, the revenue implications of the whole supply and disposal system could be covered in one bill, with sanction possibilities built in against non-payment.

---

5. The extensive experience with community contracts in Sri Lanka is described in chapter VIII.

C.   Community-based low-cost sanitation

*Which of us...is to do the hard and dirty work for the rest —
and for what pay?
Who is to do the pleasant and clean work, and for what pay?*

John Ruskin, *Sesame and Lilies*

In the past, labour-based, low-technology systems of sanitation have tended to mean the haulage of raw excrement away from houses to be tipped outside the city. The scavengers, often ostracized by the rest of society, have to creep about the city in the early morning, carrying (often on their heads) their stinking buckets to the "honey cart." In Kumasi, the second largest city in Ghana, for example, at least half the compound houses are equipped with bucket latrines designed to be emptied daily by a workforce of about 500 "scavengers"[6] who head-load the raw excrement to collection points from where it is tipped outside the city (Hellen and others, 1991). In 1987, government-imposed staff reductions led to 400 of the "scavengers" being dismissed and taken on as independent contractors operating with virtually no supervision from the Kumasi Metropolitan Authority (KMA). Their conditions of work vary between unpleasant and dangerous as increasingly austerity-struck councils economize on vehicle maintenance, washing and disinfecting facilities, and medical care. The amount of employment created by this type of sanitation system is quite substantial, and it is self-selecting toward the poorest of the poor. However, conditions may be so unamenable to significant improvement that the handling of raw excrement is not to be encouraged as an employment alternative.

By contrast, the recent United Kingdom Government-supported Kumasi Waste Disposal Pilot Project has both monitored and recommended the continuation of SSEs being responsible for running public latrines[7] and disposing of solid waste (Christie and Harris, 1992). The privatization of public latrines operated by KMA appears to have led, in many cases, to a definite improvement in service. The latrines are cleaner, facilities for children[8] are provided in some, and the customers seem to be happier about the system (Todd, 1991).

As the shortcomings of the water-borne sewerage system — especially in cost, use of water, and problems of maintaining its sophisticated components — have become obvious in developing-country conditions, the merits of other, less centralized and capital-intensive systems which separate people and their excrement until the latter is safe to handle, have been recognized. Composting systems, such

---

6.   As the local Asante people regard excrement as taboo, the scavengers come from a minority northern ethnic group and are ostracized by most Kumasi residents.

7.   In this case aqua-privies or (more rarely) water closets.

8.   Many thousands of whom routinely use refuse dumps as toilets.

as the Ventilated Indirect Pit (VIP) latrine and its various regional versions, allow sanitation to be removed from a centralized system based on large investments in pipework, water for flushing, and digestion plants. Instead, the pit can be hand-dug, lined and covered using locally available technology (bricks, stabilized soil or cement blocks), and covered with reinforced concrete sealing panels, capable of being moved by one person, and locally cast squatting plates. The superstructure can be built with the simplest of local materials. Instead of a complex flushing and removal system, requiring a city-wide network and a large (and foreign-exchange-led) per capita investment in sophisticated plant, the excreta can be removed after a safe composting period by a person with a shovel and barrow, to be used locally for compost.

D.   Waste management

It has been estimated that city authorities in developing countries spend 30 to 50 per cent of their budgets on solid-waste management (UNCHS, 1989b). Despite this, most do not manage more than keeping up with the backlog and few see general environmental improvement without some external funds specifically allocated for cleaning up the city.

For both collection and disposal, local-authority operations which use small vehicles, house-to-house collection, and some sorting and recycling will create more employment than large vehicles, collection from dumps using bulldozers, and landfill disposal. In order to appear efficient, there are attractions for local authorities to adopt highly mechanized, and foreign-exchange-oriented, sophisticated systems. These will, however, not only have a small employment component but are also liable to expensive breakdowns. Furthermore, they reach only those parts of the city that are accessible to heavy vehicles and finally, they have very low income multipliers.

In developing countries, a large proportion of the waste produced is organic. Because of this, and the activities of people collecting re-usable items, a relatively small proportion of what is dumped may have to be collected by municipal operators. In Khartoum, many low-income families keep goats which scavenge through piles of uncollected refuse, in the process feeding themselves, reducing the level of organic waste, and supplying milk to families that otherwise would not have the means to obtain it. One study carried out in 1982 estimated that of all the solid waste deposited by households in Khartoum, 35 per cent was removed by municipal garbage lorries, 21 per cent was eaten by domestic animals (especially goats and cattle), 20 per cent was removed by people (pickers or scavengers), 17 per cent was eaten by wildlife (including dogs), and 8 per cent remained as accumulation.[9]

---

9.   Joseph Whitney's survey reported in Stren, 1989.

In their study of Orangi *katchi abadi* in Pakistan where household animals are common, Akhtar and others (1992) reported that only 6 per cent of garbage delivered to the tip is of organic (but not wood or cloth) material. Table 7 shows that one would expect considerably more of this material. On the other hand, nearly 70 per cent of the 0.36 kg/day/capita refuse produced is dust, ash and mud. This is a result of the earth-dominated built environment which is swept regularly.

Some cities have a refuse-collection service, either door-to-door or from recognized tipping places. While providing a service, these operations also create a great deal of employment. In the United Kingdom, employment in refuse disposal is an occupation passed down through families and jealously guarded by those who do it. In developing countries, however, where employment conditions are less controlled, the collection of garbage is not a pleasant job at all. Like excreta-disposal labourers, people engaged in waste collection and disposal are often regarded as inferior by the majority of the population, and sometimes ostracized (Mosse, 1993). Yet, many people are prepared to do it in return for a living wage.

Many people make a living within the continuum of collecting, sorting, and recycling waste materials. Large garbage heaps the world over have their groups of people picking over the refuse in search of materials to sell. One of the most notorious, Smoky Mountain in Manila, supports a community which lives and works on the combustible heap. Individual pickers, known as "vultures" in Cali (Birkbeck, 1979) sell their material to warehouses. Prices tend to be constrained by the cost of alternative sources; for example, waste paper can never be as costly

Table 7. Composition of garbage in sampled cities in developing countries (percentages of total volume)

Material	Cali	Kampala	Low-income countries	Middle-income countries
Organic	74.3	83.5[a]	40-85	20-55
Paper	16.0	5.4	1-10	15-40
Cloth	3.0	-	1-5	2-10
Metal	2.0	3.1	1-5	1-5
Glass	2.0	0.9	1-10	1-10
Plastic	1.4	1.6	1-5	2-6
Wood	0.7	-	-	-
Bone	0.3	-	-	-
Other	0.3	5.5[b]	-	-

Source: Cali (Birkbeck, 1979); Kampala (Environmental Quality International, 1991[c]); low- and middle-income countries (Bushra, 1992).

a. Includes sawdust and tree cuttings
b. Street debris
c. Based on an ILO study.

as pulp or it would simply not be bought. The only way for an individual to make money from garbage is to handle large quantities. Yet, any attempt to scale up the operation would lead to a reduction in employment.

In Cairo, where 9.5 million inhabitants generate 6,000 tones of solid waste daily, there is a very well established waste-collection and recycling system operated by members of the Zabaleen community, a Coptic Christian minority. During the night, garbage collectors pick up about 2 tones of wastes each and take them back to their houses. There, they sort the refuse into organic waste (which they feed to pigs), paper, plastic, ferrous metal, non-ferrous metal, bone, glass etc. These are sold to other workers who sort and clean the materials. For example, plastics will be sorted into types, washed, baled and re-sold. Then, there may be a process to turn the bulk waste into a usable material, for example plastic nodules, which again adds value. Finally, the product is sold to an industrial concern or used locally to make a product, for example, plastic containers. Through improvements in working and housing conditions, assisted by the Ford Foundation and the World Bank, the Zabaleen's own area of the city is now becoming a thriving commercial and industrial zone (Bushra, 1992; Urban Age, 1992).

In India, thousands of street sweepers, paper pickers and other workers collect refuse for dumping or recycling. Efforts are being made to improve the worst features of this system and there is a long way still to go before these occupations can be given dignity. However, the basic system of labour-intensive collection has much to commend it as an employment opportunity for the poorest of the poor (*Urban Edge*, 1979; Mosse, 1993).

There are major resource and employment gains to be made from recycling refuse. While this can be organized on a large scale, it can equally well be done through individuals and SSEs each specializing in a particular function or type of waste. Thus, waste collection can be contracted out area by area, be dumped, or be deposited for sorting at sub-city or city level. Its sorting and pre-processing (washing, baling, etc.) is ideally suited to SSEs as it is highly labour-intensive and involves little capital. Even the processing of, say, baled plastic into granules for sale to casting industries, or the casting of simple items, can be done by SSEs (Bushra, 1992). Organic matter can be fed to animals raised in intensive conditions or can be composted for sale to farmers and horticulturalists. Both animal feed and compost are bulky materials with a relatively low value per unit weight. It is preferable, therefore, that they be used in the vicinity of production to avoid high transport costs.

Although it is wise to carry out a small market survey before undertaking investments in recycling activities, it should also be remembered that even if markets are not found immediately, they may be developed. Production of compost is also suitable as a side activity for women at home or underemployed people in the informal sector, who could take it up with minimum opportunity cost (Lyby and others, 1991). There are societies, however, where composting and the re-use of organic wastes are complicated by taboos. In Ghana, for example, domestic refuse contains some faecal matter and there are doubts whether it will be accepted as a material used in the growing of food (Christie and Harris, 1992).

It should be recognized that the amount and value of recyclable waste is quite limited in low-income settlements, e.g., in cities in sub-Saharan Africa (Ouedraogo, 1992). In addition, the viability of recycling depends not only on the amount and value of recyclable waste, but also on the prevailing industrial infrastructure and level of technology in use. Waste pickers salvage those waste materials for which there is a demand from industrial consumers. For this reason, in Dhaka in 1970, only waste paper, glass, scrap iron, brass, lead, and copper were salvaged and sold. By 1980, a major change in technology had occurred and, hence, many new waste materials became recyclable, including polythene sheet, hard and soft plastics, zinc, aluminium alloy and bones. By 1985, scrap tin had been added as technology improved (Ahsan and others, 1992). Appropriate technology for collection and an efficient and equitable system of revenue collection are both essential to the success because, as Birkbeck (1979) points out, the only competitive edge a recycler has over new materials suppliers is price.

On both environmental and employment grounds, waste recycling deserves continued attention (see table 8 for a summarized assessment of various methods of waste disposal and reuse). However, improvements are required to reduce the health and social costs to the workers involved. The waste pickers should be provided with training on the need for, and correct use, of protective clothing,[10] health care and education in order to minimize the harmful effects of this generally unpleasant employment and increase the efficiency of recycling (Ahsan and others, 1992).

As recycling becomes more favoured both for its environmental value and as an employment creator, members of society should be encouraged to handle waste more carefully so that collection work becomes easier and more hygienic. One of the key requirement for a community-based solid-waste system is sorting at the source. For this to materialize, a well-functioning community organization must be in place where the issues and problems can be discussed and tackled on a community basis. Lyby and others (1991) suggest that it would be sufficient to start with two bins per household — or for a group of households — one each for organic and non-organic waste[11] to work towards a system by which much of the garbage would disappear, and some people would be employed. Local markets producing large quantities of vegetable waste would be natural places to start, by providing them with split oil drums, one set for wet waste (animal feed), and

---

10. In extremely hot and/or humid climates, the wearing of rubber protective clothing may be seen to be the greater of two evils by the operatives. There is a need for climate-sensitive design of such clothing and education as to its importance, especially as AIDS and Hepatitis B continue to spread.

11. This is similar to a system in operation in developed countries, e.g., Germany.

Table 8. Assessment of methods of waste disposal and re-use

	Dumping	Sanitary landfill	Incine-ration	Com-posting	Recycling
Investment cost	None	Very high	High	High	High
Environmental effects	Very bad	Fair	Bad	Good	Good
Resource recovery	None	None	None[a]	Good	Very good
Employment	None	Few	Few	Few	High
Skills	None	Fair	Fair	Fair	High
Cash flow	None	None	None[a]	Fair	High
Operational expenses	None	Fair	Fair	Fair	Low
Use and value of land	High	High	Low	Fair	Low

a. When incineration is used as an energy source, resource recovery and cash flow could be "fair."

Source: Bushra, 1992, p. 6.

another set for compostable material. Bushra (1992) recommends the use of transfer stations, places where refuse is brought for sorting (rather like bottle and paper banks in Europe) rather than simply tipped. Owing to their small size, transfer stations allow sorting to be done more quickly, more safely, and for a wider range of components than is feasible at the large dump sites. In addition, they can be cleaned at regular intervals in order to limit the breeding of vermin such as rats and lice.

In a recent survey in Kampala, women greatly welcomed the idea of waste collection and recycling and were interested in participating in the exercise provided technical know-how and initial capital were provided (Galukande, 1991). Small collection systems in Douala, Cameroon, and Pikine and Rufisque, Senegal, have proved successful in generating work for the very poor (Diop, 1992).

E.   Transport

The construction of transport systems might appear to be, of necessity, dominated by heavy engineering using large capital equipment. However, railways have frequently been built using mainly manual labour, particularly in Great Britain and North America during last century and the early part of this. In more recent times, there have been instances of labour-intensive construction of railways and the TAZARA line linking Kapiri Mposhi in Zambia with Dar-es-Salaam was built in this way by the Chinese. Even urban systems may be amenable to labour-intensive methods, as the Calcutta Metro System has shown.

Private and informal-sector participation in public transport, and in the carnage of goods has been a feature of developing countries for many years. The *dolmus* (from the Turkish word meaning to stuff) of Istanbul; *Tro-tros* (from three-pence, three-pence) for urban trips and the *One pound, one pounds* for inter-urban travel in Ghana; and *matatus* in Kenya, are examples of the vibrancy of private transport. Although many of these modes of transport are illegal — because they ply for hire and/or because they are likely to be less than roadworthy under road traffic laws — they are a fact of life and provide the poor with a means of getting to work and carrying their goods and chattels which publicly-run transport systems fail to do.[12]

Lee-Smith's (1989) case study of *matatus* in Nairobi provides a useful base from which to explore the advantages and disadvantages of private and informal-sector participation in transport. Despite harassment, the informal-sector, privately-operated *matatus* have augmented Nairobi's passenger transport operations to the tune of about as many passengers as the formal-sector bus company. In doing so, they provide 50 per cent more jobs per passenger trip,[13] both in direct employment on the vehicles and in multipliers to the car-mechanics and other service trades. The vehicles are kept on the road through a mixture of second-hand spare parts, cheap labour and sheer ingenuity.

No-one who has visited Suame Magazine in Kumasi, or its equivalent in Lagos or Ibadan or a hundred other cities, can fail to be impressed at the hopeless cases of broken-down vehicles which emerge, brightly painted and moving though rickety and not quite straight, to ply up and down the streets laden with passengers for another few months before they break down. These groupings of SSEs often contrast starkly with the public authority or large transport company depots where lines of expensive vehicles await the bureaucratically involved procedures before a part can be replaced and their function resumed.

Road safety continues to be a major concern, not only because of the generally overladen and badly maintained condition in which these vehicles operate, but also from their conduct on the road. The quasi-legal status of informal-sector transport operations has led to problems over parking for picking up and setting down passengers. In addition, drivers and other workers must put in long working hours for fairly meagre wages, thus adding the problem of fatigue and increased human error to the passenger risk. In some countries, Ghana and Nigeria being cases in point, many vehicles used for carrying passengers and goods are imported second-hand, often as road-test failures in Europe.

---

12. It should, however, be noted that many among the poor find even these modes of informal sector transport unaffordable. The number of people walking to work in many cities around the world is thus increasing. *Matatu*-fares in Nairobi are actually higher than public busfares. A typical fare for a 7 km trip is KShs12 ($0.30 by late October 1994) by bus and KShs15 ($0.38) by *matatu*, both of which are unaffordable for the poorest groups, as a round-trip consumes more than a quarter of the income even of many formal sector employees.

13. Each *matatu* creates about 2.5 jobs. The cost of job creation is about the same as for buses but *matatus* mostly create employment for the poor.

There is a huge employment potential in the smaller, human-powered vehicles in both urban and rural areas. The humble cycle, and its three-wheeled offspring the cycle-rickshaw, have the capability of transporting a variety of loads and gainfully employing unskilled people. In Dhaka alone, there are an estimated 200,000 licensed cycle-rickshaws[14] each of which will have two drivers working shifts. Thus, direct employment is provided for 400,000 men in a city whose work-force is unlikely to be much above 2 million adults. In addition, the manufacture and repair (not to mention the lavish decoration) of rickshaws and their parts is obviously a vigorous industrial concern carried out in many small workshops, often within residential plots. Although they provide such an important service (probably handling about 40 per cent of trips in the city)[15] and take up such a large proportion of the roadways, there are no formal parking places provided for them and they must simply congregate at the side of the road, increasing congestion. As with the *matatus* of Nairobi, their status may be legal but they are treated as inferior.

Plate 8. There is a huge employment potential in labour-intensive transport (Dhaka, Bangladesh)

14. There are probably a further 100,000 without licences.

15. Dr. Md. Shahidul Ameen and Prof. Khairul Enam of Bangladesh University of Engineering and Technology contributed information on rickshaws in Dhaka.

A balance has to be found between passenger safety and the low prices which the poorer passengers require. If increased safety and regulation imposes costs which cannot be recouped within the poor's willingness to pay, the currently legitimate but informal-sector transport modes may be forced out of business. This would not reduce demand, however, and more dangerous means may be adopted, e.g., pick-up trucks and freight vehicles, for which controls are completely absent. A recent attempt in Ghana to prevent the use of wooden-bodied *tro-tros* for passengers has increased their protection from splintered wood in the event of accident but may have encouraged increased crowding in not-too-safe alternatives. As some wooden-bodied *tro-tros* can be seen once again plying for hire by passengers, the effectiveness of such measures, without a general consensus, may be limited.[16]

F.   The potential for using local labour in infrastructure works

Infrastructure works and construction — particularly those forms of basic infrastructure most likely to benefit the poor — have the potential of being both labour intensive and cost-effective, offering considerable scope for unskilled and semi-skilled workers. It has also been demonstrated that there is a congruence among low foreign exchange requirements, low cost technologies, and high employment potential for low-paid workers. As the construction industry has traditionally kept a small permanent staff of skilled workers and supplemented it with labourers to suit the jobs in hand, there is plenty of opportunity for favouring local against non-local labour in infrastructure works without having to deprive established workers of their jobs.

The division of works into "major" and "minor," with the former requiring full minimum employment benefits and working conditions accorded to formal sector workers, formalizes the relationship between an unskilled or semi-skilled (and, therefore, poor) workers and the probable lack of infrastructure in their neighbourhoods. In the absence of this distinction, some policy makers often regard service improvements to and around a neighbourhood as a valid subject for self-help, even though other, richer, households receive them as of right. To avoid such inequalities and furthermore to recognize the economic and employment payoffs to investments in poor informal settlements, minor works should not be associated automatically with unpaid labour. Rather minor works simply involve a higher degree of community participation in the choice of the infrastructure and in the organization of works and possibly of community contribution (in cash, kind or unpaid labour), whereas major works involve a normal formal sector employer/ employee working relationship.

---

16. The above having been stated, it should be kept in mind that an increasing number of people in many developing countries are facing a situation where they cannot afford even this type of public transport, but rely on their own feet to bring them to their destination.

Thus, in the Ugandan example of the road leading through a settlement but mainly used by wealthy residents of a neighbouring area, though outsiders might regard the provision of roads in squatter settlements as reasonable community action, the leaders in the neighbourhood felt that they should receive payment through tolls (Galukande, 1991). However, in his distinction of major works, Lyby (1992) moves the threshold of payment much nearer the home, so that only minor infrastructure and services (i.e., lateral drains; streets and footpaths; on-site (plot) sanitation; communal building improvement; and primary collection and treatment of solid waste) and individual house improvements can be reasonably expected to be done unpaid.

At the same time, it is obvious that the community contract concept opens up a wide spectrum of local but major works to local cooperative efforts, with benefits accruing directly to the community. As the community contract recognizes the right of a worker to his/her pay, unskilled and semi-skilled labour can be recruited just as if the contract were awarded to a private contractor. In the past, local residents would probably have seen unskilled and semi-skilled workers from outside their areas being brought in to do major works close to their homes while they continued to search for paid employment. At the same time, they would be expected to do fairly similar work on an unpaid community basis. It is hardly surprising, therefore, that contractor-built infrastructure deteriorates for want of care and maintenance while community-provided services rely on a few public-spirited individuals inspired by committed professionals in NGOs. Under the community contract, the likelihood is that (even in the unlikely event of its not being stipulated in the contract) local underemployed or unemployed unskilled and semi-skilled workers will be employed in preference to outsiders.

There are occasions when outside contractors find that they must employ local workers for their daily-paid labourers. The Capital Development Authority in Dhaka attempts to ensure this. However, there can be problems, as the Jamaican case highlighted by Laquian (1983a) shows. Where a worker is appointed by a local leader rather than by the contractor, and where the latter cannot easily dismiss the worker for poor work, bad time-keeping etc., productivity is bound to suffer. In Dhaka, problems of local politics do occur but close supervision through local team leaders under permanent supervisory staff (as with the Botswana District Roads programme) minimizes the problems.[17] The extent to which local politics play a part in labour-based works is unclear. There is no doubt that further research is required on this topic. The community contract obviates most of the problems caused when outside contractors are involved because the community leaders are then responsible for both the efficient completion of the work and for personal relations with and within the workforce.

As has been pointed out elsewhere, low-paid manual work tends to be self-targeting to the poor. This has the disadvantage that it could exploit the desperate

---

17. Source: Emdadul Islam, Executive Engineer, RAJUK.

situation of those who are most in need of reasonable pay and working conditions — the unskilled and ununionized. There must, therefore, be an element of training involved in the work, selecting the most technically able to be equipped with skills and those with suitable personal qualities to be trained (McCutcheon, 1988) as supervisors and team leaders. On the other hand, the predominance of the poor in the labour force implies that the effect of the earnings will be redistributionary. In addition, the concentration of earnings in the locality being serviced is likely to have many favourable effects both directly and indirectly.

We have seen how the installation of basic infrastructure and services is likely to increase both direct housing benefits and the ability of occupants to carry out successful economic activities. Furthermore, in the context of the theory that increasing income density leads to more opportunity for local enterprises, it is likely that increases in both the workers' spending capacity and the local multipliers would indeed be important to the economy of the area. In addition, increased earnings for unemployed and underemployed household heads may lead to housing improvements, to the founding of home-based enterprises (HBEs), and to additional rental rooms giving a permanent flow of income. Both of these latter activities would, of course, be more effective because of the improved infrastructure whoseconstruction generated the wage income for the establishment of these enterprises.

Plate 9. A great potential for using community contracts and paid employment for local residents. These badly eroded residential streets are unlikely to be repaired by volunteer labour (Kumasi, Ghana)

V. Appraisal of employment-generation potential and constraints through backward linkages

Housing investment and employment created in the housing sector give rise to investment in other sectors because the construction sector is a significant purchaser of goods and services from other sectors. Backward linkages are measures of these demands created by one economic sector (in this case shelter) for the products of other sectors. In construction, they are mainly involved in the building operation and, before that, the production of materials, transport and other activities leading up to building. Moavenzadeh (1987) details how the construction sector buys inputs from of other sectors to the value of 52 per cent of total building cost in Kenya and 51 per cent in Mexico, while Moavenzadeh and Hagopian (1983) record that a survey of 11 developing countries found an average of 55 per cent. As table 9 shows, non-metallic minerals, metals and metal products, and wood and its products are all heavy intermediate inputs to construction in the countries featured. The inputs from trade, transport and other services are also significant.

In developed economies, a very approximate rule of thumb states that for every job created in the construction industry, an additional job will materialize in the building-materials, trade, transport or services sectors (Spence and others, 1993). This constitutes an indirect employment multiplier of 2 (ILO, 1987a). Similar data for the developing countries are hard to find but a study of employment in the Mexican housing industry in 1974 showed the ratio of indirect to direct employment effects from investment in low-cost housing to be 0.7:1. A study in Costa Rica showed that 1,000 units of construction demand generate about 400 units of output in all other sectors (Bulmer-Thomas, 1982). Thus, the backward linkage effect from construction investment may be lower in developing countries than in industrialized ones. This is probably partly because of the significant imports of materials, components and equipment which seriously weakens the backward linkage effect.[1] This publication recommends that developing countries use their indigenous resources more fully through the development of their domestic building-materials industry. If such development is based upon an appropriate choice of technology, the output and employment benefits from backward linkage will be maximized (Spence and others, 1993). Klaassen and others (1987) and Moavenzadeh (1987) claim that backward linkages are greater in the human settlements sector than in most other sectors even though the data collected from official sources do not include the informal sector which is

---

1. In Kenya, input-output analysis revealed that construction ranked second among all industrial sectors in import intensity (UNIDO, 1985).

Table 9. Construction sector's domestic purchases from other sectors: share of supply sectors.

Sector	Egypt	Ghana	Kenya	Malawi	Sudan	Zambia	Fiji	Iran, Islamic Rep. of	Iraq	Jordan	Korea, Rep. of	Malaysia, Peninsular	Philippines	Sri Lanka	Syrian Arab Rep.	Argentina	Bolivia	Chile	Mexico	Peru
Agriculture, forestry, farming	–	20	–	–	40	–	–	10	–	–	5	5	–	–	–	–	–	–	–	–
Mining and quarrying	–	–	10	10	–	–	–	5	20	20	5	–	5	10	5	–	20	10	–	–
Wood, furniture, paper, printing	10	10	5	–	–	5	20	10	20	–	10	20	20	10	20	20	–	10	10	20
Rubber	–	–	–	–	–	–	–	–	–	–	–	–	–	–	–	–	–	–	–	–
Chemical, plastic products	–	–	–	–	–	–	–	–	–	–	5	–	–	–	5	–	–	5	–	–
Petrochemicals	–	–	5	–	–	–	–	–	–	–	5	–	–	–	–	5	10	–	–	–
Non-metallic minerals	20	20	10	–	–	20	20	20	40	40	20	20	20	20	20	40	–	40	20	40
Basic metals, metal products	20	5	–	–	–	–	–	10	–	20	20	5	10	20	–	20	–	20	20	20
Non-electrical machinery	10	5	20	–	–	5	–	–	–	–	–	10	–	–	–	–	–	–	20	–
Electrical machinery	–	–	–	–	–	–	–	–	–	–	5	–	5	–	5	–	–	–	–	–
Transport equipment	–	–	10	–	–	–	–	–	–	–	–	–	–	–	–	–	–	–	–	–
Electricity, gas and water	–	–	–	–	–	–	–	–	–	–	–	5	–	–	–	–	–	–	–	–
Construction	–	20	–	–	–	20	10	–	–	–	–	–	–	–	–	–	–	–	–	–
Trade	–	5	20	–	40	10	10	20	20	10	10	20	20	20	20	–	20	–	20	–
Transport, storage, communications	–	5	5	–	–	5	5	20	–	5	10	–	–	10	–	–	5	5	–	–
Other services	40	–	10	10	–	20	20	–	–	–	–	–	10	–	5	10	5	5	5	–

Key: 40 = 26–50%; 20 = 14–25%; 10 = 8–13%; 5 = 3–7%; – = 0–2% (or n.a.)

Source: Based on Reidel and Schultz, 1978, pp. 56–57.

especially strong in construction.[2] Recent reports from the ILO (1987a) and the World Bank (1993) claim that, in developing countries, about two other jobs are generally produced in response to each job generated by investment in residential construction.

Different kinds of buildings imply different capital-labour ratios and different skill mixes. Therefore, they have different consequences for local employment and use of resources (Peattie, 1987). Klaassen and others (1987) demonstrate that the beneficial effects of income multipliers gained directly and through backward linkages are inversely related to the cost of the housing. In other words, as low-income housing (especially that constructed by the informal sector) uses greater proportions of locally produced materials, higher labour to capital ratios, smaller amounts of imported machinery, vehicles, fuels and lubricants, and more unskilled and semi-skilled labour, the economy of the country benefits more from its construction than from higher-cost housing. In addition, Moavenzadeh (1987) argues that the informal sector uses fewer imported items than the formal sector and, therefore, is likely to maximize backward linkages. Table 10 shows how backward linkages and labour intensities of construction vary between different technologies.

Table 6 shows the total amount of employment generated from different types of house building in Sri Lanka, including on-site labour, labour in the production of building materials, in the supply of raw materials to the building materials industries, and in trade and services. It can be seen that the higher level of services and finishes in luxury housing generates only half as much employment

Table 10. Source and labour intensity of various materials

Material	Source of material		Labour intensity in production and processing
	Place	Sector	
Mud and wattle	local	informal	high
Sun-dried clay or stabilized soil blocks	local	informal or formal	high
Stone	local	informal or formal	high
Timber	local	informal or formal	high (skilled)
Precast-concrete panels	local or imported	formal	medium
Cement blocks with chemical additive	local or imported	formal	low

Source: Modified from Klaassen and others, 1987, p. 45.

---

2. Their argument is based on UNIDO (1985) and Moavenzadeh and Hagopian (1983). Furthermore, it should be noted that backward linkages to the informal sector might be harder to document in developing countries, although they do exist.

for each unit of expenditure as the conventional and traditional houses, which generate about the same (Spence and others, 1993). The employment per unit of expenditure in luxury houses could, however, be considerably expanded by increasing the share of locally-produced products used in the finishes and services. A policy of substituting imported by local goods could increase the employment generated in the building industry in Sri Lanka by nearly 20 per cent (Ganesan, 1975). This, on its own, would have reduced the national unemployment level from 14 to 10.5 per cent.

Table 6 shows that conventional house building creates about 0.1 work-years of employment per square metre of space. Assuming that the average amount of living space per head of urban population in low-income countries is about 6 m², and that these space standards are maintained, it is possible to calculate the amount of extra space required each year and the employment likely to be generated from its construction, as urban populations expand.

In a case where the urban population is growing at 6 per cent a year (a typical figure for many urban areas in developing countries in the 1980s), the construction of residential accommodation creates employment for 3.6 per cent of the total population (maybe up to 10 per cent of the workforce). This will be in addition to whatever employment is generated by the construction of roads and

Table 11. Labour-intensity of building-materials industries in Sri Lanka

Sector	Material	Income generated (as percentage of production)	Employment in unit production[a] (w/m)
Modern industrial	Cement[b]	15	26
	Asbestos cement[b]	13	23
	Steel products[b]	9	18
	Plastic pipes	3	7
Modern medium-scale	Cement products	21	237
	Tiles	21	137
	Electrical fittings	18	60
	Paint	7	12
Small-scale and traditional	Bricks[b]	77	1,222
	Sand[b]	84	976
	Tiles[b]	71	962
	Lime[b]	72	530
	Palm thatch	52	801

a. The unit of production is output value of Rs. 1 million (about US$100,000).
b. For these materials the labour includes indirect labour, i.e. labour generated in quarrying and transport of raw materials to the factory.
Source: Spence and Cook, 1983, p. 295 (based on Ganesan).

infrastructure. Spence and others (1993) further argue that, although these assumptions may be unrealistic in some senses, the figures do indicate the potential for employment generation through house construction. These figures are considerably higher than previous estimates in employment in construction, which suggest that, for countries with a GNP per capita of less than US$1,000, less than 1 per cent of the population may be employed directly, and a further 1 per cent indirectly, in construction of all types (ILO, 1987). The difference may point to a considerable amount of hidden employment in urban construction. The employment is hidden because it takes place largely unreported, much of it in local small-scale building materials manufacture and associated services.

Even within the use of particular materials, the technology adopted may have immense influence on the labour-intensity (see table 11). From the foregoing, it can be seen that the not unusual neglect of indirect employment effects leads to an unrealistic and too pessimistic picture of the employment that may be created by shelter investments. Even more importantly, the extent to which investments lead to increased production and employment generation depends on the way the money is spent. Public or private projects applying high standards and sophisticated techniques seem to induce the least employment in most countries.

A.   The building-materials industry

One of the most important sectors in which backward linkage occurs is, of course, the building-materials sector. This refers not only to the primary production of basic building-materials but also to industries which use the products of other building materials producers, notably cement, timber and steel in a secondary stage of production. Concrete-block making and the galvanizing of roof sheets from imported rolled steel are examples of secondary industries that produce primary elements for construction.

The World Bank (1993) identifies the common problems associated with the organization of the building-materials industry. These are systematic underproduction of necessary materials, lack of variety, and inefficiencies in production and distribution which result in chronic shortages of building materials for residential and infrastructure construction. These problems are particularly acute in countries with monopolies in materials production, import restrictions, and tariff barriers which prevent competition in building-material markets. Often, small producers cannot obtain the necessary licenses from government, and then find it difficult to enter the industry. Monopolies often extend to land assembly and subdivision, to obtaining infrastructure on site on time, and to house construction as well. Such complementary investment in infrastructure by governments is frequently necessary for the responsible harvesting of timber. Similarly, the construction of gas lines into areas where brick production can be developed may be an essential prerequisite for medium- and small-scale investors.

In view of the increased demand coupled with the decline in supply and quality of traditional materials, many governments have established large-scale factories for the production of basic building materials, particularly cement, steel, roofing sheets, bricks, tiles and concrete products. They have been heavily reliant on foreign exchange for establishment and continuing imports of factor inputs, spare parts and machinery and have often proved to be unsuitable to the local market conditions with respect to location, quantity demanded, and price.

The small-scale sector of the building-materials industry, in contrast, has shown remarkable dynamism and resilience. Despite the fact that they are often discouraged by the legal and financial environment, small entrepreneurs produce the bulk of building materials in most developing countries. Much of the activity in the sector takes place at a sub-industrial level through the work of artisans or groups of artisans. Activities such as the production of concrete blocks or stabilized-soil blocks, and the production of pre-cast roof panels frequently take place at the construction site and utilize only small amounts of plant or equipment.

However, the small-scale sector has seen little innovation or upgrading of its production processes through the diffusion of new technologies or techniques. Rather, it continues to rely on traditional production processes, which may be wasteful of raw materials and energy and suffer from diseconomies of scale. Thus, improved productivity and lower production costs have rarely been achieved.

Just as in the case of direct construction, the building-materials industry can benefit from intermediate-scale appropriate technologies which combine the advantages of small-scale technologies (e.g., flexibility in operation, the ability to use locally-available low-grade raw materials and fuel, and not demanding high initial capital investment or highly-skilled labour) with the scale-economy of larger-scale technologies. These are already available and have been successfully tried in several countries. Notable among them are down-draft brick kilns and vertical-shaft lime kilns which can replace clamp-type kilns, traditionally in use in most developing countries. They not only reduce production costs because of higher efficiency and better process control, but they also ensure better and uniform quality acceptable in the formal-sector markets (UNCHS, 1993a).

However, small-scale producers face several constraints in upgrading their production facilities and acquiring appropriate technologies. First, they do not have easy access to information on new technologies or about their suppliers. Secondly, with very little risk capital at their disposal, small producers are generally unwilling to venture into uncertain markets. Thirdly, with few exceptions, governments have been unable to provide essential industrial extension services (e.g., feasibility studies, access to credit, import of equipment, training etc.) to the domestic building-materials industry to facilitate the acquisition of new technologies (UNCHS, 1993a).

There is evidence that small workshops producing building materials are providing employment for large numbers of people in the cities of developing countries. In Central America, the industrial production of building materials, relating to the wood, chemical products, non-metallic minerals, and metal products industries alone, may amount to as much as 30 per cent of national industrial output (Aragon, 1988). The marketing of these materials generates a similar amount of value added in the commercial and services sectors, and even more in transport. Further wealth will be created through the production of the machinery, equipment and energy required in the materials production and distribution process (Spence and others, 1993).

While building materials cost developing countries between 3 and 5 per cent of their GDP per annum, they account for 5–8 per cent (not far from double the former range) of the total value of imports (Moavenzadeh, 1987). Where labour-intensive technologies are adopted in the building-materials industries, jobs are created for a very large number of people. A recent survey of building-materials production in Bangladesh estimated that approximately 180,000 people may be employed directly in the brick industry, more people than in the entire jute industry which is generally considered the mainstay of the Bangladesh economy (SKAT, 1991). As a large part of each employee's spending will be on local goods and services, further wealth is created through multiplier effects. Hence, building-materials production can be output and growth enhancing, contribute to the alleviation of poverty, and help reduce regional and income inequalities (Kaplinsky, 1990).

In order to increase housing production and employment therein, building materials must be available. This is particularly crucial at times of rapid increase in shelter construction. Accordingly, the GSS aims at "rapid expansion in the supply of basic building materials at low cost [through] promoting the small-scale sector" (UNCHS, 1990, para. 108). UNCHS (Habitat) (1991b) reiterates the need for governments to withdraw from shelter production to concentrate on facilitating the overall framework within which private and household developers can operate. In this, local authorities' planning and coordination function will be central.

While there are important economic reasons for replacing imported materials with locally made ones, many conventional building materials are made in processes that are highly sophisticated and consume large amounts of energy. Turn-key technology transfer, in which a European building-products factory is set down in Africa, has proved unhelpful because of the gross demand for electricity, the huge potential output of high-quality (and expensive) products for which demand is only developed slowly, and the tiny employment generated in the production process (see below).

Many building-materials industries, especially secondary industries, can operate at very different levels of technology and scales of production. Concrete blocks, for example, may be produced on a large-scale using mechanized processes, or in small quantities by hand — either in small workshops or on the construction site itself. Although a few large-scale plants may be found in the major cities of developing countries, it is probable that small workshops are responsible for the bulk of the production of concrete blocks and pipes. Workshops also produce other secondary products such as sawn timber for roofing, timber windows, shutters and doors, metal windows and doors, and so on (Spence and others, 1993).

Small-scale, relatively labour-intensive building-materials manufacturing technologies are generally associated with larger multiplier effects than large-scale, capital-intensive technologies for the following reasons:

- Most, if not all, the equipment (e.g., moulds, mixing equipment) may be manufactured locally instead of being imported. Production of such equipment will thus generate additional employment and incomes.
- Small-scale plants use local fuel (e.g. wood, agricultural wastes) while large-scale plants often rely on oil or electricity. If small-scale plants are adopted, the gathering and processing of fuel wood or other local materials will generate additional employment. However, this might have negative effects on local biomass resources and may be inappropriate in some regions, e.g., Kenya (Syagga, 1992).
- The marketing and transport of materials produced by small-scale units should also generate more employment than those of the output of large-scale plants (ILO, 1984).

According to Hansen and Williams (1987), most of the imported materials currently in wide use in developing countries can, in principle, be replaced by locally-produced, cheap materials. For example, lime and various pozzolanas[3] can replace Portland cement in a number of applications,[4] while fired-clay roofing tiles and fibre-cement roofing sheets can substitute for aluminium and galvanized-iron roofing sheets (see also table 11). This is already occurring in some countries, such as China, India, Indonesia and Malaysia. The problem is that knowledge about the production and use of innovative building materials which can be locally produced is limited to a few laboratories and research institutions. The gap in technology transfer, within a country and between countries, for wide-scale adoption of innovative materials is a result of several related factors. For instance, most building research institutions in developing countries lack the comprehensive structure required to translate their findings into commercial production. The communications required amongst investors, manufacturers, building contractors, and research institutions is at times non-existent (UNCHS, 1987).

---

3. Pozzolanas are substances made from natural (mainly fine volcanic earth) or artificial (e.g. fly ash combined with water-quenched boiler slag) materials reacting and creating a binding effect with lime in the presence of water. It can be used as an additive to or a substitute for cement.

4. When three technically viable options for mortars were compared, it was found that a lime-pozzolana mortar (commonly used locally) was able to generate over four times as much employment in local industries as the cement mortar option (Centre for Development Studies, 1975).

Production in small units close to markets creates local employment while also reducing transport costs. This is a particularly important consideration as they tend to have low value to weight ratio (Moavenzadeh, 1987). In Botswana, Honduras and the Sudan, the cost of transporting cement 100 miles exceeds its value. Thus, the economies of scale available from a centralized production system may be more than lost if markets are widespread and the transport infrastructure undeveloped.

In addition to transport advantages, locally-based small-scale production units can train labour cheaply and on the job, providing opportunities for women and youths. In addition, the capital investment per worker is only 1 per cent of that required for large-scale production (JUNIC, 1987). In Sri Lanka, the capital investment in the production of tiles was less than 0.6 per cent of that required to produce galvanized-iron sheets in a large-scale industrial process (UNIDO, 1985).

B.   Some examples of labour-intensive building-materials production

It is not feasible to provide a comprehensive discussion of a wide spectrum of building materials in a publication like this. Instead, a small selection will be discussed in order to draw lessons which may be applicable to them and to others.

1.   Stone

Quarrying can be a very labour-intensive operation. In an analysis of laterite quarrying in Burkina Faso, Kaboré (1991) found that a team of two labourers could cut 50 blocks of 15 x 15 x 40 cm per day with a capital outlay (one large pick and one hoe per team) of CFAF 7,500 per worker. The blocks would sell at CFAF 35 to 45, the lower price being profitable when the laterite crops up at the surface. Where stone is in use as a building material, its quarrying provides many opportunities for employment. In Nairobi, there are 350 quarries employing a total of 7,000 people directly and many more indirectly (Syagga, 1992). Production from a quarry employing 20 people is about 220 metres of stone per day. Even so, demand runs ahead of supply in Kenya.

In Nairobi, dressed stone walling can be cheaper than cement blocks. Laquian (1983b) reports that, when stone was locally available for builders in the Dandora sites-and-services scheme, small-scale contractors could produce houses cheaper by using stone from a local quarry than using cement blocks for which the project was designed. In addition, the stone houses have a special character and appeal not available from the more utilitarian concrete blocks. About 8 per cent of the owners of plots were stonemasons who gained considerable employment in the construction of houses in the scheme.

In Uganda, squatters around quarry sites have organized small-scale stone-crushing units using simple hand tools as a way of eking out their inadequate formal earnings (Mukunya, 1992, p. 3). On the outskirts of Accra, Ghana, local stone is broken up into pieces suitable for decorative application to walling.

2. Vibrated-cement and fibre-cement tiles

The small-scale production of tiles, using cement reinforced with fibres such as chopped sisal, has been developing over the last few years, largely through the efforts of J.P.M. Parry and Associates. Such tiles have since been made in projects in more than 70 countries across the developing world, using a variety of fibres. Production and use are not without problems, especially over the amount of timber required to support the roof compared with corrugated-metal sheets, and over the underwater curing required during manufacture. However, the product remains "the closest which the Appropriate Technology movement has come to a clear product for construction to be sold on the free market" (Spence and others, 1993, p. 60). The concern here is with the employment effects of manufacture and use.

A study in India, which compared tiles on timber roof with steel reinforced-concrete slab roofing, found that the total labour component of the two systems was similar. However, the tile roof generated three times as much employment in local industry as the concrete slab roof for which both cement and steel had to be imported from distant production plants (Centre for Development Studies, 1975).

The potential for the labour-intensive production of fibre-cement tiles is demonstrated by the Humama women's group in Nairobi. It was founded in 1988 after the women had watched a film, screened by staff from the African Housing Fund (AHF), depicting women living in very poor conditions but working hard to improve their lives. The Humama women identified their own needs as job training (for none had formal skill), credit to start up viable businesses, and secure land for their businesses. With a loan of about US$56,000 from AHF, the women started the first phase of their building-materials production by producing roofing tiles for commercial sale.

The first phase involved organizing and training the members in various skills (e.g., business management, housing construction, social organization and development) and setting up the Humama business. Within a year of its existence, the project had paid the women about Ksh 900,000 in salaries and had generated a net profit of about Ksh 1 million which is to be used for the members' own housing. Some of the houses are under construction and use tiles and other materials when there is a lull in sales. After a six-month grace period, Humama started paying back the loan. From AHF business loans totalling Ksh 1.3 million the project had generated over Ksh 2 million (about US$ 87,000) in only one year. The factory produces about 4,200 tiles every day, with the women working in two shifts.

Though there have been difficulties along the way and AHF help has been essential, the Humama women have in all aspects fulfilled the requirements of their business contract, making a large-scale business operation in tough competition with

Table 12. Yields from the vibrated-mortar and fibre-mortar tile
manufacturing process

Scale of production	Number of tiles per week	Type of machine	Number of workers	Number of tiles per worker per week
Small	500	Small mobile vibrator	2	250
Medium	2,000	Electric	3	667
		Manual	4	500
Large	5,000	Full-scale plant	7	714

Source: Modified from Kaboré, 1991.

professional large businesses, a phenomenon which has encouraged government officials to plan for new approaches in the development. The Humama factory has also turned into a training ground for other AHF-supported cooperatives from all over Africa (Katumba, 1990).

The investment needed to set up a production unit is quite small and the only item which must be imported is the spring-mounted vibration table operated by a small 12-volt motor. The materials used consist of 1 part cement, 3 parts sand and 10 grams of chopped sisal fibre for each tile. The small-scale producers can typically sell them at 50 per cent of the price of larger concerns' tiles (Syagga, 1992). Production claims vary; Syagga (1992) claims that two workers can produce 200–250 tiles a day whereas Kaboré (1991) claims only 250 to 500 per worker per week depending on the size of operation (see table 12). Vibrated-mortar tiles combine a number of economic advantages over other materials with respect to both the cost price of covering materials and the reduction possible in the scale of the load-bearing structure (Kaboré, 1991).

3.　Low-cost brickmaking

According to the ILO (1984), small-scale brickmaking techniques should be favoured as they generate substantially more employment than the technologies used in large-scale turn-key factories. This is especially the case where:

- low wage regimes exist;
- foreign exchange is in short supply;
- no well-developed industrial base exists;
- infrastructure and technical skills are not well developed;
- the market is small or widespread.

If these factors are not present, small-scale technologies may not be appropriate (Keddie and Cleghorn, 1978). Thus, project evaluators should properly consider all available alternatives prior to promoting one technology or another.

A study of brickmaking techniques in Santafé de Bogotá (Colombia) shows that large-scale brick-manufacturing plants produce 83 per cent of the national brick production although they use only one third of the total labour force in the brick

Table 13. Labour generation in large- and small-scale brick production

Method	Output per plant (bricks/day)	Labour input per 10 million bricks (work-years)
Small-scale, traditional manual	2,000	160
Small-scale, intermediate technology	2,000	200
Soft-mud machine, otherwise manual	14,000	76
Moderately mechanized	64,000	20
Highly automated	180,000	8

Source: CNC, 1976.

industry. In other words, small-scale units, using relatively labour-intensive techniques, require from 10 to 20 times more labour than large-scale plants per unit of production (CNC, 1976, and see table 13). Another study carried out in Colombia (Baily, 1981) shows that the labour-capital ratio in small-scale brick-making units is over 100 times greater than that for large-scale manufacturing plants (ILO, 1984). In other words, for a fixed sum of capital, 100 times more jobs can be created in labour-intensive brick-making than in large-scale mechanical plants. Table 14 shows that, from a foreign exchange and capital-investment point of view, small-scale brickmaking technologies are much more appropriate than large-scale, automated plants. Similarly, the import component of these investments is 5 to 15 times larger for the automated plants than for small-scale units (ILO, 1984). In fact, whereas the small-scale traditional manual process spends some $2 of foreign exchange per 10,000 bricks produced, an advanced mechanical plant spends $3,000, i.e., 1,500 times as much! Capital investments in large-scale plants are 6 to 100 times larger than those for small-scale plants.

Not only is the generation of work through brick-making important — as a major component of the cost of a house is that of building materials (particularly in low-cost and self-help housing) — it is also important to keep their prices down. Brick-production techniques and scales of production which minimize unit production costs should, therefore, be favoured. Although reliable estimates of

Table 14. Capital costs and foreign-exchange inputs

Description of brickmaking processes	Total cost for 10 million bricks per year (US$ thousands)	Proportion of costs (percentage)	
		Import	Local
Small-scale, traditional manual process	34	5	95
Small-scale, intermediate technology	578	15	85
Mechanical plant with Hoffman kiln	3,880	75	25

Source: Parry, 1983.

Table 15. Unit production costs

| Classification of brickmaking process | Unit production cost (US cents per bricks) | |
	Medium-wage regime[a]	Low-wage regime[a]
Capital-intensive, all year round	6.5	6.2
"Least-cost", all year round	3.1	2.3
"Least-cost", seasonal working only	2.9	2.0

a. Medium- and low-wage regimes refer to assumed wages for unskilled workers in middle-ranking and poorer developing countries in 1977.

Source: Keddie and Cleghorn, 1978.

these costs are not available, studies tend to indicate that small-scale plants, using intermediate technologies, produce bricks at a cost two to three times lower than that of bricks produced in large-scale, capital-intensive plants (see table 15).

Experience on the ground has been generally good. In Lusaka, the cost of bricks is estimated to have been reduced by a half, without reducing the quality, through the use of informal production techniques (LHPET, 1978). However, clay is not always of a suitable quality for bricks. In Nairobi, there is a reject rate of 30 to 50 per cent because of the low quality of clay (Syagga, 1992).

There is a strong demand for terracotta bricks in Burkina Faso following a period of labour-intensive industrial production in Comoé Province. Although industrial production stopped in 1982 because of desertification following the heavy use of wood for burning, small-scale production still exists in fertile parts of the country. The manufacture of a batch of 25,000 bricks employs 20 people for 10 days (Kaboré, 1991).

4.   Cement- and stabilized-soil blocks

Cement- and stabilized-soil blocks are hospitable to small-scale and labour-intensive production. Both solid and hollow cement blocks can be manufactured centrally or on the building site using labour-intensive methods and simple moulds manufactured locally. Their apparent simplicity to manufacture can lead to problems of quality owing to unclean sand, economies with cement, and lack of curing, as unskilled entrepreneurs catch the ready market.

Stabilized-soil blocks have been manufactured for many years using several proprietary presses such as the CINVA ram, the TEK block press, and, more recently the sophisticated BREPAK press which has a hydraulic ram to increase compaction to prevent cracking. The problem facing proponents of these materials is not their strength and durability, which are well-documented and proved, but the social acceptability of using a soil-based block when a "modern" cement-based equivalent is probably little more expensive in use.

Kaboré (1991) reports that, in Burkina Faso, producing stabilized-soil blocks with a TEK block press involved a team of seven; two storing and crushing, three mixing soil and stabilizer, and two moulding and pressing the blocks. This team produces an average of 625 blocks per day for a cost of CFAF 38.3 per block, of which CFAF 10.61 is labour cost (Kaboré, 1991).

Wherever low-cost technologies are used in large projects, opportunities exist for small enterprises to manufacture components. The simple technology for manufacturing stabilized compressed blocks in the Cissin project in Burkina Faso caused small artisanal groups to spring up on the site. In spite of the scale of demand for blocks for the project and the novelty of the technology, a large stock was built up before the work began, the average rate of production being 400 blocks per day per group (Kaboré, 1991).

C.   The potential for using alternative building materials

The development of local building materials has been documented and promoted by local research establishments for several decades. Despite their ease of production by SSEs there are very few instances of their being used on any large scale. Not only are they constrained by market distortions in favour of imported "conventional" materials, they also suffer from inappropriate building regulations, consumer resistance to "old-fashioned" ideas, and problems balancing supply with demand. The poor diffusion rate of these and other appropriate building materials is also partly due to a simple lack of awareness on the part of key decision-makers, that is builders, professionals, government officials and aid officials, of viable alternative technologies.

Even where new and cheaper products are introduced, experience shows that they are met with a suspicious and slow response. Housing is a very long-term and very substantial investment and builders are reluctant to adopt new or untried building materials. Thus the durability of a new product needs to be demonstrated over a substantial period of time before it will be adopted widely. Absence of any failures in one or two rainy seasons may not be enough. Government departments (which might be expected to be taking a lead in encouraging low-capital import-saving technologies) are even slower to respond. This is because the building professionals and officials do not wish to take responsibility for any resulting failure, and tend to rely on existing formally defined standards. This is where aid agencies, particularly NGO aid agencies, have played a vital role in the promotion and diffusion of new technologies, as the case of fibre-reinforced-cement tiles demonstrates. Local standards organizations clearly have a role here too, in defining standards for promising new products.

Many governments have announced their intention to alter the building codes to allow the use of stabilized-soil blocks, pisé, and other labour-intensive low cost-local materials. However, few have actually implemented the changes. Consumers in the lower income groups are less adventurous than building technology researchers might encourage them to be. They need to know that their materials will be reliable, they will use what is easily to hand (usually cement blocks), and they value easy transport (so metal roof sheets score above clay roof tiles).

There is a problem of acceptability with earth-based materials. Earth or mud has always been lacking in glamour and prestige. A mud house is a synonym for poverty. While attempts to introduce new uses for traditional materials are limited to small-scale trials, on or close to the campuses of building research establishments, their success in influencing public opinion is likely to be low. It follows that efforts should be made to construct prestigious public buildings receiving as many visitors as possible in order to convince the sceptical and neutralize the system's detractors. If the government gave a tax break to the manufacturers of building components made with local materials, or if new schools are built using them, or if the Prime Minister's summer residence is built in rammed earth, the effect is likely to be much greater (Kaboré, 1991).

Similar statements could be made about roofing and many other building materials and components. The technology is available; the materials to use directly, or from which to manufacture building materials, are present in most countries. What is lacking is a commitment by governments and local authorities to be active in promoting their use so that a building-materials supply system will come into being as entrepreneurs see the demand and become involved.

D. Alternative building technologies in use

A notable attempt to involve labour-intensive methods and/or SSEs in large-scale building of new houses has been the Million Houses Programme in Sri Lanka. Started in 1984, it is one of the very few government-directed housing programmes aimed at the true scale of the housing supply issue. Through easing land availability, granting small loans, a technical information service, and skills training, the Government has succeeded in enabling the construction of great numbers of houses through local SSEs. Although potentially a self-help programme allowing for owner-building, most households have opted to employ local semi-skilled labour to assist, or a small-scale contractor to undertake the whole construction work. Because the amount of money in each loan available is very small, the technology used in house construction and improvement is inevitably local and labour-intensive. As a result, there has undoubtedly been a great increase in employment in SSEs in the construction sector through artisans taking on and training assistants (UNCHS, 1989b).

There are recent innovations in the use of pisé within the context of both contractor-built and self-help low-cost housing in tropical Africa. So successful have been the pilot projects in Ghana, Kenya, Malawi and Sierra Leone, that the first large-scale commercial developments are being planned. Pisé consists of a mixture of good-quality soil (of which laterite, found almost ubiquitously in tropical areas, is probably the best) and water which is pounded in a series of thin layers between metal shutters. The soil and water are mixed in a very specific ratio so that the material is friable and crumbly. The pounding action binds the laterite particles together in a physical bond; shutters both restrict outward movement under the pounding and leave a smooth, weather-resistant surface. When the shutters are full, further sets are fixed above them until the wall height is achieved, they are then removed and used in the next location virtually indefinitely. The skill involved in pounding is familiar to most people and can be perfected for pisé applications in a few hours. In the recent innovations, the metal shutters are bolted approximately 300 mm apart, they are of new light construction and are faced with renewable plywood, and the panel ends are tongued and grooved to restrict lateral displacement. Window and door openings are simply blanked off with removable boxes. The wall surface is very hard and it can be built through wet seasons if the exposed tops of walls are protected from heavy rain during the construction period. In common with all uses of earth for building, pisé has much better thermal insulation qualities than an equivalent cement-block wall.

Through the use of good development practice and a virtually free raw material, great savings can be made which are passed on to the future owner of the house. In a joint British Council and Africa Housing Fund-sponsored project at Kauwi in Kitui, Kenya, women of the Kauwi Muungano Women's Cooperative built new houses in their existing village for an average cost of $600 for 40 m² ($15 per m²). They are now able to build as many more houses as they wish using the shutters which were left with them.

The technique has considerable commercial potential as the technology is extremely simple with a very basic skill (pounding) at its centre. Though supervision over thorough compaction is axiomatic to the technology, it is so straightforward that it is quickly taught and easily understood. In addition, very little mechanical plant is required, greatly reducing front-end costs and overheads. Thus, compared with to a conventional construction company also capable of building dwellings by the thousand, a company using the pisé building technique can maintain very low overheads while employing large numbers of people and transferring technology in a very effective way.

Compared with conventional techniques, contractors using the pisé building technique are capable of responding to rapid fluctuations, especially increases, in demand for housing. As conventional building relies on masons (and their equivalents in brick and block laying), building capacity can only respond to upward fluctuations in demand as rapidly as the supply of masons can be increased. In pisé construction, however, there are nine unskilled pounders and one supervisor in every gang, and one skilled mason-equivalent can control two gangs. This is a huge increase in productivity per skilled worker over the mason-plus-mate team in conventional contracting and a much shorter lead-time for moving into high levels of production (Tipple, 1993).

In a recent project to build 100 "economy" dwellings in the 16th Sector of Ouagadougou, Burkina Faso, traditional *banco* (sun-dried mud bricks) were used as the main building material. The aims of the project were not only to offer a decent and inexpensive type of dwelling, but also to keep running costs to a minimum (less than 5 per cent of the purchase price) over a period of 20 years. The Design Office of the Directorate General of Architecture recommended *banco* bricks as the basic building material making it possible to minimize the cost of construction, to provide adobe-brick manufacturers with substantial levels of income, and to ensure the survival of artisans skilled in brick-laying.

Thus the policy of the Government laid stress on the activity and energy of skilled workmen, the very ones whose private-sector activities have made it possible to cope with the housing of 26,000 and 11,000 people per year migrating to the cities of Ouagadougou and Bobo Dioulassou, respectively from the country during the last 20 years. Furthermore, the large-scale use of this kind of material has helped in the short term to reduce the rate of urban unemployment; the only skill on which the young people who make up the exodus usually possess is a good knowledge of the use of *banco* for building purposes (Kaboré, 1991).

VI. The potential of various actors

...the full potential and resources of all actors in the shelter production and improvement process [must be] mobilized; but the final decision on how to house themselves is left to the people concerned

UNCHS, 1990, p. 8

It is evident that there are many actors involved in the housing process, particularly when the government does not assume the role of provider and landlord which it does in the former command economies. In the enablement process, actors ranging from individuals to governments and international agencies have important roles which complement each other if the process is operating smoothly. In the current housing provision environment, complementarity is less common than conflict and so it is appropriate to examine the roles of the various actors and identify, where possible, the constraints which hold them and their weaknesses so that policy can be directed to assisting them. As a starting point, the roles suggested by Lyby (1992) and set down in table 4 are taken, but others will suggest where appropriate.

A.   Individuals

Buildings can be created by human labour with hardly any capital to speak of

Arthur Lewis (1954)

In the distinction between major and minor works (see table 4), individuals are seen to have a role as paid workers and as taxpayers in the former (Lyby, 1992). In minor works, individuals are seen to contribute unpaid labour through communities and to act individually to improve their own houses. However, just as in major works, individuals can take paid employment in minor works where their skills are required to supplement community unpaid labour. While trenches can be dug and pipes laid by unskilled labour, there is a need for some skilled people to supervise within the building process and in other types of public works; to establish levels, install pipe joints, and similar complex parts of the operation. These inputs, which must usually be paid for, should be sought from local paid labour rather than bringing workers in from outside.

Because people's individual activities are organized through their community system, it is difficult to separate individual activity from community activity except in the building or improvement of their individual house and in the operation of SSEs. The individual householder's perception of benefits accruing directly to his or her household is probably important in mobilizing people in a self-help housing project (whether for upgrading or for new construction), especially in improvement to individual properties and the minor works which involve groups in unpaid cooperative effort. These will be weighed, in an intuitive manner, against the costs which will probably be well understood and probably over-estimated by affected householders. These costs will be greater if regular building and planning codes are to be followed by participants. Thus, as Mhenni (1987) points out drawing from experience in Tunisia, projects which rely on a significant self-help component could benefit from the following:

- a reduction in planning and building regulations;
- the strengthening of people's participation in the conception of the project as well as its execution;
- an integration of improvement of housing conditions with real improvement in living conditions through jobs and income-generation opportunities.

In some cultures, individuals are not able to make independent decisions or take care of their own concerns before those of the community. In these areas, it is essential to work through the decision-making unit. Examples of this can be found as widespread as in West Africa and Indonesia. In West Africa, village and neighbourhood chiefs, in council with their elders, take decisions which the rest of the community will stand by. At the house level, there will be a representative who is regarded as the father of the house whose decision carries executive power. In Indonesia, village headmen (*Kepala Desa*) represent the loyalty structure of village people and are the appropriate agents with whom to negotiate.[1]

Probably the most important individual in any development scheme, particularly when undertaken by the private sector, is the developer; the person who conceives the idea in his or her mind and translates it into action. Without the developer, development will be stalled. Currently, in the absence of large-scale housing developers building ahead of demand in most developing countries, the role of developer is taken by each householder who, deciding to build a house, takes on the role of the instigator in his or her own small project. In this one-off situation, they gather together the inputs (land, finance, materials and permissions), arrange for the utility undertakings to provide infrastructure, engage contractors, make payments, run around solving problems and making contacts, etc. At the end of the project, when the learning curve has been scaled, the newly experienced developer puts his or her skills into cold storage, probably swearing never to do it again. Thus, all the tasks which could be undertaken more economically and efficiently by a professional developer must be done by the individual. Furthermore, all the training and skills gathered are lost to society.

As in the small operation of having a single dwelling built, so in the larger development the task of the developer is to turn an idea into a reality through gathering together all the inputs and managing the project. In comparison with the scale of a project, a developer does not need a large amount of money because the

---

1. Archer (1992) found that, in a typical Guided Land Development Project, decisions regarding servicing and subdividing traditional land needed to be made in consultation with the landowners and village headman.

amount of resources that are expended before income begins to flow through the sale of the first products (houses) is usually a relatively small part of the total investment. Part of the developer's skill is to borrow money in such a way that the project is moved forward with as little of the developer's capital laid out as possible. Successful developers can make large profits in real terms and truly gigantic ones in relation to their own initial investment.

There is a need in developing countries for the training of developers. The skills of a successful developer are learnt largely through experience, therefore training on the job is a necessary part of their formation. Successful developers are necessary not only to ensure that development is efficient but also to save the banks from losing money, because development is a risky business in which many people can gain and, if it goes wrong, many can lose. Within the context of this publication, however, it is important to train developers in labour-intensive techniques and in the art of handling workers, paying them fairly, treating them in line with international labour standards, and training them to become supervisors and, possibly, developers in their own right.

Ismael and Marulanda (1992) discuss the role of individuals whom they call "development consultants." They are professionals from many disciplines who are committed to supporting the improvement of the living conditions of the poor. One of their major roles is the promotion of "co-development" or development through partnerships involving public and private sectors and communities, to use existing resources and mobilize new ones, to assist the parties and to defend the interests of the weaker groups. The role of the development consultants is seen to involve assistance to the low-income communities, to try unconventional approaches which could provide them with better access to resources, and to utilize the ones they have in more efficient ways in order to strengthen their position as one of the main actors in development.

B.   Communities

In its simplest form, the distinction between major and minor works made by Lyby (1992) regards the community as having no role in major works. However, the success of the community contracts programme in Sri Lanka and experience in Soweto demonstrate that there is a potential for community contract organizations to bid for major works projects. If they can successfully carry out engineering and construction work in their own residential area, they can build low-trafficked roads, lay paved parking spaces, dig and line major drains, lay water mains, build dams and construct schools, clinics and other public buildings.

An additional way of looking at works which are suitable for community activity can use the "ultimate level" of service (Cotton and Franceys, 1991) as the indicator of the end of public-sector responsibility and the beginning of autonomy within the community. In the full servicing provision, where each plot is provided with a connection to publicly maintained infrastructure lines, this ultimate level is the plot boundary (or even within the dwelling, the place where the service is metered for charging). This is, undoubtedly, the ideal, which all would prefer if they could afford it. However, the reality of the late twentieth century is that the majority of citizens cannot afford it and most governments cannot cope with such provision. In the absence of the best, therefore, it is reasonable to argue that second-best solutions not only should be accepted but should be welcomed as a way forward to gaining the major improvements in living conditions which can result from limited improvements or no servicing at all.

In the context of community responsibility for provision, maintenance and revenue collection, the ultimate level can be moved upwards to the boundary of the area occupied by the group whose members agree to act in concert. The area concerned may be a compound house (as in West African cities at present), a house group formed around a single cul-de-sac or alley, or even a whole neighbourhood or settlement. Thus, the public authority could contract with a community to provide piped water to a point on the main pipe at which the supply is metered. From that point on, the community can provide the level of service which its members demand (i.e., need and can pay for), and can accrue the profits (or carry the losses) contingent on revenue collection. The public sector can, instead of paying for the service provision, simply subsidize the community's own provision with a grant to cover the cost of installation. For very poor communities, whatever subsidy option is chosen on social-welfare grounds can be applied at the ultimate level, by charging sub-economic prices for the water delivered to the meter (or the wastes collected from the dump).

Thus, UNCHS (Habitat) (1990) recommends that communities, represented by CBOs, have a role to play in assisting in the implementation of local-authority strategies, especially as local authority resources are insufficient for all the tasks they must fulfill. CBOs would be ideally placed to undertake the day-to-day implementation of policies affecting their neighbourhoods, to act as intermediaries between individuals and the local authority, and with finance agencies (in which role they can act as honest brokers, or as the corporate entity with which proceedings for distraint may be joined), and to encourage groupings of artisans or entrepreneurs who can negotiate successfully for infrastructure provision or contracts.

Lyby (1992) characterizes the CBO in an area as standing between the Town Hall on one side and NGOs and SSEs on the other, describing their role as:
- identifying local needs;
- mobilizing human and financial resources;
- negotiating contracts with the municipality for execution of works and for maintenance;
- carrying out the works in accordance with the contract.

Communities have a role to play in financing shelter improvements, both through organizing savings and through acting as an intermediary in the borrowing process. There is a long tradition of community savings schemes; some very simple and involving no interest payment but, instead, a turn in collecting the combined contributions of the pool (either by lot or by regular turn).[2] The role of intermediary has also been important as an interface between individuals and formal financial institutions.[3] The need for the intermediary arises from the presumption of bankers that low-income households with no collateral are a poor risk. If these households are to break out of the need to use cash only or borrow from the usurious private money lenders, the brokerage of the community as an intermediary may be essential. However, Peattie (1990) warns that there are conflicts of interest inherent in expecting a CBO or any NGO both to collect user fees (financial policing) and represent community interest and solidarity at the same time.

It is noteworthy that a cohesive group of poor people appears to hold more sway with governments and bankers than the individuals who comprise the group would if acting alone. As communities may be conflict-ridden and heterogeneous, the creation of an organization to act as a joint platform for negotiation and organization is vital. The Community Action Planning approach and community contract system which have been in operation in Sri Lanka for several years exemplifies this. When a community has decided it wants to undertake a physical improvement programme, NHDA (National Housing Development Authority) will introduce the Community Action Planning approach through a two-day workshop. During this, a development programme for the settlement is prepared and an implementation schedule is agreed upon. Where issues require detailed planning and discussion, special half-day workshops are organized to work out how the problem can be resolved.

Community construction contracts are written agreements between a government agency and a community to carry out the construction of simple public facilities in its area. The community is regarded as a partner in the development process. Before this can happen, the community should be represented by a legal entity — in Sri Lanka's case a Community Development Council (CDC). It should be involved in the planning and design of the proposed facility, and must open a separate bank account for the funds involved in the contract. NHDA pays the community the cost of the construction (materials and labour) plus a small profit, more or less equal to the costing of a commercial contractor.

It is left to the community to decide how to organize the work. It has to buy the materials, but can ask NHDA for advice. The community can decide on the rates for its own skilled and unskilled labour and on the use of remaining funds (or profits) for other community activities. A technical officer of NHDA supervises

---

2. *Susu* in Ghana and *arisan* in Indonesia are examples of such schemes. Others involve more sophisticated banking techniques. SEWA in Ahmedabad has set up such a scheme for financing small businesses, training, housing, etc., among the low-income group.

3. The Roof Loans Scheme in Ghana loaned money through community groups and further loans to the members were contingent on full payment of previous loans.

the construction, checks its quality and gives technical advice. In some cases the CDC management may be too weak and inexperienced to handle a fairly large contract. In that case, an NGO can assist the CDC in carrying out the contract and NHDA funds will be channelled through the NGO.

In the period January 1986 to December 1988, a total of 83 community contracts were awarded to 70 different CDCs. The range of works included residential roads and drains, toilet blocks, water-supply standposts, community buildings and repair and maintenance for buildings and infrastructure. Since that time, however, the number of awarded community construction contracts has declined. The major reason for this is the NHDA's increasing reluctance to issue contracts without sufficient guarantees from the CDCs (UNCHS, 1991c).

It has been found in Sri Lanka that contract procedures are much easier with community contracts than with the conventional process (UNCHS, 1994f). There needs to be no calling for tenders, as the community sends their request to the project staff and the plans and bills of quantities can be prepared by NHDA. A construction committee is appointed consisting of the technical officer from NHDA, and three or four members of the community. The construction is always done under the guidance of NHDA.

There are several advantages to be obtained by this system. Community construction contracts have a positive effect on the employment situation of the beneficiary community. Not only are (temporary) jobs provided to skilled and unskilled workers, but their skills increase due to their involvement in infrastructure works. These improved skills foster employment opportunities. In a study commissioned by the Training Programme for Community Participation, it was found that as long as clearly defined developmental activities were required in the communities, the CDCs were active. As soon as some of the basic facilities were provided, the councils became less active or even disintegrated (UNCHS, 1991c).

Community participation is an end in itself. Through the system of community construction contracts, people are involved in the planning and design of facilities in their own neighbourhoods and take part in the implementation. This involvement increases the community's responsibility for the condition and maintenance of these facilities, ensuring longer economic life (UNCHS, 1991c).

In minor works, Lyby (1992) points out that community initiatives have three major contributions:

- Urban upgrading based on community initiatives may be the only way to make something happen.
- The community contribution would reduce costs to government.[4]

---

4. Watermeyer (1993, p. 12) considers the laying of 460 m of 160 mm diameter piping and concludes "community-based construction was significantly cheaper than labour-intensive construction and compared favourably with plant-based construction."

• Community-based maintenance of minor works could be organized following their provision by the community.

It is important to include community-based minor works in an urban upgrading strategy not so much because the government saves in proportion to the community contribution, although this in itself is potentially significant as well. What is probably more important is that the community, which has built and maintained the neighbourhood (albeit to a fairly low level of provision, perhaps) before the government showed any interest, is involved in the improvements and regards them as their own (Martin, 1983). However, this is more than an exercise in instilling pride through individual home-ownership which then leads to individual action. It is a process of involving the community as a group rather than as a number of free-wheeling individuals. Attempts have been made at flood prevention, water supply, sanitation and garbage collection at the level of the household rather than the community. However, using the community's combined energy and resources can make the difference between success and failure (Lyby and others, 1991).

The local population forms one of the main resources available for undertaking housing improvement. Although household heads may be employed full-time, there may be a good number of adults who are either unemployed or underemployed. Experience in the Lusaka Upgrading Project points to the importance of community leaders in mobilizing residents to participate in self-help public works (Pasteur, 1979; Martin, 1983).

In the Dodoma upgrading programmes, there were local leaders, especially "Ten Cell Leaders" and "Ward Leaders", willing and able to participate effectively in the mobilization of labour in their units, and supervise self-help labour at the site. In most cases, the Ward Leaders announced the task(s) to be done on a specific day, and residents voluntarily worked until the task was completed. Usually the local leaders plan when the work should be done and the residents are notified through their Ten Cell Leader two to three days in advance. This having been said, however, it should be noted that many residents find life so hard that they are reluctant to give up their time to carry out community projects such as drainage, access improvements etc., even though they regard them as priorities (Kombe, 1992).

Community-based works involve a community contribution in labour or cash. Their ability to directly create paid employment is, however, subject of some debate. Lyby and others (1991) argue that community-based works create fewer jobs than contractor-executed works. However, this applies more to those in which minor works carried out through voluntary contributions constitute the whole or a major part; in that case only skilled jobs will be paid for. Infrastructure works executed through community contracts are likely to be labour-intensive by nature, as against a more mechanized construction approach of commercial contractors (UNCHS, 1991c). Both approaches do, however, stimulate the business of small contractors or artisans who tend to carry out those tasks demanding any degree of technical sophistication. Thus, even relatively simple drainage and earthworks can generate a reasonable amount of employment. It should be added that in most communities there are members who would prefer to give their contribution in cash instead of labour. This can be a particular useful source of funds for payment of wages to artisans and for the purchase of materials. The level and method of contribution are questions to be discussed and decided within the communities themselves (Lyby and others, 1991).

Marxist writers would argue that community involvement in shelter or service provision is only a means of exploiting the poor. Mesa (1987; 1990) argues that individual or group responsibility for the construction of housing, community or social space, or cultural environment in general adds unremunerated work to an already long working day. In addition, the role of tenants in community-based upgrading is inevitably a difficult one. They may welcome the improvements sought through upgrading but, unlike the owners within the area, they receive no financial reward in the shape of increased property values and may be reluctant to join in the hard work (Tipple, 1988; Kombe, 1992). Indeed, as values rise, their rents are likely to be increased, perhaps resulting in economic hardship or a move to another, unimproved location. Tenant participation in upgrading may be contingent upon their receiving rent holidays or other rewards.

In view of the high degree of willingness among residents to participate in improvements of their settlements, there is a great need to shift from the current unrealistic assessments of public resources, to a partnership between the community and public sector. However, the process cannot be managed without the support of experienced professionals. A sustainable process requires considerable training and institutional development efforts within the local authorities and ministries concerned. Steps towards this goal are currently being taken under the UNDP/ UNCHS (Habitat) Sustainable Cities Programme in Dar-es-Salaam. One of the most important processes required is the restoration or establishment of trust between local people and local authorities, and between local authorities and the central government. As the Lusaka Upgrading Project (Martin, 1983) and that in Hai es Salaam (Davidson, 1984) demonstrated, there is a need for the local authority to establish local offices from which to initiate participatory planning and implementation of neighbourhood upgrading (Lyby and others, 1991).

It is possible to base infrastructure improvement and sustain the development through local efforts and funding. However, it is necessary to assist the community to formulate and institute a locally-generated fund for maintenance. The community should also be assisted to form locally-based maintenance groups to undertake some of the maintenance tasks (those which need paid labour). These groups could be paid from such a fund.

It must be remembered that a community is a very fluid entity in most urban areas. While there may be unanimity among the people and an able and sympathetic group of leaders one year, after five years the initial personnel and fervour may well have disappeared from the scene. Thus, it is axiomatic to community participation to have a supportive local authority or NGO working closely with the people and their leaders to ensure the continuity of the systems necessary to maintain the services. Herein lies some of the work which will replace that of direct provision in the demands laid on local authorities and central government.

C.   Small-scale contractors

Much of the discussion in the previous chapters has concentrated on the role of SSEs and there is no need to reiterate the material here. It is appropriate, however, to concentrate briefly on the requirements for utilizing the potential of SSEs for carrying out public works programmes.

There is a need for a great increase in the number, variety and scope of SSEs in the fields in which public works take place. This is unlikely to occur spontaneously, ahead of demand. Much more likely is the birthing of enterprises in response to policies to hive off particular functions. If, for instance, the local government works department begins demanding building materials which can be produced locally, SSEs are likely to be set up to supply them. However, in the past, specifications have tended to be very specific, even to the manufacturer of a component, thereby excluding one which could be manufactured locally.

In order to avoid political repercussions, the SSE sector will need to be more cooperative with regulations covering taxes, health and safety, and conditions of employment. While an artisan pays neither income tax not property rates, he/she is unlikely to be popular at City Hall. Politicians responsible for substantial budgets cannot afford to be linked to tax defaulters even through the fair award of contracts properly carried out. Voters will be unimpressed if public works projects are carried out by welders who are not equipped with masks, or sanitary workers whose death rates remain high from excreta-related diseases. Furthermore, contractors benefiting from public money should not be seen to avoid pension contributions or sickness benefits for their workers. Similarly, SSEs must increase their reliability in terms of quality and value for money.

It might be expected that, of all labour-based contracts, those for rural road building are the most difficult for successful small-scale enterprise participation. The problem lies in the geographical spread of the work. Supervision, inspection and payment may all be difficult if the length of road is great. Recently, however, programmes have been successfully carried out in Ghana, Kenya and Lesotho and to enable SSEs to take over from the public works department staff (Miles and Andersson, n.d.). ILO experience in Ghana with small-scale road contractors has shown some promise and exposed some problems, most of which are common for SSEs in the construction sector in general. In the past, SSEs were unable to register as contractors for roads programmes because they could not raise the financial backing required to be considered. However, in the ILO project those who came forward for training in estimating, tendering, bookkeeping, road construction etc. were then registered as labour-based contractors with the guarantee of one contract each to enable them to gain the experience needed to register as a contractor.[5] In return, the SSEs are expected to follow the methods taught in the training course and, particularly, to remain financially transparent so that trust can be established. Experience has shown that one of the main problems of SSEs is the lack of financial management skills. In response to this, a training package is now available from the ILO.

D.   Large-scale contractors

There are a small but, seemingly, increasing number of large contractors who are willing and able to use labour-intensive methods to build housing and infrastructure in developing countries. The case of road construction in Dhaka has already been mentioned. In addition, the contracting companies which are being set up through IPDS (a United Kingdom based company using the pisé building method) will also use labour-intensive techniques as if they were large-scale SSEs, i.e., a large contractor using the methods and having the advantages normally associated with SSEs (Tipple, 1992a).

Large contractors who do not use labour-intensive techniques will probably always dominate the very large projects, especially where high technology is required or speed is of the essence. Yet, if current trends continue, the cost of labour-based methods will probably continue to undercut those of capital-based methods, and increasingly so if fiscal austerity continues alongside increasing populations requiring work. In addition, as labour-based approaches prove their commercial worth, it is likely that some large contractors will adopt them, either directly or through sub-contractors.

There is an important role for large contractors in enabling and encouraging labour-based contracts through sub-contracting. In Soweto, large contractors have been engaged as managing contractors in control of labour-based sub-contractors. Their role is to bring experience, management, training and finance to the works and, through their involvement, allow the development of able labour-based contractors. Table 16 describes the changes in responsibilities as this training and enablement process evolves and the fledgling labour-based contractor takes on more of the duties and obligations of a full-scale contractor.

E.   Local government

Governments and local authorities have increasingly been seen as obstacles by the millions of householders who, through the informal sector, have erected

---

5. This "chicken and egg" situation is a common bar to entry into contracting and many other fields of work.

Table 16. Levels of contractor development under a managing contractor

Level	Labour-based contractor's contractual responsibilities	Managing contractor's contractual responsibilities
1	• Provide labour • Provide small tools	• Offer advice, practical assistance and training • Provide and distribute materials • Provide plant other than small tools • Finance fortnightly wages
2	• Provide labour • Provide small tools	• Offer advice, practical assistance and training • Issue bulk materials • Provide plant other than small tools • Finance fortnightly wages
3	• Provide labour • Provide small tools • Provide all materials • Provide transport • Finance fortnightly wages	• Offer advice, practical assistance and training • Offer materials for purchase • Provide plant other than small tools
4	• Provide labour • Provide all materials • Provide all plant and transport • Finance all contractual aspects including the provision of surety	• Offer advice, practical assistance and training • Offer materials for purchase and plant for hire
5	• Provide all labour, materials, plant and transport • Finance all contractual obligations	• Offer advice and consultancy services

Source: Watermeyer, 1993, p. 9.

semi-legal structures in and around the cities of the developing world. Many, however, are now coming to the realization that the task of central and local government in enabling construction, and making it more efficient, can be achieved, giving a new impetus to public authorities' housing activity. While this is a major change in direction from the production role, it does not involve less responsibility and care on the government's part; it is not a recipe for *laissez-faire*. Strong and cohesive government action is required to ensure responsive supply markets and hospitable policy; particularly with respect to legal and regulatory reform and housing finance. Local authorities are needed to apply active management to the cities and towns in their care. They must be diligent in collecting taxes and revenues so that they can function effectively as they have a vital role in infrastructure provision and coordination of agencies and community groups involved in the supply of housing.

Under the UNDP/UNCHS (Habitat) Sustainable Cities Programme, training and institution building efforts are aimed at increasing the ability of city authorities to undertake functions which are supportive and facilitating rather than directive and implementing. It is recognized in the GSS that the shift from implementing (or rather failing to implement) to enabling does not mean that governments abdicate their responsibilities. It will, however, pose new and largely unfamiliar demands on planning, management and policy-formulation tasks at both central and municipal government levels. The key element will be sensitivity to the specific nature of local priorities and perceptions.

As already noted, there is a need for public authorities to develop the skills of a facilitator rather than an executor, so as to assist others to do the tasks which, traditionally, it did itself. There is ample scope for public authorities to transfer some of their executing responsibilities to other actors and to enter upon the facilitating role. Furthermore, there is likely to be significant potential for employment in such changes.

Watermeyer (1993) confronts the issue of providing professional assistance to labour-based contractors, in his case in Soweto, through either a professional team or a managing contractor. In the professional-team approach, professionals who may be employees of the local authority assist labour-based contractors with the administering and financing of their contracts, offer technical training, engage specialist contractors, and supply necessary materials and equipment. The professional team is engaged separately by the same employer as engages the labour-based contractor. Thus the professional team can be regarded as construction facilitators, arranging for the provision of resources which the contractor lacks.

In the managing-contractor approach described from the Soweto experience (Watermeyer, 1993), an experienced conventional contractor contracts with the employer to administer, manage, finance, train and supply materials and equipment to a labour-based sub-contractor. In this case, the sub-contractor enters into a contract with the managing contractor, who in turn contracts with the employer. This approach is best suited to work where the expertise of established contractors is required to execute certain aspects of the work.

As seen above, Soweto City Council has been involved in facilitating community involvement and labour-based public works. Following three small projects in which experience was gained, the Council decided on a labour-based approach because it would create employment opportunities for Soweto residents and it would stimulate the development of competent, conventional contractors among the Soweto people (City of Soweto, 1992).

The local authority provided the professional team and, with it, carried out the tasks of the managing contractor outlined in table 17, with the intention of progressively reducing its role as the individual contractors became more capable. On a major water-supply project, there had been 55 level 1 (see table 17) contracts awarded up to 1 January 1992 and two level 2 were being called for. In general there has been successful completion although managing many contracts at once (32

Table 17. Public management styles for urban services

Function	Management styles	
	State as provider	State as facilitator
Needs assessment	Surveys, census, field visits and statistical analysis, centralization of information	Communities' self-survey direct consultation, dispersal of information
Determination of requirements for services	Professionally established regulations; uniform and high-level technical performance	Incremental upgradable requirements based on adaptation of existing situation and technologies
Financing	Greater dependence on national government grants and international loans	Local governments and communities generate revenue
Planning	Professionals in government and parastatal agencies	Communities and local governments with guidance of professionals
Implementation	Centrally controlled and managed by authorities, directorates and public corporations	Controlled and managed by communities with local government support
Financial and quality control	Monitoring and evaluation by central authorities through reports, auditing, and strict adherence to numerous and uniform rules, regulations, procedures, codes, and designs	Service providers accountable to community residents and local officials and judged on final effectiveness of service rather than adherence to procedures, etc.
Service personnel	Few professionals assisted by large support staff	Community volunteers and para-professionals supported by small groups of professionals
Cost reduction	"Efficient" management, competitive bidding, and "economies of scale"	Community self-help, adapting regulations to local situation and affordability; elimination of "overhead" costs
Relationship of service providers to users	Separated and often opposed to communities' demands; government controls	Merging of providers and users; communities control government supports

Note: Most successful experiences of urban services involve elements of both management styles.

Source: Rondinelli and Cheema, 1985, p. 183.

were running simultaneously) severely strained the authority's resources (City of Soweto, 1992).

For governments, constrained as they are for skilled labour, the managing contractor or development consultants mentioned earlier in the chapter can be seen as "extension partners" to assist with professional non-routine, non-bureaucratic work in an effort to develop alternative planning, implementation and management mechanisms which can respond more efficiently and realistically to the complexity of the current development.

Other local authorities have mobilized residents to improve their shelter very successfully, albeit in a small way. For example, according to the local leaders involved in squatter upgrading in Dodoma, the United Republic of Tanzania, the local authority has played an important role by contributing construction materials, including iron bars and cement. Without this, local leaders contend that it would have been difficult to implement the projects, because most households are just too poor to contribute enough cash for buying the building materials. The support given by the local authority was also considered by many residents to represent political approval, commitment and recognition of their informal settlement. In addition, it provided a basis for private-public partnership in the improvement programme and established a yardstick of the amount of assistance residents could expect from a government which has serious financial constraints (Kombe, 1992).

Local government can play a major role by creating a climate of support based on promotion rather than the regulation of the informal sector (UNCHS, 1990). Support strategies for SSEs are required which are appropriate to the specific circumstances of the area. The formulation of such strategies will entail the staff of the local authority in a learning exercise which should encourage stronger and more sympathetic links between them and the operators of SSEs. The strategies should be mindful of those regulations which inhibit the development of SSEs in housing areas and in the construction sector. In addition, the projects launched for the local authorities; school and other public buildings, and housing for the poorest who may continue to need direct support; should be built in cooperation with small-scale construction enterprises wherever possible, using local raw materials.

Rondinelli and Cheema (1985) discuss the difference in approach which local and central government need to take towards development if they adopt the enabling role rather than that of provider. Table 17 sets out the two ends of the continuum rather succinctly. The management style for the State or local authority as provider of services is radically different from that for the State as facilitator of services. It requires reorientation of policy and the way the bureaucracy operates. Public administrators and politicians must change their attitudes to service provision so that, instead of providing what they regard as suitable or nothing at all, they take the lead from local people in what services are provided, where and by whom. Service delivery organizations need restructuring so that they concentrate on what they do best and successfully encourage others to participate in the rest. This may require agencies to be promotional and training organizations as much as deliverers of services.

Axiomatic to all this is identifying with the urban poor; eschewing "standard packages" of services and adopting those which the residents of poor neighbourhoods recognize as being important. This will require considerable training inputs. Thus, there is a need to strengthen municipal administration for the successful implementation of the enabling approach. All too often, national governments starve local authorities of resources, preferring to keep the power in the centre. An essential principle of the GSS is decentralization, both in political terms (of where decisions are made) and in financial resources. Local authorities should be able to set, collect, and allocate their own resources (Ljung and Farvacque, 1988). Unless local authorities have up-to-date records, they cannot hope to collect revenues, maintain and extend services, or predict development potentials. Without assistance from the centre, these issues are unlikely to be addressed.

Mawhood (1983) argues that local governments should have autonomy in managing development projects in their localities, including the collection and use of taxes, rather than being treated by central government as though they were just another government department. For their part, argues Kombe (1992), local governments should provide the necessary support to self-help initiatives in upgrading programmes, cultivating an environment for continuous partnership where both the local authority and residents play effective roles. This may be something as simple as provision of basic tools such as shovels, wheel-barrows and pick-axes to the self-help groups, but followed by more adventurous partnerships (Kombe, 1992). Although no direct correlation is implied, Kasongo and Tipple (1990) found that upgrading efforts in Kitwe, Zambia, which flourished under the support of an autonomous council during the mid-1970s, faltered and were replaced by a harder line after the City Council became an arm of central government in the "decentralization" exercise of 1980.

The choice of technology can have significant effects on employment both in construction and in maintenance of public services. Furthermore, it has been seen that the adoption of local materials and technologies, and the construction of simpler houses, creates more employment per dollar invested in construction than other approaches. As local authorities and national governments are major actors in the construction sector, their potential for influencing employment through switching from one technology to another could be considerable. Most government buildings can contain substantial labour-based components and can maximize maintenance rather than capital cost if there is a will to do so. Classrooms, clinics, administration and payment offices, depots and other buildings can be built in labour-based materials both for their own sake and as examples to legitimize otherwise unaccepted technologies.

The shift to SSE participation in public works programmes demands that the rules for tendering should be changed so that the size of enterprise which qualifies for tendering procedures, through some prequalification vetting procedure, is lowered to include SSEs. The rules governing tendering, and the procedures used for selection of contractors, needs to be much more transparent and this may be politically difficult.

While the transfer of services and functions to outside organizations, especially SSEs, will reduce the burden of executive activity, the new function of facilitator and enabler will pose new and largely unfamiliar demands on planning, management and policy formulation tasks at both central and municipal government levels. As Rondinelli and Cheema (1985) indicate, there is a need for local authorities to develop multiple modes of service delivery, sensitive to local conditions, and the strengths or weaknesses of community organizations and local formal agencies.

VII. Forward linkages: Shelter as a workplace

> *If there is one lesson for planners in the massive literature on slums and squatter community life, it is the finding that housing in these areas is not for home life alone. A house is a production place, market place, entertainment centre, financial institution and also a retreat. A low-income community is the same, only more so. Both the home and the community derive their vitality from this multiplicity of uses. The imposition of artificial restrictions on both, would only hinder their growth and development*
>
> Laquian, 1983a

In this section, forward linkages[1] arising from construction of housing and its infrastructure are discussed in some detail. It will be seen that the contribution of the house as an environment within which economic activity takes place is so significant that it can be regarded as part of the production process as, along with infrastructure, a product whose purpose is to foster other activities. The stream of benefits arising simply from being well-housed are important, but the opportunities housing gives for commercial activity, storage, small-scale manufacturing, service industries, and retailing are also very valuable. Thus, the argument follows, to value a house simply on its physical worth is only as logical as valuing a factory in the same way (Chatterjee, 1981).

While the provision of space to work forms the focus of this section, it should be remembered that increases in the housing stock create jobs in such industries as textiles, furniture and household fixtures as the occupants turn the house into a home. In addition, an array of service trades establish themselves around housing areas (repairs, maintenance, domestic services etc.).

A.   Home as a workplace

Despite regulations in many countries to the contrary, it is not uncommon for people to use their home as a workplace. In pre-industrial societies, this was

---

1. Forward linkages are described by Moavenzadeh and Hagopian (1983) as consumption encouraged by the production of intermediate goods. For example, toughened glass is an intermediate product in the production of motor cars. While it is relatively simple to value the contribution of a toughened glass windscreen to the motor car industry, Moavenzadeh and Hagopian (1983) hold that it is "next to impossible" to value the construction industry's product from the value of the activities carried on inside. Attempts at evaluation have produced very varied results. Reidel and Schultz (1978) claimed that construction supplies almost nothing to other sectors of production. On the other hand, Wheeler (1982) attempted to value the contribution of at least part of construction's products — infrastructure — as inputs to other sectors. His findings were inconclusive showing some benefits in Israel and Singapore but no discernible benefits for Malawi and Zambia.

the norm.   The beginnings of the industrial revolution in Great Britain can be traced to the move from home-based manufacture to factories.   Until recently these small shops and cottage industries were the dominant mode in the world, often part of sophisticated and complex production and distribution systems. Peattie (1981) found that the shoe industry of Santafé de Bogotá is reliant on numerous small producers working from their dwellings.

The design of dwellings to allow for economic activities has rarely been considered in official housing projects although housing is very often necessary to sustain specific trade and manufacturing activities (Fass, 1980).   It is, however, quite common for residents to alter their housing units to accommodate some form of home-based economic activity.   Sarin's (1982) work on Chandigarh, India, and recent introductory work on self-help transformations (Tipple, 1991; 1992b) show the extent to which poor people are willing to go to make their housing environment productive.   A study of the transformation of dwelling units by residents of a public housing estate in New Delhi (Dasgupta, 1987) demonstrated that the main reason for their adaptation of the layout and use of dwellings was to accommodate changing economic activities (UNCHS, 1989b).   Bhatt and others (1993) describe and illustrate a variety of alterations to dwellings in China to accommodate activities such as tailoring and noodle making.

Farbman (1981) found that poor neighbourhoods in San Salvador were filled with economic activity, with an estimated 85 per cent of the households engaged

Plate 10. Home as a workplace: small-scale handicrafts industry (India)

in tiny businesses which often provide 50 per cent or more of a household's income. Carpenters and furniture makers, using simple hand tools, laboured in their homes or in the alleys between the houses; food sellers had set up small eating places consisting of a small table wedged into a tiny room, with a gas or kerosene stove and possibly a refrigerator; candy makers worked on wood-fired stoves using large metal kettles, wooden stirring ladles and cutting boards; street vendors were everywhere selling fruit, vegetables, clothing and lottery tickets. In addition, bottles were collected for resale to bottling companies by people carrying burlap bags or pushing small carts; shoemakers worked out of their houses or a booth in the street; laundrywomen work at public washbasins or in the home; tailors and seamstresses used treadle sewing machines set up in any available space at home; and retailers (small food stores are most common) sold off shelves in a corner of one room of the home.

Fass's work on informal settlements in Port au Prince, Haiti, found that the use of dwellings for making, storing, and/or selling goods was so universal that he decided to treat the dwelling unit as a piece of productive infrastructure rather than as predominantly part of household consumption (Fass, 1977). It takes so little capital to start a shop in a room in the house, that many low-income households make their first foray into earning a living this way. By buying items (even at retail prices) and splitting them into small lots (single cigarettes or pieces of fruit) or adding a small amount of value (hard boiled eggs, sandwiches), or simply making them available near people's homes, the space in the room can provide some income. Given the smaller amounts of capital used, it is likely that men and women setting up small retail establishments in the home prefer to obtain relatively stable earnings and would forgo relatively higher and less stable earnings. Another possible reason is that many women prefer not to work far from home because of obligations to children and/or to the protection of their dwelling unit from theft (Fass, 1980).

In this way, the link between housing and employment in the informal sector is both close and (as will be seen below), symbiotic, in that economic activities enable housing improvements and the latter improve employment prospects and productivity. It is well documented that the informal sector provides employment, products and services for a large proportion of the population of the developing world. Furthermore, a large majority of informal enterprises, particularly SSEs, are either based in the home, attached to the home on a residential plot or on the land adjoining, or are within residential areas (often informal residential areas).

B.   Types of income-generating activities found in houses

Income-generating activities in the home have been catalogued by several writers, notably Strassmann (1986) writing about Peru; Gilbert (1988) reviewing the literature and empirical data from Santafé de Bogotá and Valencia; and Raj and Mitra (1990) and Mehta and Mehta (1990) on HBEs in India.

In the HBE studied by Strassmann (1986) in Lima, people bake, cook, sew, print, repair, photograph, give injections, cut hair, sell drinks, rent lodging, keep chickens, and sell other goods and services. All through the low-rent areas in Santafé de Bogotá, residential façades conceal a multitude of small firms, operating almost invisibly in the interior of dwellings, where they can avoid regulations on minimum wages and fringe benefits. Thus, they can charge the low rates which create the economic logic for sub-contracting by larger firms or for selling to customers who would otherwise buy in city shops. The low rents sought by small firms can, in practice, most easily be found in low-income housing where those with minimal resources can be "independent" (Peattie, 1981).

Nientied and others (1987) found a very wide range of undertakings in people's homes. About one third of all enterprises were retail, as is common, but 22 per cent kept livestock, even a few buffaloes were kept in front of the house and milk sold in the home. Piecework for the garment industry, food processing, plastic moulding etc. were also found. Contrary to findings elsewhere (McGee, 1979), there was no evidence of any illegal trade.

Home-based piecework characterizes what the ILO calls "home work." By this is meant only the manufacture of items in the home on contract to an intermediary or industrialist. The types of product manufactured in India, for example, include *beedis* (or *bidis* — hand-rolled cigarettes), garments, textiles,

Plate 11. A wide range of products are made in or next to the home: informal-sector locksmiths in a residential area (Kumasi, Ghana)

footwear, food products, and handicrafts (Bhatt, 1989). The workers, usually women, may work on their own as artisans or on piece rates from a contractor or intermediary, or they may do both at different times of the year. Mehta and Mehta (1990) found uses such as manufacture of incense sticks and diamond polishing being undertaken in their study area in Ahmedabad.

Small shops in dwellings are an almost universal phenomenon. In Indonesia, food, cookies, and breakfast dishes are sold from houses in and around low income housing areas (Batarfie, 1987). In Brazil's *favelas,* small shops known as *biroscas* sell refreshments, alcoholic drinks, food and many other goods. They also function as meeting places, with recreation options like television, tables for billiards, cards and other games (Treiger and Faerstein, 1987). In Brasilia, Epstein (1973) found that more than 90 per cent of the commercial enterprises were bars, groceries, or general stores.

The preparation of cooked food in the home for sale outside from a stall, in a market, or wandering the street is a common home-based industry all over the developing world. Many of the poorest people have no accommodation other than the streets, or have rooms in which it is impossible or inconvenient to cook, or need food at times when they are far from home. For these, home-based food sellers provide a cheap and remarkably hygienic supply of food.[2]

A large number of households also raise guinea-pigs, rabbits or ducks for their own consumption and for sale (Lobo, 1982). Even in the most inconvenient locations, i.e., flats high up in multi-storey blocks, the keeping of pigeons, chickens, turkeys, and even sheep, can be found.

Raj and Mitra (1990) classify HBEs according to "skills"[3] in three broad hierarchical groups:

- HBEs that require "little or no skill"; these are such tasks as stitching and knitting, and petty retailing;

- HBEs that require "some skills" or a few resources; including cycle repair, tailoring and dressmaking, and simple metal, leather, or wood working;

- HBEs which are either entrepreneurial or require a "moderate to high level of skills" and/or resources, including fully-fledged retailing with bookkeeping, etc., medical practitioners, dentists.

---

2. As Gokhale (1992) found in a study of Pune, India, street food may be no more contaminated with bacteria than restaurant food because it tends to be produced inside houses rather than on the street where it is sold.

3. It should be noted that this classification is based more on the capital and/or entrepreneurship and/or professional education needed to complement labour than on the skills of the workers.

C.   Characteristics of HBEs

1.   Size and occupation of space

Seshachalam and Rao (1987) divided urban informal activities in Hyderabad, India, into the following eight categories according to their use of space:

- a shopping front with a residential dwelling in the backyard;
- a dwelling unit in the front with a workplace in the backyard;
- the ground floor as a business place, with upstairs as a residential unit;
- the ground floor as a residential unit with the first floor as business space;
- a rental residence and own shop;
- own house and a rental business space;
- own house and an encroached business space;
- own business space with encroached *katcha* (poorly built) or semi-permanent residential structure.

Nientied and others (1987) found many HBEs even on very small plots in India; some even had two. In Raj and Mitra's (1990) sample in Delhi, a large number of households have not allocated separate space in the house for the HBEs (renting, regular retailing and specialist services are exceptions). Indeed 50 per cent of HBE operators acknowledge that the possibility of mixing the two kinds of uses is the main advantage of HBEs. In the case of 12.5 per cent of HBE operators, the public space in front of the plot has been appropriated for petty retailing and rearing livestock.

The relationship the between amount of floor-space used by the business and its income was found to be highly significant (Strassmann, 1986). In the Lima sample, the average household with an HBE used 30.6 per cent or 1.2 out of 3.6 rooms for the business. With 1.9 rooms for the business, providers of lodging gave the most space, followed by makers of metal and food products with about 1.5 rooms or over 40 per cent of their space. The women who wove, knitted and laundered used the least space for business, 13 per cent, yet these were the most dependent on the dwelling.

2.   Frequency and distribution

As Gilbert (1988) points out, although there are many HBEs, they are only present in a minority of houses. His data on Santafé de Bogotá, Mexico City and Valencia show about one in 10 households with some enterprise in or attached to their home. Retail/commercial ventures outnumber others. According to Strassmann (1986), from a tenth to a quarter of dwellings in the cities of developing countries have an enterprise on the premises, usually one that the operators prefer to unrelated outside work. His study of Lima, Peru, shows that their location is non-uniform; they tend to concentrate in certain neighbourhoods. In the city as a whole, one in nine dwellings (10.8 per cent) had an HBE, but in *pueblos jovenes*,[4] they occurred in one in six dwellings while in conventional residential areas, HBEs were found in only one in 16 dwellings. Mesa (1987) found that 40 per cent of houses in *pirata* settlements[5] contained business of rental activity but only 22 per cent in the invasion settlements.[6] The reasons for the differences are hypothesised as a combination of consolidation of the dwelling allowing more economic activity, and the more established population generating local markets in the older *pirata*.

In resettlement blocks in South Delhi, Raj and Mitra (1990) found that 20 per cent of all plots were used for income generation. Of these, 11.5 per cent were wholly or partly rented out while 9.7 per cent of households operate business, service and manufacturing enterprises on the plot.

The characteristics of neighbourhoods determine where the greatest proportion of households have HBEs, what type they tend to be, and where they are most lucrative. These neighbourhood characteristics either raise (or lower) the demand for the goods and services produced by HBEs and raise (or lower) the availability of inputs (Strassmann, 1986). The way such demand and supply factors affect different neighbourhoods will change the composition of output produced by HBEs located there.

The underlying view of writers like Strassmann (1986) and Raj and Mitra (1990) is that, being home-based, these enterprises have been the most viable alternative to the formal sector with its instability and factor-price distortions. The HBE core of the informal sector has ease of entry, small scale, labour intensity, and unregulated competitiveness. However, its strength also lies in the ease of shifting labour, funds, equipment, materials and space from making one product or service to another, from the market to the family, and to dwelling expansion itself, what Lipton has called "extended fungibility" (Lipton, 1980).

The density of income per square kilometre may be seen as a major determinant of the incidence of many types of SSEs, particularly those which provide retail and other services. The occurrence and the profitability of HBEs will change according to such factors as transport, proximity to formal-sector enterprises, and degree of unemployment in an area.

Strassmann (1986) found 15 different types of home businesses in seven types of neighbourhoods. Nearly half the HBEs were in the retail trade and these were disproportionately located in *pueblos jovenes*. Second came the manufacture of clothing, and this went on especially in conventional neighbourhoods and in the

---

4. Formerly called *barriadas*, these "young towns" are the unauthorized areas occupied by low-income people.

5. Settlements taking the form of unauthorized subdivision of privately-owned land.

6. Invasion settlements are often known as *barrios* and are equivalent to the *barriadas* of Peru (see footnote 4 above).

quintas[7] and *callejones*.[8] Though not as lucrative as some other HBE types, selling manufactured goods to businesses was generally much more profitable than work in the formal sector. These businesses depended on access, just as the retail stores in the more remote *pueblos jovenes* depended on lack of access of operators to job opportunities and of buyers to better shopping possibilities (Strassmann, 1985b).

In addition to retail stores, personal services were important home businesses in *pueblo jovenes*. Manufacturing of "sturdy" products (footwear, furniture, and metal goods) occurred in areas where there is both space and good access. HBEs serving food or drinks, renting rooms, dispensing health services, and making repairs of many types were most common in conventional/standard neighbourhoods, probably as a function of income density creating demand for such services. In a typical two-block area in Lima, Strassmann (1986) found seven dry-goods stores and two repair shops, two bars, four prepared-food stands, one soccer clubhouse, one political club and one pharmacy. There were also many artisans involved in the repair and creation of articles.

While HBEs are a crucial part of the economic and social fabric of most cities in developing countries, their role varies greatly with the type of neighbourhood. Petty retailing and cooked food production tend to be present in poorer neighbourhoods, often those where access is also poor. In areas where transport, proximity to formal-sector enterprises, availability of space and other neighbourhood characteristics allow, enterprises with a city-wide clientele tend to be found. These would be light manufacturing (food, clothing and textiles) and a variety of services, above all medical and dental clinics. To function here, the HBE has to be able to compete with nearby large or modern enterprises. Larger enterprises which require space, good access to utilities and many skilled workers among the resident population can operate here. (Strassmann, 1986).

Raj and Mitra (1990) found that each type of HBE is linked to particular income groups and each income group in turn enters specific kinds of HBEs. From their survey, they note that movement of households from lower levels in the hierarchy to higher ones is not common. Many reasons were advanced for this, one being that each type of HBE has its own market conditions, requiring a given level of resources and mix of competitive conditions. Although, in theory, HBEs in manufacturing could expand, there are barriers to entry into higher levels of operation by the nature of their establishment in the informal sector and in residential areas. In addition, the wider market is more competitive, and HBE operators tend to lack negotiation skills or working capital, or they do not have the production environment to achieve the desired results. On the other hand, Benjamin (1990) offers two cases to show that such progress is possible in the context of an improved housing stock. He describes the changes made by owners

---

7. Tenements in old subdivided inner-city mansions.

8. Small permanent dwellings along an alley or courtyard.

of flats in New Delhi originally rented to refugees from Pakistan. The original two-roomed flats, built in two-storey blocks around a square central courtyard, have been extended by their occupants by up to 130 per cent to provide both more room for the original occupants and space for renting and business uses.

In the first case, a schoolboy named Singh set up a stall selling sweets and soft drinks outside one of the block's communal toilets which adjoined his home. Through the years this expanded, eventually taking over the toilet block, now unused because residents had generally added toilets to their flats. As economic circumstances changed, including a growth in such shops leading to reduced profit margins, Singh switched to selling sports goods and is now (in his thirties) an employer and a city-wide supplier to both retail and wholesale customers. In addition, relatives have swapped flats in other parts of the blocks to join him in the corner so that their extensions and commercial activities can be done cooperatively.

In Benjamin's second case, a retired civil servant, Kapoor, had extended his flat to its maximum extent to house his household of 11, but could not sacrifice the living space in the front room for commercial purposes despite its profitable location. However, every Tuesday when the market came, he set up a stall on the pavement and sold toys. On other days he made wooden crates on the pavement during the day. By mid-1986, contacts made and contracts awarded allowed Kapoor and his son to join the market on its travels round Delhi and sell toys full time. In both of these cases, it is unlikely that the employment for each household would have developed without the opportunity to use the home and its immediate environs.

3. Profitability

Gilbert (1988) reports that, while a few HBEs are large and profitable, most are small and only assist in eking out a marginal income. Retail outlets often have only a minimum of stock; indeed the proliferation of tiny enterprises, sharing out what little income-generation there is among many people (McGee, 1976), is seen by many commentators as a sign of poverty.

Strassmann (1986) found that activities producing for only local neighbourhood sales are likely to yield the lowest incomes because of easiest entry, least skills and lowest capital intensity. They brought in $75.90 less monthly than others. Their operators were found to be from households which experience twice as much unemployment (12.8 per cent) as the average of all households with HBEs (6.7 per cent). The most lucrative HBE operators, city-wide providers of food products or personal services, earned over $700 dollars per month, and one retail store had earned $2,500.

Strassmann (1987) found that, for his Lima and Sri Lanka samples, earnings per HBE worker were about half of what workers from these households would have earned had they had outside jobs instead, although HBE work was full-time for 93 per cent. However, the vast majority of home workers seemed to accept

Table 18. Type of HBE, average household income per month, average space used and annual household income per m² of space used for HBEs (Delhi)

Type of HBE	Income/month (Rs.)	Average space used (m²)	Annual income (Rs./m²)
Renting	230	16.0	168
Retailing I (small shops)	320[a]	1.5	2,556
Retailing II (regular outlets)	1,190[a]	9.0	1,587
Livestock rearing	300	20.0	180
Hawking and storage	825	3.0	3,300
Tailoring/knitting	579	4.2	1,654
Service I (repairs, laundry etc.)	500[b]	6.0	1,100
Service II (doctors, dentists etc.)	1,000[b]	11.0	1,134

a. Mean for all retailing = Rs.795.
b. Mean for all services = Rs.876.
Sample size = 57   Rs.10 = US$1.00
Source: Raj and Mitra, 1990.

that differential as reasonable. In Sri Lanka, more than 80 per cent of home workers would require a higher wage to switch employment, and more than 60 per cent considered an HBE inherently superior to wage or salaried employment. To earn the equivalent income on the outside, over half of HBE workers expected that at least an additional hour would have to be spent working and travelling, and 38 per cent thought an extra three hours or more would be needed.

The overall pattern seems to be that HBEs everywhere make up around 40 per cent of income among the households that have them. Strassmann (1987) found 40 per cent for Lima but in excess of 45 per cent for his Sri Lanka sample. In the South Delhi case, the contribution of income from HBEs was higher, at 56 per cent of the total income. An average worker engaged in HBEs earned Rs.777 (US$78) per month (see also table 18). It may be that typical households feel that diverting space from family use (or building an addition) would be worth it only if so much is earned. However, the rate of return on total capital invested in HBEs is phenomenal. At the lowest rung of the investment ladder, the rate of return is as high as 20 to 50 times of investment made. Invariably no taxes are paid on the establishment or workers' income and no costing is made for work-hours devoted by family members (Raj and Mitra, 1990).[9]

The more sophisticated retailing and services activities can be seen to be the most lucrative, followed (perhaps surprisingly) by storage and hawking. In St Martin, Haiti, Fass (1980) reports 29 per cent of traders selling from the home but 83 per cent storing goods there. Renting is the least profitable activity, both in total and in return per unit area (see below) but it is more than twice as common

---

9. Whether, on balance, it is beneficial or harmful that tax is not paid is outside the scope of this publication.

as other economic activities. The attraction of its meagre income probably has everything to do with its almost total lack of time commitment.

4.   Characteristics of workers in HBEs

Raj and Mitra (1990) found that 36 per cent of the individuals engaged in HBEs are heads of households. In these cases the entire household income is drawn through HBE activities. In 30 per cent of the cases the activities are undertaken by housewives, other family members and even distant relatives from the workforce. The mean number of household members involved was 1.6 per household. All except one of the HBEs were operated with the help of unpaid family members.

Strassmann (1986) found that low-income HBEs were more likely to be operated by women.[10] No male household head washed clothes at home while no female household head ran a business in repairs or making leather, wood and metal products.[11] The tailors were all men and each generally specialized in one article of clothing. Most worked in their homes, although some were in clothing factories. Male-operated industries with a city-wide market in Lima were found to give the highest income, followed by retail trade, restaurants etc., with a city-wide market. Both are more profitable than making leather, wood and metal products. A number of women posted signs by their doors indicating that, for a small fee, they would administer an injection. Some of these practitioners had taken a short course from the local public health nurse. A few individuals, primarily women, also cured the traditional illnesses of *susto* ("soul-loss" often caused by a bad dream).

D.   Advantages

The chief advantage of HBEs, which tends to overshadow any other, is the contribution they make to the household economy of low-income people, and the opportunity they provide for growth in poor people's incomes. In a time of unprecedented population growth against a background of fiscal austerity and inability to create formal sector jobs, developing countries can benefit from the employment potential of HBEs. As premises are either free, or accounted as such in the business, overheads are kept very low and the householder face a lower marginal capital investment for setting up operation at home than in setting it up elsewhere.[12] In Lima, Strassmann (1986) estimates that there were about 106,500 households (10.8 per cent) with home-based businesses in 1983 and with them they

---

10. Laundries and other services with only a local neighbourhood clientele were particularly unprofitable.

11. 80 per cent of the operators of these businesses were male household heads, compared with 24 per cent for the entire sample of HBEs.

12. It also allow marginally profitable businesses to be established and continue to operate where they would otherwise be uneconomic.

produced 3.9 per cent of metropolitan household income. In addition, as the enterprises are in the residential areas, they impose no transport costs with respect to journeys to work and save transport for local clients.

Settlements tend to evolve and develop in response to the income-earning capacity of the residents. If this capacity is enhanced, the residents will be able to undertake all types of improvements to their living conditions including improvements to their houses (UNCHS, 1989b). There is evidence to suggest that, though HBEs tend to be more prevalent in low-value housing areas than high, the presence of HBEs in low-income settlements increases the quality of housing there.

Strassmann (1986) found that, in poor, informal neighbourhoods, dwellings with HBEs were of better quality than others without them; their value was one third higher, they were on larger sites, had more floor space, and were more likely to be sewered.[13] Since 68 per cent of Strassmann's respondents in 1983 said that they needed the HBE in order to afford the dwelling, it is clear that housing conditions would have been worse without HBEs. Conversely, 70 per cent of HBE operators said that their enterprise would not exist if the dwelling space was not available. Many of the operations were regarded as inseparable from the houses. Dwelling expansion and improvement, however, depended not so much on what type of activity went on there as on total household income, which depended more on HBEs in some cases (the manufacture of "sturdy" products) than in others. Tenants rarely made improvements, and owner-occupants of the most expensive housing in better districts also made fewer improvements than others. In the low-income neighbourhoods, HBE operators were the elite, while in the conventional neighbourhoods, the HBEs belonged to relatively poor households trying to keep up (Strassmann, 1986). Both of these suggest that HBEs act to redistribute income progressively.

In India, the housing conditions of households with HBEs have been shown to be better than the overall conditions, indeed Mehta and Mehta (1990) suggest that they can be the reason for and enabler of settlement upgrading. Raj and Mitra (1990) found that 91 per cent of houses with HBEs had permanent structures and 72 per cent had more than one storey. They argue that, without HBEs, both the incentive and the income for making improvements would be lacking, and housing and neighbourhood conditions throughout the city would be worse.

E.   Disadvantages

However, the disadvantages arising from HBEs should not be forgotten. They tend to be a result of the more general malaise in housing and in employment conditions rather than the result of working in the home *per se*. They provide opportunities for housing problems and worker exploitation to occur in the same

---

13. However, in better-quality neighbourhoods, dwellings with HBEs were worth 26 per cent less, were on smaller sites, and were less likely to be sewered, than dwellings without HBEs.

place. It would, however, be unhelpful to point to the disadvantages as a reason for condemning HBEs; rather they should be dealt with as housing or employment issues within those general sector policies.

The first group of disadvantages arise particularly from the isolation and lack of visibility in which the workers carry out their tasks. Factories are liable to inspection much more readily than HBEs whose nature is to blend into their residential environment in conscious or unconscious anonymity. While factory workers can benefit from group solidarity in order to campaign for better working conditions, home-based workers are isolated and less able to improve their lot. The exploitation of workers inherent in the outwork system is now generally recognized. It has been said that —

> it allows the manufacturer to pay wage rates which imply an intolerable level of exploitation of the worker, frequently lengthening the working day, and forcing the worker to work in conditions which present not only safety but health hazards to herself and other members of the family (Young, 1981).

The persistence and spread of exploitation has, however, been attributed to the large-scale existence of poverty and surplus labour in third-world countries. The meagre earnings of outworkers are often crucial for family survival; the majority of outworkers are women, who are particularly vulnerable to this form of labour exploitation. The roots of exploitation in the outwork system can be traced to its organization of production. The fragmentation of the production process not only keeps home-based workers isolated and in competition with each other, thereby militating against workers' identity, but home-based workers are not able to see the entire production process and the extent of their deprivation in terms of returns to their labour. The common practice of specialization in the making of a part of a product leaves the workers ignorant of how to make the whole product on their own, and also about matters like sources of raw materials and market outlets, which do not allow the workers to begin independent production (Bose, 1990).

Mies (1982) studied lacemaking in Narsapur in India. An estimated 100,000 housewives are engaged in this occupation which accounts for 90 per cent of export earnings of the state. However, the earnings of outworkers were found to be as low as Rs. 0.56 (about 6 US cents!) per day with wages having remained practically constant since 1931, partly due to the proliferation of agents and sub-agents all of whom take a cut off the direct producers' wages. The constant fine work in dim light inevitably has harmful effects on health and eyesight (Bose, 1990).

Similar problems occur in other traditional industries in India such as *beedi* making, in which 35 million *beedi* rollers and 17,000 tobacco processors are involved all over India. Nine out of 10 of the workers are women but the trade is controlled entirely by men. The homes of *beedi* rollers are generally in poor condition with barely enough space for all the family members. The houses are damp, usually full of smoke, and have open drains outside full of discarded and stinking *beedis*. Only 50 per cent of the houses are electrified and the women must work by the light of kerosene lamps (Bezboruah, 1985).

Home-based workers in India have been found to earn less than labourers or street vendors; and many can be said to be living below the poverty line (Schneider de Villegas, 1990). Burra (1989) found that young women and girls working at home in low-paid sub-contracting were liable to miss out on any training as it was regarded as of no economic value. However, the counterfactual situation is argued by Nha (1987) in Viet Nam where the "family economy"-based production is regarded as an effective environment for passing craft skills from the old to the young.

The second group of disadvantages concerns the effect of economic activities on the residential environment. This may be measured in monetary terms through dwelling values, though these may react unevenly or only partially reflect increases or decreases in residential quality, or they may be more affected by factors other than the presence of HBEs. It has already been seen that HBEs are more prevalent in poorer neighbourhoods than in richer. Thus, it is no surprise that Strassmann (1986) found that, in neighbourhoods where there are many HBEs, the value of the building was considerably lower, especially in comparison with household income, than in areas where they were less frequent. However, it is likely that this reflects the effect of the HBEs on housing less than the propensity of poorer households to need HBEs to survive.

There are some externality issues which need to be faced. An externality is an effect which a land use or activity has on neighbouring uses and occupants.[14] HBEs may have considerable negative externalities which may be tolerable for some and intolerable for other residents. The fumes from fish smoking, charcoal burning and other smoky or smelly enterprises may cause nuisance. Fire and boiling liquids can cause dangers beyond their immediate users, especially to children. Tinsmiths and other metal workers, car repairers and engineering activities cause noise. All activity tends to increase the need for access by larger vehicles than are simply used for the occasional passenger journey.

There is a need, therefore, to assess the advantages of HBEs, especially in their creating work and providing services in the neighbourhood, against the disadvantages, both in connection with exploitation of workers and with the dangers and nuisances they cause.[15] Using the sort of analytical techniques assembled by

---

14. A new golf course is likely to have positive externalities on house prices as people would like to live near a large, well-tended open space frequented by the elite. On the other hand, a chemical works will have some positive externalities (improved infrastructure) and some negative (pollution).

15. Not least in order to set some order of magnitudes on the dangers and nuisances which tend to be the main reasons why planning authorities resist them and keep them in uncertainty about their continued existence.

Tipple and Willis (1991a), analysis of the costs and benefits of various activities could be carried out in order to recommend policy which would decrease the incidence of problems while maintaining the viability of HBEs.

F.   Passive HBEs: renting

In contrast to what might be termed "active" HBEs, in which non-residential activities invade the housing areas, renting out rooms does not insinuate any non-residential use[16] but does create income for those involved. It can, therefore, be dealt with separately.

Rental rooms are important, both for supplying accommodation for the poor and for generating some income for the not-quite-so-poor.[17]   Because home-ownership is becoming more difficult, there is a substantial and growing demand for rental housing, particularly in the rapidly growing urban settlements of developing countries. The symbiotic relationship between house-ownership and rentals, where the money from renting out rooms allows the ownership to become a reality for relatively poor households (Woodfield, 1989) and similarly between house-ownership and HBEs (Strassmann, 1986), may be regarded positively or negatively. It is clear that there is still some resistance in the minds of government officials to the renting of rooms by low-income households. Their attitude towards landlords,[18] and towards renting out part of an owner-occupied house for tenants, should be urgently reviewed. The message of the last few years, and the context in which this publication is prepared, is that this symbiosis should be embraced positively and wholeheartedly by beleaguered government housing agencies as therein lies at least part of the solution to both the housing-supply and cash-flow problems affecting the poor in developing countries.

The extremity to which housing has sunk as an investment attracting private capital (traditionally the major source in most countries) is expressed eloquently by landlords in Mexico: "it's the worst business I ever got involved in; right now, renting is the worst, really the worst, business you could name" (Gilbert and Varley, 1990). Although renting of rooms or whole houses is being avoided by entrepreneurs seeking profit in the 1980s and early 1990s, it is still popular with low-income groups and many owners are more than willing to rent out a room or more in order to make a little extra income. Studies of Lusaka squatters (Schlyter, 1987, for example) show increasing levels of renting. Work on Kumasi, Ghana,

---

16. Except in the minority of cases where they are rented to non-residential users.

17. See for instance Peattie, 1987; Gilbert and Varley, 1990; Malpezzi and Ball, 1991; Tipple and Willis, 1991b; UNCHS, 1994f.

18. Landlords are often characterized, officially or merely covertly, as officious, greedy, and profit motivated. Many recent studies (brought together in UNCHS, 1989c) have shown that landlords are often very supportive of their tenants and many do not charge as much rent as they could.

shows that owners of houses shared by tenants have lower incomes than those who own single-household houses, in fact they are closer in income and other characteristics to their tenants than they are to owners who do not share with tenants (Tipple and Willis, 1991b; 1992a).

The symbiotic relationship between owners and tenants has been seen to be the chief motivator for much of the low-income housing construction and consolidation which has taken place in recent years (Woodfield, 1989). Indeed, the renting of rooms appears to be the most common income-generating use to which dwellings are put.

In low-income settlements in India surveyed by Vaidya and Mukundan (1987) and by Raj and Mitra (1990), renting was the most common economic activity. Vaidya and Mukundan (1987) found that, while only 6.8 per cent of the houses had visible home-based economic activities, 39.5 per cent of units had rented rooms. Raj and Mitra (1990), however, found only 27 per cent of their Delhi sample engaged in renting but every class was involved in some way. Table 19 represents their findings and the link between income on the one hand and rental-housing quality and other activities on the other.

From evidence from two low-income housing areas in Ahmedabad in western India, Mehta and Mehta (1990) found several levels of rented space and almost one third of the units having a renter. Many houses have extensions; those in the backyard are usually for the households' own use but those in the front and especially on the top are essentially for rental units. Units located on the access roads and the end units in each block have encroached upon a much larger area and occupants have rented or sold these to commercial users; thus benefiting more than owners of interior units. About 25 per cent of the original owners have sold their houses and these exhibit far greater extensions and improvements than the rest. Mehta and Mehta (1990) see the creation of a rental market through upgrading the houses, assisted financially by HBEs, as a part of the households' survival strategy.

Table 19. Type of rental accommodation offered and other HBEs

Income class (Rs./month)	Type of rental accommodation offered	Type of HBE
0-600	Substandard	Services (ironing of clothes etc.)
601-1,000	Relatively good quality	Petty retailing, storage for hawking, tailoring
1,001-2,000	Good quality	Retailing through separate shop, livestock rearing (milch cattle), tailoring, manufacturing, services (skilled jobs, i.e., plumbing, electrical repair)
2,001 +	Good quality	Shops, storage, garment manufacturing, services (doctor, dentist)

Rs.10 = US$1.00

Source: Raj and Mitra, 1990, p. 174.

Nientied and others (1987) report that, on the very small (down to 25 m²) plots at Jahangipuri, New Delhi, renting was not common but, where it did occur, it was usually a first floor added for the purpose. Thus, it appeared that if a household on a small plot wanted to generate some income through renting, they are compelled to invest a substantial amount on construction.

Tipple (1991; 1992b) found that the renting of space to another household was a motive for extensions to government-built housing in some cities. In Mirpur, part of Dhaka, Bangladesh, households who had only a single room themselves tended to rent out extra space they built. As they were paying highly subsidized rents but their sub-tenants paid market rents, their profits were worth the sacrifice of space (Ameen, 1988). The extensions to flats in India reported by Benjamin (1985) and Dasgupta (1990) were frequently rented out, not only as residential space but also to commercial and other establishments. Thus the doctor's clinic, the nursery school and the pharmacy were all paying rent to flat owners. Where rented housing is very scarce, single-roomed additions are in great demand. This was observed in Harare, Zimbabwe, where the addition of a simple wooden room (designed as a garden shed for wealthy residents) could be rented out for one quarter of a labourer's wage.

As Hansen and Williams (1987) and Tipple and Willis (1991b) argue, growth in the supply of rental housing frequently depends on the growth of owner-occupied housing often at the lower end of the market. As most cities in the developing world are likely to double and triple in size over the next two or three decades, rental markets will assume an increasing share of the housing supply. Policies which will encourage owners to rent out rooms, and which will encourage ownership by the expectation of some rental income, will be a vital part of a government's arsenal of enabling policies.

G.   The link between housing and infrastructure investment and future income

The link between time and money is universally recognized; time-consuming tasks have an opportunity cost even for the poorest. Thus, any reduction in the time spent fetching water or walking to a distant bus stop could be turned into economic activity. As the poorest tend to live in unserviced, unhealthy areas, marginal improvements in services can be significant in saving time in addition to the more obvious, and vital, effects of reducing mortality, improving nutrition, and discouraging high birth-rates to compensate for infant mortality (actual or expected).

Low-income housing and employment opportunities within and around it tend to form an environment in which the poorest members of society can eke out some sort of living, and in which low-paid workers can supplement their formal incomes. It follows, therefore, that policies and programmes which seek to improve housing conditions through relocation to resettlement areas are likely to disrupt the economic activity patterns set up in the former environment. The point was well made by Turner (1976) in his case of the semi-invalid mason whose move to a peripheral higher-quality government housing area implied that the household lost the security of his wife's income from selling from the house.

Nangia (1987) describes the resettlement of three settlements in Metropolitan Delhi and the effects the move had on real wages (wages less transport to work costs) and on entrepreneurial activity round the home. Housing conditions in the former settlements were poor; mud buildings and some of flimsy materials such as old cloth, tarpaulin and thatch. In the new settlements, security of tenure and loans encouraged rapid improvement of housing conditions on plots 50 to 100 per cent larger than in the squatter settlement. However, the inhabitants immediately experienced a decline in their income of between 10 and 25 per cent. This was caused by waiting time for work near the new location, lack of opportunities near home for children to work, and disruption of child care. At the same time, an increase in expenditure was experienced because of increased distance to work. Contrary to the general experience, manual skilled workers and those engaged in services registered an increase in their income after moving. The income took three to seven years in the new area to be restored after which it showed a rising trend as the new work-centres provide increased opportunities and, with skills acquired, the bargaining power of labour has also risen.

It could be expected that upgrading would be less disruptive to employment opportunities than relocation and more likely to be advantageous to HBEs. Strassmann (1980) demonstrates the importance of access to water in determining the value of dwellings in his study of Cartagena de Indias, Colombia. He found that not only was the house value reduced by a lack of water by much more than the cost of fitting it, but the dwellings without water were much less likely to be improved or enlarged than those with a water connection. He suggests, therefore, that fitting water supply to a settlement may be the single most effective upgrading task.

Electricity can also be important for HBEs. Gilbert (1988) points out that settlements with many clandestine electrical connections are more likely to suffer from blackouts than settlements where most electrical connections are legal. These cause problems for workshops and for cafés where refrigeration is required.

There is some evidence that the impact of the upgrading process can be both positive and negative, with the net effect difficult to quantify. Leynes (1987; 1990) carried out an analysis of the effect of reblocking[19] being carried out as part of the

---

19. "Reblocking [is] a term coined to describe the activities of planning the physical layout of the road network and land allocation for residential, commercial and institutional use, subdividing the residential area into individual lots for awarding to eligible beneficiaries and realigning the existing structures so that they fit into generated lots and infrastructural networks can be laid" (Leynes, 1990, p. 17).

Zonal Improvement Programme in Metropolitan Manila, the Philippines, between 1981 and 1984. The survey of 2,160 households found that those with incomes from entrepreneurial activities had increased by 25–36 per cent while renting showed only a marginal increase by 11–12 per cent. Those households who have experienced some form of disturbance from the reblocking have found that the improvement has had relatively positive effects on home-based income-generating activities. However, the history of such effects may be characterized by a negative effect in the short term due to disruption which, following mobilization of the coping mechanisms inherent among the informal settlers, is surpassed by positive improvements. Depending on how the settlers react to the temporary dislocation, the consequential effect could either be positive or negative (Leynes, 1987).

> For those who are unable to cope with the dislocation, any or a combination of the following events may happen: a change in their means of livelihood, a change in status of occupancy for those who opted to sell their 'rights' to settle again elsewhere, and/or totally losing their home-based income generating activity. For those who are able to make the necessary adjustments, an induced home-based income generating activity is expected (Leynes, 1987, p. 24).

Batarfie (1987) reports that the Kampung Improvement Programmes (KIP) encouraged a general increase in the incidence of places selling food, cookies and breakfast dishes which are run to earn supporting or additional income. The upgrading of Pavao-Pavaozinho in Brazil appeared to lead to an increase of 100 per cent in the number of *biroscas* (Treiger and Faerstein, 1987). These examples indicate that the upgrading process itself can improve conditions for trade and, thereby, contribute (albeit temporarily) to raising the standard of living of the inhabitants.

H.   The case for intervention in HBEs

The challenge to policy-makers is to attempt to maximize both the employment-creating potential of the informal sector, in this case HBEs, and the degree of social protection and regulation extended to it (ILO, 1991). The GSS requires formal intervention to encourage the informal shelter sector through, *inter alia*, a radical reappraisal of laws and regulations governing land holding, planning and building, property leases etc., with a view to amend, simplify and streamline those which present obstacles to growth and employment in the informal sector (UNCHS, 1990). Both of these international recommendations bring the informal sector, and HBEs, within the general supply system as part of an overall economic policy.

The progressive "legalization" of the informal sector is clearly an essential requirement for its integration into society. But it is more likely to take place in a positive environment where the obstacles to legal entry are reduced to a minimum, where the costs of being legal are not prohibitive, and where there are clear benefits to becoming legal. The classic case recorded by de Soto (1986) of 289 days being required to complete all the formalities required to start up an enterprise is by no means an isolated example. It would seem important, for example, to distinguish between regulations that are essential for public health and safety, for instance, and those that are less essential and place unnecessary obstacles to the operations of HBEs.

The ILO has a particular concern over the non-compliance of the informal sector with labour legislation and basic labour standards, owing partly to the fact that a majority of informal sector workers are self-employed or unpaid family workers who are not subject, in practice, to many legal obligations of this nature. The empirical evidence is inadequate to assess the costs in employment terms of imposing controls over the excesses of poor wages and working conditions, lack of safety precautions, etc., evident in the informal sector as a whole, or in the home-based part of it. Yet it is possible to hypothesise that the difficulties of introducing some regulation, and of preventing excesses, will be greater in the HBEs than those in more public places. As they are concealed within homes (sometimes with the intention of secrecy from the authorities), locationally scattered, unregistered, and often away from motorable roads, they are extremely difficult to control even in comparison with other informal enterprises located in the industrial equivalent of squatter settlements.

In the case of informal-sector enterprises which do hire labour, compliance with the full range of labour regulations, including those governing hours of work, weekly rest, holidays with pay, minimum wages and social security contributions, might absorb the very low profits made by such enterprises and wipe them out of business altogether. In addition, as a high proportion of workers in HBEs are self-employed, they would stand to carry the full cost of the improvements in conditions as well as enjoying the benefits. However, there is currently no way of knowing what the effects would be, nor of the amount of cost (in lost employment) which any particular benefit (in regulation of working conditions) might impose.

Within the progressive spirit, however, fulfilling some standards could be encouraged as a first step towards regularization of the informal sector. Three types of such standards would appear to deserve priority attention.

- Basic human rights such as freedom of association, freedom from forced labour, and freedom from discrimination.
- The most exploitative types of employment relationships in which many children find themselves trapped — often at a very early age — such as bonded labour; the employment of children in particularly hazardous occupations or industries; and the employment of very young children.
- Basic standards of occupational safety and health.

Meanwhile, it would seem counter-productive to inhibit economic activity within the home. On the contrary, it should be actively encouraged. Afrane (1987) points out that policies formulated by housing authorities have failed to give adequate attention to the viability of employment and income-generating ventures in housing areas. However, this review demonstrates that the separation of home and workplace is likely to be counter-productive for many of the world's poorest people who understandably refuse to behave in a manner congruent with town planning law, preferring to increase productivity (often just to scrape a living) than to move the workplace out of sight of the living-room.

I.   Measures to assist HBEs

Measures which might be successful in enabling or encouraging HBEs would include the following: reversing the trend for smaller plots; revising regulations governing the use of plots and the type of structures to be developed on them; making small-scale borrowing available for HBEs; and stimulating the production of rental housing. These measures are discussed below. Other measures, such as the positive impacts of improved infrastructure and the establishment CBOs have been discussed above.

1.   Reversing the trend for smaller plots

Small plots are often being adopted in order to make the services provided affordable. However, they may be inappropriate where space is needed for income-generating enterprises. The lack of adequate and suitable space can be as much an inhibiting factor as lack of credit in the development of income-generating opportunities (UNCHS, 1989b). Nientied and others (1987), however, writing from Indian experience, maintain that limited plot size is no bar to activity and cite a case of a cycle repair shop on the roof of a 22 m² house. There are, however, cases where space is crucial, for example for vegetable growing, animal husbandry, storage and protection of raw materials or customers' articles in for repair, weaving, and rented rooms. Bhatt and others (1993) advise that private yards in Chinese housing should be large enough to allow for extensions or gardening, or commercial activities.

2.   Revising regulations governing the use of plots and the type of structures to be developed on them

This should include a removal of the locus of control over planning issues within a neighbourhood from the urban authorities to neighbourhood groups. This implies that the community has the potential to be a more effective watch-dog against environmental pollution by local enterprises than the public authorities (UNCHS, 1989b). Gilbert's (1988) experience in low-income settlements in Colombia, Mexico and Venezuela suggests that the establishment of neighbourhood councils, to act as development control agents and arbitrators in disputes, is likely to result in locally sensitive judgements on the level and nature of economic activity in residential areas. He also proposes more tolerance of HBEs in government housing areas.

Where commercial activity is encouraged in residential plots, potential arises for cross-subsidy. For example, corner plots where main routes meet can be particularly highly priced because, upon development, they would be well-suited to commercial activity. On the other hand, smaller plots deep within the residential area can be sold more cheaply to the poor and are less likely to filter upwards. Strict zoning laws and unimaginative planning tend to remove the possibility of using well-located sites for economic activity. Bhatt and others (1993), in their proposals for residential areas in Fangtin, China, propose the promotion of mixed uses in residential areas in line with UNCHS (Habitat) (1993d). In order to increase the number of households with the potential for owning businesses, they propose narrow frontages on streets suitable for commercial uses.

3. Making small-scale borrowing available for HBEs

The new UNDP Micro-capital Grants Programme (UNDP, n.d.) recognizes that the poor deserve an opportunity to enlarge their income-generating options. The requirements for building the capacity in the informal sector are typically very small amounts of capital in the form of materials, cash or credit — a vendor may need $100 in start-up capital, or a prospective food seller may need a water tap within the house. At this level, it would seem reasonable that governments could consider making many tiny grants to reinforce productive capacity in a group of existing small-scale and home-based enterprises rather than concentrating industrial seed capital on a few large-scale enterprises. Since returns can be expected to be quite rapid, short-term loans may be appropriate (Nientied and others, 1987). As Fass (1977) advises, there shall be a liberal attitude towards the use of such loans for housing extensions or improvements if there seems to be a good chance of establishing or improving the viability of HBEs.

4. Stimulating the production of rental housing

Relatively low-income households should be encouraged to add rooms for rent to their dwellings both informally, such as the renting of rooms in a house, and in more formal rental units (such as apartments). The message of the last few years is that the symbiosis between owners and renters should be embraced positively and wholeheartedly by beleaguered government housing agencies as therein lies at least part of the solution to both the housing-supply and cash-flow problems affecting the poor in developing countries. Rent controls may prevent profitability and should be progressively withdrawn (UNCHS, 1994f; Malpezzi and others, 1990). Tax benefits on rental income would be helpful in places where landlords routinely pay tax,[20] especially in formal-sector houses or in areas where informal housing is being formalized.

---

20. It is not uncommon for rental income to be more heavily taxed than "earned" income. In Ghana, for example, theoretical tax levels are much greater on rents than on other income (Tipple, 1988).

The efficiency of extensions made for renting out, in areas where services are already in place, deserves more attention. As extensions are discouraged by planning regulations on maximum use of plots or by estate owners, occupants of relatively well-built and well-located housing may be discouraged from supplying rooms for rent which they can well afford to build (Tipple, 1991; 1992b). Adding rooms to an existing house is comparatively inexpensive — possibly as little as half the price of new building as no new land is required (Hansen and Williams, 1987) and at least some of the structure is already in place.

J.   Conclusions

Many HBEs are bound to be unsuccessful, others start small and stay small, operating quite successfully for years, yet, others will grow and form the basis for larger, successful companies. Meanwhile, their cycle of founding and floundering or survival sustains a level of economic activity which is intrinsically valuable. Gilbert (1988) recommends that the best policy for government to adopt is tolerance and non-intervention. Within this, however, there are approaches which are likely to impose some control on the problems while allowing the potential to be developed.

The promotion of home-based income generation, as proposed above, requires that housing units, provided either by the public or the private sector or built by self-help, should be designed in such a way as to be able to accommodate income-generating activities. This means that designs which allow for the multiple use of space and opportunities for occupiers to adapt and extend them should be provided and not discouraged by lease or tenancy agreements.

HBEs are so common and of such value to the economy, at household, neighbourhood and government levels, that housing should be treated as productive infrastructure and be eligible for loans on the same terms as factories. If governments begin to value full employment, especially for the poor, with the vigour which the Employment Policy Convention, 1964 (No. 122), implies, it is likely that HBEs will be given a better deal.

Although there are a number of useful studies on several aspects of HBEs in some cities, no overall picture is available on their costs and benefits. The balance of the argument so far appears to be in favour of allowing them (Gilbert, 1988), and Peattie (1987) went so far as to propose their enablement after her study in Santafé de Bogotá. Whether the balance is well enough established to encourage them, not only to cease harassment but also to enable, is less easy to assert. Their presence argues a greater benefit than cost for those in whose home they occur; whether the benefits would be greater and costs less if they were separated from, but still close to, the home, is not known. What their effects are on neighbours (their externalities), and the balance of pros and cons of particular uses, are also unknown.

In addition to research to establish values for some of the variables in the cost-benefit equations for particular uses and neighbourhood types, it would be useful for a series of pilot projects to examine the modalities of establishing mixed-use areas as proposed in UNCHS (1993d) and explored by Bhatt and others (1993). These projects could test the logistics of integrating work-place and residential space in a variety of house types in differing cultures, examine the economic relationship between expected income and willingness to pay for housing and services, and determine whether residents without economic activities would choose to live in such areas, because they offered employment or services, or simply because they were unconcerned about the externalities.

VIII. Experience with employment generation and poverty alleviation in poor communities

It is appropriate at this time to review some of the experience gained by national and international organizations, donor agencies and NGOs with specific support programmes concerned with reducing unemployment and improving shelter, infrastructure and services provision. Much of this is described in policy documents and project reports which are not widely circulated. In addition, it may be unknown to readers outside the sectoral specialism. A good example of this is the literature on employment programmes aimed not only at providing infrastructure but also at poverty alleviation. It is likely that readers in the shelter field would have little access to the experience gained through such projects. In addition, shelter sector workers may be unaware of relevant experience gained by agencies whose past concerns have tended to be tangential to housing. It is suitable, therefore, to begin this section with experience gained by the ILO.

A.   ILO projects

The ILO has, for decades, been involved in projects aimed at improving employment in developing countries, particularly among the poor.[1] Accumulating evidence from most developing countries shows that an increasing proportion of employment and output is originating from what is known as the informal sector (see Sethuraman, 1981; Maldonado and others, 1987). It is this sector in which more and more poor and new job seekers are finding opportunities to earn an income. The ILO recognizes that the informal sector has made a substantial contribution to national economies, providing employment and incomes, developing human resources through being a training ground for millions to acquire productive skills at low cost and no public cost. Despite low incomes, participants in this sector have mobilized considerable savings both in cash and in kind — with no burden on the public sector — and have made maximum use of indigenous resources. The sector does not receive any public subsidy (unlike many public-sector units) and yet has expanded. It has therefore passed the market test of viability and it generates goods and services of value to society (ILO, 1990).

The 77th Session of the International Labour Conference (the top policy-making organ of the ILO) held in June 1990 adopted a resolution concerning self-employment promotion which implicitly referred to the urban informal sector. In its introduction and the concluding part, the resolution acknowledged that many of the working poor in urban areas are self-employed, and that the promotion of productive self-employment is a means for raising incomes. This has guided the

---

1.   A review of those activities has been presented in ILO (1990).

formulation of a programme targeted upon the urban informal sector. The main objective of the programme is to assist member States in the design and implementation of policies, action programmes, and projects to create additional employment and raise incomes and productivity of workers engaged in informal enterprises. Among other objectives are dissemination of knowledge and experience on how to integrate the urban informal sector into mainstream economic development and on the creation of favourable economic, regulatory and institutional environments.

More specifically the programme aims at:

- increasing awareness of the need to promote the informal sector;
- enabling countries to create the appropriate policy and institutional environment to favour growth of output and employment in the informal sector;
- encouraging governments to allocate greater credit, training and other resources to the informal sector;
- assisting governments in improving the functioning of various markets and in reorientation and strengthening concerned institutions;
- assisting governments in the design and implementation of informal sector projects.

Various means of action are utilized in promoting the above objectives. Perhaps the most important are the short-term advisory services to member States and longer-term technical cooperation aimed at strengthening the national capacity to design policies and implement programmes. Others are aimed at strengthening dissemination of knowledge and information on experience, undertaking studies in order to identify emerging problems, designing appropriate policies and strategies, and helping to discover the problems in implementation and suggest remedies (ILO, 1990).

Two complementary approaches have been taken based on different conceptualizations of the informal sector. The first looks at the sector as consisting of individuals and seeks to eliminate inefficiencies in the labour market. In other words, the interventions seek to improve the allocation of labour among various sectors/activities and the returns to labour of different categories (men/women) by eliminating market segmentations and distortions. This has been labelled "the labour market approach".

The second approach regards the informal sector as consisting of enterprises which in turn provide employment to individuals. This approach (called "the sectoral approach") suggests that any improvement in income of workers in the informal sector can only be brought about by intervening at the source of employment, i.e., at the enterprise or the sectoral level. Although micro-level characteristics — the amount of physical capital, the level of education, skills and experience of workers and the level of technology — affect earnings, conditions at the macro or sectoral level may be more influential to profitability. These would include the level of aggregate demand for informal-sector goods and services, the relationship between informal and formal sectors, the policy and regulatory environment, the efficiency of various markets, and the general policy environment. The aim of interventions in the second approach, therefore, would be to raise the level of output and employment, productivity, investment and technology in the informal sector.

Both approaches seek to maximize the returns to labour. In the first this is achieved through elimination of labour market distortions and encouraging the mobility of labour towards occupations yielding higher return. In the second, labour is enabled to realize higher returns (and productivity) through improved access to factors complementing labour as well as through creating a more favourable macro-economic framework. The two approaches thus complement each other. The sectoral approach is confined to micro-enterprises only (and through them the workers) in contrast to the labour market approach which covers all individuals irrespective of whether they are engaged in micro-enterprises or as wage labour in casual work and domestic service.

The interventions currently taking place through ILO technical assistance fall into three overlapping categories:

- direct support to the grass-roots level including NGOs;
- strengthening the capacity of governmental institutions assisting the informal sector;
- improving the policy and institutional framework to encourage expansion and growth in this sector.

Though some of these interventions are channelled through national governments, most involve dealing directly with the target groups or their organizations or other NGOs. They include:

- Access to credit (complemented by advice and assistance with skills acquisition) for the poor who run their small business or wish to set one up (known as income-generating projects). These projects have a strong equity orientation and are generally implemented in close collaboration with NGOs.
- Assistance with management skills, improved technologies, tools and equipment, marketing, product design etc., for micro-enterprises with few wage workers and/or apprentices. These projects are more concerned with raising productivity rather than equity. Such direct support activities emphasising improved credit or input delivery mechanisms often call for intermediary institutions (e.g., NGOs) as a channel for delivery and communication with the target groups. One of the objectives of these interventions has, therefore, been to create such intermediaries where they are absent or deficient — for example, artisan associations or other equivalent self-help groups. Besides facilitating links with support institutions (banks, training/technology institutions etc.), they also serve as a means to defend the interests of the target groups and exert pressure on policy makers. Thus, organization of the target group and improving their collective capability forms an added objective (see Maldonado, 1986). The end result of

these interventions has been not only to encourage participatory development but also to strengthen the capacity of the target groups to help themselves.

Strengthening the capacity of government and other institutions takes various forms. It generally implies strengthening the staff capacity of the institutions concerned through training, preparation of manuals and teaching materials, or in the case of banks and other support institutions, it may involve improving their financial capacity (ILO, 1990).

It has been found advisable to have a preparatory phase in a project, lasting between 12 and 15 months and typically reviewing sociological conditions, institutional and legal constraints, and ongoing interventions and projects by other actors. Following this, ways to mobilize internal resources are identified and the beneficiaries' willingness to commit themselves to common objectives are assessed. This approach has been followed in Benin, Burundi, Cape Verde and Haiti.

A distinguishing feature of technical cooperation projects in francophone Africa has been the promotion of participatory development. Informal-sector producers (or artisans) are encouraged to organize themselves into flexible groups, taking into account their socio-cultural characteristics. Local participation has been promoted through self-learning and self-evaluation. The artisans are encouraged and assisted to manage on a collective basis (e.g., managing the common workshop facilities) and to improve their technical know-how. They are encouraged to discuss the problems concerning their activity among themselves and with the government representatives in order to find suitable solutions.

By strengthening the organization of small producers and by promoting mutual credit/savings groups, it has been found that artisans can undertake the investment necessary on their own. This implies that the role of the ILO is one of catalytic agent, mainly confined to motivating and guiding the artisans in making productive investment (ILO, 1990). Assessments have shown that incomes of the artisans have increased and conditions of life improved (Maldonado, 1986). For example, significant improvements have been registered in housing, clothing and personal belongings, and nourishment of the family. An important supplementary indicator is the observed increase in individual savings. Perhaps a more significant indicator is the improved capacity of informal artisans to negotiate with the institutions, to contribute to the project design and implementation, to explore new markets and to obtain greater access to credit and other resources.

Since 1988–1989, the ILO has been active in assisting the informal sector. Project documents have been prepared and advisory services provided following requests from member States, employers' and workers' groups. The projects have included employment creation through promotion of micro-enterprises (Chad); and women in food processing and catering (Côte d'Ivoire). The scope of technical cooperation has expanded to improve policies and regulatory practices in support of the informal sector by carrying out studies in Benin, Tunisia and Zambia.

Pilot projects have been set up to generate action at the national level). In addition, employers, workers and NGOs interested in promoting the informal sector have been assisted (for example, through a training programme for workers' cooperatives in Indonesia, the strengthening of NGO capacity for training the urban poor in Bangladesh). Also women's enterprises in the tourism sector have been supported through such funds.

In the ILO's experience (von Braun and others, 1991), as the potential for public works programmes becomes clearer and as the most urgent problems are more clearly defined, a narrowing of investment takes place both by location and by type of project. In Senegal, for instance, rather than attempting to supervise activities all over the country, as in the past, priority targets are being defined. Public works programmes are being limited mainly to areas of severe land degradation, high irrigation potential, and urban settlement. The country-wide effort has given way to greater targeting. Recently, there has been a relative shift in emphasis from rural to urban areas.

B. The UNDP/ILO Employment Generation in Urban Works Programmes

This Programme (INT/89/021) addresses the creation of employment opportunities and improving living conditions for the poorer strata in urban areas in the least developed countries. Its immediate objectives can be summarized as the formulation of employment-intensive policies for urban upgrading based on studies of local resources. Employment is seen to be one of the issues which is raised rather starkly in the current level of urban growth; migrants are not seen as attracted by the jobs in the city but rather pushed out of the rural areas by a lack of opportunities. Because so much employment is required, new approaches are needed. In the context of the recent promotion of a local resource-based approach, enabling strategies, and new public-private partnerships, the Programme recognizes the importance of the involvement of all appropriate actors in the development of urban works.

The Programme suggests that the most efficient, equitable and sustainable approach to delivery and maintenance of urban works programmes can be found through a clear distinction between major and minor works (see table 3), as a means of dividing the work for which workers should be paid and those which they can be called upon to do voluntarily. The argument underlying the Programme is that, though minor works may create relatively less paid employment (mainly in skilled components), turning them over to the community and its organizations may be the only way to achieve improvements in local infrastructure and keep them maintained. On the other hand, recognizing the principle that labour components in major works must be paid for, efforts should be made to increase the labour component in proportion to capital.

A positive feature of labour-based approaches is their self-targeting nature among the poor. As wages for unskilled work are low, an increase in activity at that level benefits the poor more than the richer without any additional conditions being attached. This is in contrast to many other efforts to target assistance to the poor. However, it is recognized that low wages are not necessarily an advantage to those who receive them. Thus the Programme is to be carried out in the context of overall ILO policy which aims at a productive and motivated work force, eligible for training and subject to good employment practices.

The Programme recognizes the need for acceptable standards based on sustainability, affordability for the users, and adaptability to local conditions. Thus, urban infrastructure and housing projects should be designed with the use of local natural, human and waste resources in mind. Wherever possible, wastes should be recycled, partly because it makes ecological and economic sense (sustainability) but also because it provides a rich vein of jobs for the poor (poverty alleviation). These functions are set within a series of human relationships. Prerequisites for their success are that it must be recognized that it is the community which owns the project, not the municipality; and that negotiations between CBOs and public authorities must be conducted as between equal parties. This constitutes a major change, since the relationship between the two parties quite often is based on mutual distrust. In other words, it switches back to the basic idea of a "civil service" — the professional in the service of the people.

Emphasis is laid on the ability of communities, through CBOs, to enter into contracts to execute public works in their areas with any paid work being allotted to SSEs based in the areas themselves. NGOs can be useful in acting as intermediaries between CBOs and the Town Hall. In addition, focal-point institutions can be identified to provide research and development expertise, pointing to suitable technologies and procedures. The increasingly important role identified for SSEs in public works calls for training and other means of encouragement to be set up around the functions of construction, building materials and refuse collection and recycling.

One of the projects sponsored by this programme, a small block-paving project in Kampala, exemplifies the effectiveness of labour-intensive projects in urban works (see chapter IV).

C.   The UNCHS (Habitat)/DANIDA Training Programme for Community Participation in Improving Human Settlements

The primary resource of a country is its people who, individually and in communities, are a source of ideas and motivations to improve their living conditions. This Programme is aimed at helping governments to incorporate community participation into their national strategies. Within the Programme, community participation is defined as "the democratic and voluntary involvement of communities in decision-making which directly affects their living conditions" (Yap, 1988). The Programme is currently in its third phase but a recent document (UNCHS, 1991b) has reviewed the previous two phases which have been operating since 1984. Activities have been concentrated in three countries: Bolivia, Sri Lanka and Zambia where they have been concerned with training and with encouraging national strategies for community participation.

The training approaches consist of:
* offering courses in organizing and facilitating community participation;
* testing methods and tools for use by motivators in community participation;
* introducing methods to monitor and evaluate training courses;
* providing on-site advisory services for countries requesting assistance;
* organizing regional seminars to collect, exchange and disseminate information on community participation.

Phase one concentrated on developing the expertise of community leaders and project staff and established the need for, and positive perception of a programme in community participation. In this phase a series of training modules were developed, dealing with technical, social, financial and communications issues in relation to community participation. From 1988, the second phase of the Programme tested out the training methodology and modules developed in collaboration with local institutions in the three target countries: the Ministry of Urban Affairs in Bolivia, the National Housing Development Authority in Sri Lanka, and the Chalimbana Local Government Training Institute in Zambia.

In use, the modules were found to be effective for guiding training in the issues involved in community participation in settlement-upgrading and sites-and-services schemes. The institutional requirements for their success were that government supported the enabling approach, that human resource development was recognized as being important (including a recognition in local authorities that they should establish rapport with NGOs and CBOs), and that community participation should be institutionalized. The training materials themselves showed that there is a need to develop country-specific materials using the centrally prepared materials as references; that locally prepared materials reflecting local idioms are a necessary basis for interactive learning; that gender analysis of materials, staff and training needs are required; and that inter-regional exchange of experience can be helpful.

In assessing the success of the programme, Bolivia can be taken as an example. The training there has concentrated on the teams of architect, engineer and social worker (known locally as *contratistas*) who are engaged by the numerous housing cooperatives to help them to carry out their building operations. The *contratistas* were trained in involving the community in all aspects of the planning and implementation of their housing areas and in the management of them after they are finished. Materials in local languages were prepared to pass on information as varied as how to organise a group and the contract of credit, using media as varied as story telling, booklets, posters, and calendars. A cartoon magazine *"My House, My Health"* spread the word on good housekeeping and building practices. In addition, training workshops were held with government personnel in how the community participates in housing, and special attention was paid throughout to the involvement of women as equal partners with men in housing and home-making activities.

The outputs of the project are impressive, not only numerically in the sheer numbers of participants, projects affected, and beneficiaries of know-how, but also in the evidence of increased awareness of the people about what is possible in housing and what should be expected — in other words creating a more discerning clientele for housing services. The communities' organizational bases have been strengthened so that they can now negotiate with the authorities on all aspects of service provision. In addition, their traditional forms of cooperation and self-help (the *pasanacu*) have been reinforced. By training the *contratistas* to be trainers, the project's effects are self-perpetuating.

Perhaps the outwardly most impressive outcome of the Programme internationally can be seen in the community contracts procedures which have been introduced in Sri Lanka and which can point up ways forward for community involvement in public works and housing programmes in other countries. Sri Lanka was very fertile soil for the community training programme as, before it began, community development councils (CDCs) had been established extensively through a UNICEF programme. In addition, the Million Houses Programme had established enablement as the key to environmental improvement for the poor. Through training members of CDCs and staff members of the National Housing Development Authority, the foundations were laid for the CDCs to be awarded community contracts to renovate and build services. As Yap (1988) and others recount, the careful training of community members and staff of NHDA, and attention to detail in division of responsibilities, methods of payment, etc., allowed sufficient mutual trust and confidence for successful community contracts to be awarded and implemented. The CDC is the contracting entity, payments are made as if the contract were an ordinary commercial one, workers are hired locally by the CDC and paid a standard rate for the job, and NHDA keeps a careful eye on quality. However, unlike an ordinary commercial contract, the future users are involved in construction, thereby improving the quality of work. Furthermore, they have a sense of pride in the finished item in use (so maintenance is less of a problem), and the community receives the contractor's profit. The case of the large squatter settlement of Wanathamulla has been held up as a model (e.g., through UNCHS (Habitat)/Danida video presentations) of the potential of the community contracts system. Here, not only have the members of the community successfully completed contracts, but they have also negotiated new designs for such facilities as washing places with NHDA. The community contracts have led CDCs to bid for work outside their own areas and for groups of artisans to form legal cooperatives and carry out work as contractors. Even complex tasks such as sewerage mains have been successfully tackled.

D.   The UNCHS (Habitat)/UNDP/World Bank Urban Management Programme

During the 1970s and early 1980s, governments of developing countries were encouraged by international donor agencies to address urban growth, urban poverty, and the degradation of the urban environment mainly through projects: settlement-upgrading and sites-and-services schemes, provision and renovation of water mains, sewerage systems, and updating of urban transport systems. Not only did these inputs tend to be sectoral, they also tended to concentrate efforts in particular areas, usually with the intention of replication.[2] They did not markedly strengthen municipal government, apart, perhaps, from a special unit set up to implement the project.

Various conclusions have been drawn in the preamble to the Urban Management Programme from an assessment of the experience of those projects:

*   Little recognition was given to the political dimension of urban issues and the interplay of political frameworks and policy reform.
*   There was little understanding of the link between macro-economic policy and urban economic activities.
*   The effects of urban projects on macro-economic performance and urban dwellers' long-term economic well-being were not understood.
*   Little attention was paid to productivity.
*   Poverty was considered as a welfare issue with little attention to increasing urban efficiency and productivity from the poor person's point of view.
*   The informal sector was largely ignored.
*   Not enough attention was paid to capacity-building in local government.

In other words, the Urban Management Programme recognized the need for a multi-sectoral approach to urban development and for encouraging sustainability in improved urban conditions. To this end, UNCHS (Habitat), the World Bank and the United Nations Development Programme joined forces to combine their specialisms to strengthen the contribution which urban areas make towards economic growth, social development, and the alleviation of poverty.

Originally, there were three strands; urban land management, municipal finance and administration, and infrastructure. Then a fourth, urban environment was added; and finally (in 1991) the alleviation of poverty. The alleviation of urban poverty is to be addressed in three related ways:

*   to bring demand orientation to the issue;
*   to encourage policy reviews and regulatory audits to find and correct problems of an institutional and financial nature leading to inequity, inefficiency, and ineffectiveness;

---

2.   The replicability did, however, depend very largely on the effective recovery of costs.

- to help define the most effective roles and policies for government and the private sector (including community groups and NGOs) in alleviating poverty.

The conventional approach to helping the urban poor has been through public-sector agencies with particular sectoral concerns who compete for funds on the honourable ground of helping the poor. However, this encourages the idea that the poor are homogeneous, to be acted upon by different interests, and as clients with needs amenable to short-term political solutions. Despite growth in services for the poor, poverty continues to increase.

The Urban Management Programme introduces a demand orientation into the approach, recognizing that the poor represent a series of markets, just as the non-poor do. However, unlike the latter, their inability to buy (to generate effective demand for) current goods and services through lack of money disallows them from making their needs known through the market. In this context, the public sector responds by being a provider and supplier of services but, as the poor are usually not able to make their needs known through the political process either, the services offered are not always those which are required the most.

The Urban Management Programme plans to promote policy reviews and studies to assess and revise inappropriate regulations, institutional arrangements, fiscal operations, and other interventions which work against market efficiency and ineffectiveness. As urban services become more market-oriented, the urban poor will, of necessity, become more involved in their planning, delivery and management. Some interventions in the form of well-targeted subsidies and services will be included to assist the very poor and enhance their opportunities for improvement.

The institutions involved in the various parts of urban management tend to have confused and overlapping roles, and the NGOs tend to be under-resourced to cope with the calls on their expertise and influence. In order to assist, the Urban Management Programme has identified five levels at which institutional actors affect urban poverty: macro, sectoral, local, community, household and intra-household. An important part of its analytical work is to identify the levels at which the various actors are most effective, and in what roles. If the commercial private sector is a more efficient provider of a particular service than government, it should be encouraged. If government is more effective, especially if markets are distorted or the very poor are a major consumer, then it should be recognized and empowered to continue. NGOs have proved that they operate well at community level but usually do not have the resources to operate national services as efficiently as others.

Each actor can be seen to have comparative advantages in addressing the needs of the poor. The Programme will focus on bringing international experience into the analytical task so that comparative advantages are maximised in the business of poverty alleviation.

E. Urban Poverty Partnership: the UNCHS (Habitat)/ ILO/UNV/UNDP Programme on Improvement of Living Conditions and Expanding Employment Opportunities in Urban Low-income Communities

The preparatory assistance phase of this joint Programme was launched in the context of the need to increase inter-sectoral cooperation to confront the problems of living conditions and employment in developing countries. The Programme recognizes that the consequences of poverty go beyond the inability to acquire a desired set of goods and services and often lead to grave and long-lasting economic and social difficulties which can become inter-generational. Poverty's multi-faceted dimensions become evident through the settlements which provide the living environment for the urban poor: inadequate shelter and services, very limited access to sources of gainful employment, poor environmental health conditions, low levels of literacy, lack of social security, and often no legal claim to the land the poor occupy in the urban areas.

The Programme recognizes that it is important to address urban poverty alleviation in three related ways:

- to look at the issues from the perspective of the urban poor;
- to encourage policy reviews and audits of regulations to determine and correct contexts where artificial barriers, institutional deficiencies and inappropriate fiscal operations promote inequity, inefficiency and ineffectiveness;
- to help define the most effective roles and policies for government at various levels focused on facilitating and enabling strategies designed more effectively to mobilize the resources and capacity of the private sector, including NGOs and community groups.

Investment policies on urban infrastructure and basic services should be geared towards producing the maximum amount of employment which is economically and technically feasible. However, changing public policies and programmes and the existence of market weaknesses and distortions have created a confused institutional climate in many cities. The levels at which institutional actors affect urban poverty are, for analytical purposes, identified as macro, sectoral, local, community,[3] household intra-household, and individual. The Programme stresses the importance of determining at what levels each actor is most effective, and in what roles.

As economic austerity overtakes more countries, it has become more obvious that there is simply no other option than locally-based, participatory and employment-intensive technologies and approaches. However, many institutional,

---

3. The word "community" is being applied generically but judiciously to population groups that reside in definable geographic areas, and act frequently in a collective manner to confront common problems.

legal, regulatory, market and technological constraints still persist. These frustrate the full development of the local resource potential. The effects are exacerbated by biases towards large foreign construction companies, and other biases resulting from aid being tied to procurement of goods and services from the donor country. Yet, despite these constraints, policies are being developed in some countries which promote locally-based, employment-intensive and enabling strategies for urban development. A good example is found in the community contracts scheme in Sri Lanka which was discussed above.

Following the GSS, the "enabling" approach is regarded as a process in which development efforts are based on constructive partnerships between all actors in development both in government and in NGOs (private-sector, both formal and informal, NGOs) and individual communities. The role of government is redefined as that of coordinating and facilitating through consultation, community participation, accountability, and well-trained and motivated professional staff. This policy shift has, in turn, been explicitly accepted as a framework for action by governments and a number of their external support agencies. This approach is in line with a recent World Bank policy document which recommends measures including increasing the demand for labour through government policies to encourage labour-intensive productive activities; and recognizing and supporting the efforts of the poor to meet their own needs through community initiatives and local NGOs (World Bank, 1991).

While the need to build on local initiatives and cooperative partnership is recognized as essential, it is obvious that it would be unrealistic to leave all urban development to self-help efforts. Public-sector priorities towards undertaking functions that are supportive and facilitating, rather than directive and implementing will, of course, pose new and largely unfamiliar demands on planning, management and policy formulation tasks at both central- and municipal-government levels. The key element will be sensitivity to the specific nature of local priorities and perceptions.

The Programme was conceived with a view to developing a programme-level capacity and defining necessary routines for jointly identifying and supporting country-level interventions. In line with the UNDP/ILO Programme mentioned above, activities will be focused on CBOs, NGOs, SSEs in the construction, building-materials and recycling sectors, municipalities and focal point institutions. Examples of the latter might be centres like the Housing Research and Development Unit in Nairobi, or the Building and Road Research Institute in Kumasi — centres with interest, expertise and contacts in the development process.

The main programme elements are envisaged as four supportive foci, as follows:

• Support to urban low-income communities for improvement of infrastructure and basic services through local-level labour-intensive initiatives in infrastructure works, community services, construction using local materials, domestic energy development, settlements planning including land tenure issues, issues concerning women in development, and awareness-raising programmes for environmental health improvements, etc.

- Support to small- and medium-scale enterprises comprising credit, management and technical support, development of community-based credit schemes, contractor training in labour-based technologies, gender-specific business services, development of small-scale waste collection, sorting and recycling businesses, and informal-sector employment planning and marketing.

- Human-resource development and institutional capacity-building in public authorities to enhance their enabling and facilitating roles to strengthen community involvement in urban low-income settlements planning and management and employment creation. This would comprise:
— On-the-job and formal training programmes for civil servants.
— Women-oriented training courses.
— Expert reviews of procedures, regulations, and financial management with action programmes for improvements, realignment of institutional responsibility and streamlining of the internal organization of public authorities.
— Review of new investment proposals for urban infrastructure works and provision of alternative employment-intensive options.
— Improvements of records of infrastructure and basic service facilities in urban low-income areas and improvements in management information and monitoring systems in public authorities, parastatals, etc.

- Support to focal point institutions. This would comprise:
— Development of specialized expertise relating to community-based, decentralized urban improvement.
— Increasing the capacity of focal point institutions to deal effectively with the private sector, NGOs and CBOs, including the establishment of contracting instruments and procedures.
— Increasing their capacity to support research in new technologies and marketing of products, and to monitor and evaluate the support programme.

It is envisaged that the support programme's main phase (which may be characterized as a continuous, learning-based process) would be implemented and developed progressively over the longer term (10 years). The financial resources of the Programme would be devoted, in the main, to providing direct benefits to the communities in the form of technical information and training, in credit and capital, and in demonstration processes for appropriate technology development.

F.   UNDP's small and micro-capital grants

The 1988 World Conference on Micro-enterprises referred to the informal sector as "the major development agent for employment creation, income generation and social stabilization in the next decade." Substantial room exists for expanding developing-country government and donor attention and inputs to the millions of subsistence and small farmers, and the rural and urban micro-entrepreneurs who make up this sector.

It is increasingly being recognized that the millions of poor people who make a living through small-scale petty businesses and services are, in fact, part of the integrated whole, contributing in a dynamic way towards the growth and sustainability of many economies in the developing world. The poor have a demonstrated ability to undertake self-help initiatives but they require help in the form of very small amounts of materials, cash or credit — a farmer may need fertilizer, a vendor may need some start-up capital, or a community may need a clinic or access to clean water.

Currently, most formal credit schemes are directed at small- and medium-scale industries in the formal commercial sector, and rarely target the lower-level "micro-enterprise" entrepreneur. The process of obtaining credit often involves a certain degree of literacy, complicated paperwork, minimum credit allotment ceilings, and collateral, all of which inhibit poor peoples' ability to participate. The poor are then left to deal with informal capital lenders who provide cash and materials at exorbitant lending rates. Apart from credit schemes, grant assistance for social infrastructure or capital inputs tends to be extremely scarce relative to the demand.

UNDP is involved in extending small-scale capital assistance in three main ways:

- through projects supported by United Nations Capital Development Fund (UNCDF) capital investments;
- through small-scale, free-standing programmes utilizing NGOs and grassroots organizations, and domestic and international specialists through UNV;
- through UNDP-supported projects which are primarily technical assistance but contain a relatively small component for direct capital assistance, or more commonly, credit facilities such as revolving or guaranteed loan schemes.

Capital assistance can be channelled to the micro-level through formal financial institutions, NGOs and CBOs, or by a partnership between both financial and non-financial institutions such as a government department, a bank, or a CBO. Funds are provided by UNDP as a grant to government, but can then be channelled by these agencies on a grant or credit basis to recipients. In the past, experience has been gained on administering very small grants to entrepreneurial endeavours. For example, trickle-up grants of US$100 channelled through village groups and other small-scale grants have benefited more than 10,500 micro-entrepreneurs.

In addition, UNDP has channelled micro-capital assistance in support of grassroots initiatives through NGOs with its Partners in Development Programme. This Programme, which was established only in mid-1988, was initiated to build upon the increasing acceptance that NGOs can play an effective role as partners in promoting and carrying out people-centred development activities. Among the 271 projects supported to date, 222 have promoted community-based development; 44 have involved strengthening NGO associations, NGOs and CBOs. Of the projects focusing on the community, approximately 70 per cent involve income-generating activities (micro-enterprises) or skills training for self-employment.

UNV normally places volunteers as specialists within the context of UNDP-supported projects. In a recent study conducted by UNV of a sample of 15 countries where a total of 150 UNVs were working, 90 per cent of the UNVs were in some way assisting in the channelling/monitoring of micro-capital funds, sometimes in very innovative ways. Examples of projects supported in Sri Lanka are community goat-rearing farms, cottage industries such as bread baking and blacksmithing, and family-managed community stores. The support per project falls in the range of $100 to $2,500.

In a report to the Council on the role of UNDP in the 1990s (DP/1989/14), a new special fund for micro-capital grants was proposed; a Microfund. This would enable UNDP to provide small capital grants and loans at the micro-level to fill an important resource gap as a complement to its efforts at mobilizing underutilized human potential — the poor. This coincides with a growing recognition of the importance of the human factor in national development, and an overall rise in demand from UNDP for small capital grants and loans at the micro-level (below the UNCDF minimum of $200,000).

The UNDP Microfund intends to channel small capital sums to local communities and organized groups; it would put capital into the hands of poor people quickly as either grants or loans. It could finance self-contained small capital projects or capital components of larger projects. It could be a funding source for micro-project initiatives such as the Partners in Development Programme, or it could be for free-standing initiatives.

Four funding criteria have been suggested:

• The micro-project should be for a capital investment, either productive or for social infrastructure. Examples are a hand pump, a grinding mill, a production credit loan, or a community health post.

• It should be for a group of low-income beneficiaries, such as a community development committee. An agreed definition for each country of a "low-income beneficiary group" would apply.

• Projects should have a demonstrated need, cost-effective, measurable impact, and beneficiary contribution and/or participation. These elements should be described in the submission document.

• The funding request should not exceed $20,000 for each project.

The schemes for which funding are sought should be identified by the community members themselves independently, through an NGO, or as part of a larger UNDP-supported project. Administration costs are to be kept to a minimum by using existing UNDP personnel and decentralizing to country resident representatives.

G. Some relevant experience by NGOs

Over the last 10 years, NGOs[4] have grown up as significant actors in the shelter process, a role which is supported and institutionalized by the GSS. They tend to stand between governments and people either as national intermediaries, or as more local groups. The latter are often based in particular communities as CBOs. Each has its own advantages in facilitating community action and mediating between people and government but, like government, they are not efficient in shelter provision (UNCHS, 1991b). The exception to this is the CBO level and in this volume seeks to show how effective they can be in enabling, encouraging and organizing supply efforts in housing and related services.

1. Human Settlements of Zambia (HUZA)

This NGO provides assistance in skills training, marketing and product development to assist in the creation and expansion of small-scale businesses. Most of the new businesses concentrate on the provision of goods and services to the neighbourhood level. Women produce school uniforms, soap and candles, while young people have been trained to produce building components from timber and soil-cement blocks. Residents have established tree nurseries and tinsmiths have been assisted to develop units for producing improved charcoal stoves.

This small-scale local production of building materials, goods and services has a dual aim: it provides income to some and reduces the cost of acquiring essential items for others. HUZA concentrates on providing sustained support to small-scale entrepreneurs and development is taking place slowly but steadily. Some women's groups are now attracting buyers from outside the neighbourhood.

The value of such assistance is not only that it provides some people with skills from which they can earn a living but also that it raises the general knowledge and awareness of the whole community. As the coordinator of the exercise expresses it, "building people before bridges is a must if sustainable development is to be assured in any future human settlements provision and improvement" (Jere, 1989; in UNCHS, 1989b).

---

4. "The inability of the public sector to meet the needs of the growing number of urban poor has led to the development of a new institutional sector represented by the NGOs. These non-governmental, non-commercial, and non-charity (sometimes) institutions in effect fill the gaps in market orientation and mitigate the effects of market and government failure. Working closely with the poor, local, often community-based, NGOs refine and articulate the needs of the poor and organize a response to those needs more efficiently than the public sector and at a more affordable cost than would commercial interests. In addition, they can contribute to the empowerment of the poor" (World Bank/UNCHS/UNDP, 1991).

2.   The Undugu Society, Kenya

This NGO is engaged in community development in three neighbourhoods in Nairobi which the society terms "slums." Undugu encourages people to take responsibility for shaping their own future, providing assistance in community organization, low cost shelter, and employment creation. Shelter, defined to include planning, flood control, and sanitation, as well as houses themselves, is at the centre of Undugu's operations, being central to living conditions for the poor.

The Undugu Society works with local community groups (community committees) providing organizational and technical support for villagers' efforts to build improved housing, both for existing squatters, and for new ones moving in as a result of clearances elsewhere in Nairobi. For example, Kinyago village (phase three of Kitui-Pumwani settlement) was planned by the Undugu Society to receive squatters cleared from a sewage works site. They planned houses in groups of four round a courtyard, nursery school, kiosks, latrines and paths, and water catchment.

Later activities have included improving the houses already constructed by responding to the community's wish that houses should be plastered with cement, and building a community centre in pisé. In addition, health programmes, including assisting construction of latrines and drains, promoting nutrition, mother and child health, hygiene, family planning, and first aid, and the prevention of drug addiction and AIDS, have also benefited from Undugu Society assistance.

The house improvements have all been conducted using labour-based technologies and local materials. Skilled workers are drawn from within the community. In providing water points within the settlement, 15 water kiosks have been established where the City Commission meters the output and community members staff the kiosks for a month on a rotating basis and receive payment for it.

Through these activities, the Undugu Society is involved in helping the poorest people improve their own living conditions at the lowest possible cost and increasing people's sense of worth and ability to act cooperatively at the same time (Muchene, 1992).

3.   Other NGO activities

In Mirpur, Dhaka, the Bangladesh Small and Cottage Industries Corporation has inaugurated a scheme to improve the condition of silk saree weavers by recommending that an estate be established for the weavers, consisting of housing and home-based factories for each of the families. The Housing and Settlement Directorate has the responsibility for the provision of structures and water supply, electricity, sewage disposal, gas, etc. (Haque, 1987).

This housing and home-based enterprises scheme is the first of its kind in Bangladesh. Its objectives are to enable the low-income weavers' households to own a house and a HBE; to provide a more hygienic environment; to produce silk sarees using local raw materials, local labour, and applying the traditional hand-loom production for which medieval Dhaka was famous; and to train new skilled workers (Haque, 1987).

UNICEF has been involved in enabling communities to provide basic education, water and sanitation, community health and nutrition, and women's economic activities, for themselves. In Mombasa, Kenya, for example, UNICEF is supporting an NGO called Tototo Home Industries in the development and implementation of a feasible credit system to individual women through existing women groups. In Nairobi, UNICEF is supporting the City Commission in a women's skill training programme. Six training centres have been rehabilitated to give tailoring, dress-making, housekeeping, home economics, weaving and spinning courses. In Kisumu, the programme has supported four women's groups composed of very poor women (one group is composed of former street beggars) with materials to improve their rental houses within very poor areas to accommodate income-generating activities (Mirikau, 1992).

In their work in Kebele 14, Addis Ababa, Redd Barna (1992) found a large number of unemployed and underemployed people, mainly unskilled, eking out a bare living, using their time and energies relatively unproductively. Their economic position makes it impossible for them to afford decent housing and related public utilities. At the same time, the construction of dwellings and utilities could be one of the most effective ways of using this wasted labour forces. In response to this, the objectives for Redd Barna's activities in Kebele 14 are aimed at:

  •   absorbing the unemployed and underemployed residents into the stream of economic life so that they may have the income needed to afford decent housing and public utilities;
  •   facilitating the development process itself by mobilizing the underutilized human resources in the construction of dwellings and related infrastructure;
  •   assisting residents to adapt to urban life through programmes of training in health and urban community development (Redd Barna, 1992).

In the above interventions by international donors and NGOs, common threads of empowering people, using the informal sector and SSEs for tasks for which they are suited, and treating government as a facilitator and enabler, can be seen. These are in line with the literature reviewed in this publication and will be taken up in the next section in recommending support for employment generation in the process of development.

IX. Scope for support to employment generation in shelter, infrastructure and services provision

The promotion of urban development should be a holistic process, involving all actors in the processes at which they are effective, and each sector (housing, workplaces, servicing and social facilities) in an integrated way. The bringing together of the concerns of UNCHS (Habitat) in shelter in all its aspects, and the ILO in employment and welfare, provides a unique opportunity for an approach to development which matches a priority for physical conditions with the need to be economically productive.

The shelter problem, for those it affects and for the governments who try to assist, is basically a poverty problem. Governments should devote attention to improvements in the general standard of living, creating a hospitable environment for people and for large-, medium-, and small-scale enterprises to be productive in all legitimate ways. This may, however, only create improvement in the medium to long term. It is also necessary for governments, as a matter of urgency, to direct attention to shelter and employment issues as they affect the poor. That leads to one of the main conclusions of this publication: the informal sector is worth supporting not only because it is capable of being economically productive but also because any help given to SSEs is likely to benefit poorer households than similar benefits applied to the formal sector.

A. The need for a change of political culture

A serious change in culture among government and local government personnel is required. In the current movement towards democratization and empowerment of the people, the hierarchical rule from above is proving not only inefficient and ineffective, but also unpopular and counter-productive. If central government pulls the strings of local authorities (regarding them merely as agents of the centre), and local authorities, in turn, take responsibility for all activities in their areas (but do not carry them out), the current crippling inactivity is likely to continue and intensify as fiscal austerity bites deeper. A change is thus required from executing, which is mainly a technical function, to facilitating, which is mainly organizational. In addition, there is a need to develop a willingness to deal with CBOs representing the interests of residents in low-income areas. This requires that local authority officials are able to negotiate effectively and equitably with CBOs and other organizations. Local authority officials cannot be expected to have these political skills; they will have to be learned through training.

As Rondinelli and Cheema (1985) and Royat (1992) point out, the staff of governments, both central and local, are trained to act predominantly as regulators rather than as enablers. A new set of professionals should be trained or recruited, or the existing staff retrained in the skills required which are promotional and managerial; those of community organization, communication, publicity, and the ability to manage large numbers of people by consensus. There will be less need for the traditional skills represented in local authority and government sectoral departments; engineers, physical planners, architects, etc. However, people in such professions may well be suitable for training in promotional and organizational skills to complement their professional expertise and so become competent in the urbanization process in general. The professionals and technicians need to respond to the needs of the urban poor and be rewarded in their careers according to their success in assisting community-based action (Rondinelli and Cheema, 1985).

In their involvement with new approaches to spending resources in a more labour-intensive way, governments should eschew imposing development from above. Residential development should take place within the framework of a public/private partnership in which planning control is replaced by a dialogue which is based on mutual responsibility for future development. Planners should anticipate the emergence of income-generating activities in residential areas and see their role as promoting rather than constraining them. Such an approach is promotional rather than restrictive and will involve a considerable change in attitude among planning authorities and implementers whose conventional role is regulatory. The re-orientation not only of professional planners but of all who have a decision-making role in the planning process will be required through training programmes which are based on field experience (UNCHS, 1994f).

Such strategies, recommended by UNCHS (Habitat) (1989b), imply that individuals and the neighbourhood community will have more control over their environment than the local authorities. This is deliberate because it is more likely that people will be concerned with the development of their immediate neighbourhood if they consider it to be their responsibility. The community has the potential to be a more effective watch-dog against environmental pollution by local enterprises than the public authorities, and can be the focus of responsibility for the provision and maintenance of infrastructural services which serve the immediate neighbourhood (UNCHS, 1989b).

B. Support through the legislative, administrative and planning environment

Recent UNCHS (Habitat), ILO and World Bank work (e.g., UNCHS, 1989b) has focused on the need for particular actors in the development process to concentrate on the functions for which they are best suited. The most appropriate role of central governments is to create a wider policy environment in which SSEs are encouraged; to remove or adapt regulations unhelpful to them and to labour-intensive works, and to employment in the home; to give them chances to carry out projects; to encourage research leading to greater efficiency; and to support the foundation of cooperatives and trade organizations which will strengthen the negotiating power of SSEs.

At the same time, local authorities should ensure that the local policy environment is also supportive. This involves devising appropriate bye-laws and enabling building regulations; licensing and other requirements and practices which allow and support local raw materials, contracting by SSEs, and labour-intensive employment (UNCHS, 1989b).

As the GSS proposes, the first requirement for a healthy shelter sector is a bundle of well chosen policies at the national level within an effective macroeconomic strategy, being implemented by the formal sector, government, NGOs and CBOs, and the informal shelter sector, in order to increase production of housing and to improve and maintain existing housing. However, these policies must address the supply side of development. Demand for housing in developing countries tends to be much greater than supply; people are consuming little housing largely because not enough is available. The inputs of land, finance, labour, materials, and a regulatory framework should be the currency used in order to increase the capacity of developing countries to improve shelter and employment at the same time (Malpezzi, 1990).

By contrast, much of the housing effort of governments and some donors in the past have been concentrated on the construction process itself or on interventions on the demand side, by providing allowances and subsidies, often to income groups for whom they were a luxury rather than a necessity. The fact that subsidized housing has been allocated to relatively well-off households is now a matter of record and no more need be said here.[1] The lessons to be drawn from this experience are mainly directing governments away from spending their small housing budgets in building a few, excellent-quality but small bungalows. Early experiments with spreading the direct construction incentives more widely through sites-and-services schemes, core housing, and other semi-complete structures, have met with limited success. While it cannot be doubted that the beneficiaries have often done very well indeed out of them, that considerable employment opportunities have occurred through their development, and that the standard of housing produced has been high in comparison to the wealth of the plot holders, it is also true that their recipients have rarely been numbered among the poor.

The efforts over sites-and-services schemes and their self-help variations have concentrated, as was pointed out in chapter III, on the interface between the household and the house; in encouraging individual households to understand and cope with the process of housing themselves. They paid little attention to the greater productivity gains to be harvested from lubricating the contractor/house and householder/contractor interfaces. It is these which now concern us.

The Employment Policy Convention, 1964 (No. 122), which over 70 ILO member States have ratified, declares that Members should adopt policies to promote full, productive and freely chosen employment with a view to stimulating

---

1. See for instance UNCHS, 1991a.

economic growth and development, raising levels of living, meeting workforce requirements and overcoming unemployment and underemployment. Governments should, therefore, strive to create conditions in which there is work for all who are available for and seeking work; that such work is as productive as possible; and that there is freedom of choice of employment and the fullest possible opportunity for all workers to improve their skills. In addition, the policy adopted should specifically take account of the stage and level of economic development and the mutual relationships between employment objectives and other economic and social goals.

As Mayer (1991) points out, the Employment Policy Convention, 1964 (No. 122), concerns not only work carried out within an employment relationship but all ways of earning a living, including self-employed work. This interpretation is particularly important because it recognizes the contribution of the informal sector of many countries as creating more jobs than the formal sector.

The ways in which governments respond to the current opportunities determine success or failure. The challenge to policy-makers is to attempt to maximize both the employment-creating potential of the informal sector and the degree of social protection and regulation extended to it. It can only be integrated into the economy as a whole if it is treated as part of an overall economic policy. Broad policy and institutional reforms, in addition to programmes of direct assistance to the informal sector, are required to increase the integration of the informal and formal sector of the economy and enhance the capacity of the sector to generate incomes and employment for larger numbers of people (ILO, 1991).

It is in the context of a positive attitude towards the creation of employment, the informal sector, and the particular needs of the poor, that this section seeks to outline the scope for improving the employment potential of the shelter sector.

1.   Assisting the informal sector

The ILO (1991) argues that the disadvantaged position of the informal sector cannot be remedied only by creating a less discriminatory policy environment or by throwing public money at it. It will also require a wide range of special measures to overcome certain inherent weaknesses of the informal sector itself, and to strengthen the productive capacity of informal-sector units. Without such measures, it is difficult to see how the informal sector can compete, or establish mutually beneficial complementary relationships, with the modern sector, and thus become more fully integrated into the mainstream of the economy. In particular, he argues, it is important when designing policies to distinguish between the relatively viable small enterprises in the informal sector which appear to have a potential for growth and employment creation. and those units[2] which clearly have

---

2.   Most of which are no more than precarious jobs performed on an individual basis, such as many street-vending activities.

no such potential. In an attempt to increase the positive potential, the ILO has been pioneering training and capacity-strengthening in government institutions and local governments.

In a recent ILO seminar to determine the most appropriate ways to promote the informal sector, the recommendations included the following (ILO, 1990):

- to adapt the legal and institutional framework to the sector's characteristics taking care of its internal dynamism and its mode of self-organization;
- to propose economic measures which will ensure the creation of a favourable environment for the development of small crafts by setting aside for them some markets including those currently supplied by imports;
- to provide flexible technical and financial assistance focusing on appropriate technology development, product improvement and diversification, control over market networks and strengthening of local financing;
- to establish a national structure aimed at discussing and coordinating employment promotion and to set up a national fund specifically geared to financing projects for the informal sector;
- to decentralize as much as possible the assistance to this sector by transferring skills to local communities.

There is little doubt that increasing help to the informal sector as a whole, in ways similar to the above, would further the cause of employment in and connected with shelter. Recommendations can be rationalized to two levels of activity which only government can effectively influence:

- the formation of a legal, institutional and economic framework within which enterprises can flourish and employment be created (some of which is in public works provision);
- some forms of assistance to the informal sector operating within shelter, and connected with its provision and maintenance, in the way of servicing, finance, training and involvement in government contracts.

2. The legal, institutional and economic framework for housing supply

In order to address the supply issues, the institutional structure for the delivery of urban services will need to be streamlined. Currently, institutional weaknesses are a serious constraint to the delivery of infrastructure. Too many ineffective agencies, sometimes with overlapping or competing interests, an inadequate framework for encouraging and supporting community participation and a lack of motivation for efficient performance-oriented service delivery have been identified by the GSS as constraints to the supply of shelter services. The GSS suggests the following strategies to overcome these problems:

- streamlining local-government institutions and strengthening their organizational capacity to deliver urban services;

- introducing reforms in organizational structures and mandates to encourage community involvement;
- increasing organizational efficiency, perhaps through the use of performance agreements that allow private enterprises to provide some services under governmental supervision of quantity and quality specifications.

The GSS further recommends a radical reappraisal of laws and regulations affecting the shelter sector, especially what is currently classified as informal. Reforms of land legislation, planning and building regulations, property leases etc. should be undertaken by governments with their likely economic impact taken as a major determinant of their acceptability. In the short term, governments should examine their regulations and administrative practices with a view to amending, simplifying and streamlining those which present obstacles to growth and employment in the informal sector.

(a)   Land

In land administration, clarity of title and sound registration practices seem to be lacking in all too many countries so that land is difficult to acquire even where a developer can pay the market price. Land-administration systems need to be installed which are, at the same time, more precise and less rigid; more precise in the record keeping so that all parties can be aware of who owns land and what the extent of their rights are; less rigid in that there is scope for more than one level of ownership being regarded as valid for financial purposes.

Speculation in land is driving the price of housing and urban services out of the range of an increasing proportion of the population every year (Rondinelli, 1986). Few countries can afford interventions like land banking, but many could improve the situation by making decisions about land use, density, and location of government uses in a way which increases the efficiency of urban land use, rather than simply through sectoral preferences.

Interventions in the supply of land which do not involve massive government expenditures but are likely to increase equity include freezing of land values (though this would probably distort development by causing new construction activity to "leap-frog" to non-frozen areas), and the adoption of special taxes or levies on land held out of development and on windfall profits from increases in land values due to installation of public services nearby. The precise strategy will depend on country circumstances but the purpose of interventions should be to ensure a smooth and adequate supply of land for housing and other development needs, at least some significant proportion of which should be accessible to the poor.

(b)   Planning and building regulations

The imposition of rules and regulations, based on a "blueprint" of how life should be rather than a response to how life is, has tended to be the norm in the past. Housing solutions which result from this "top-down" process not only reflect official interpretations of demand but can be a drain on the income of residents without giving them what they need.[3] In contrast, Hake (1977) speaks of urbanization "from below", while others (e.g., Turner, 1976; Turner and Fichter, 1972) refer to building cities "from the bottom up." As Peattie (1987) recognizes, the reality is that most housing is provided by people outside the controlled environment of planning anyway. The approach required in order to assist the efficient supply of low-income housing is not simply one of allowing people's participation in implementing some sites-and-services or upgrading scheme; it is providing support and resources to allow lower-income groups to undertake what they see as the priority in improving their housing and living conditions (UNCHS, 1985b).

Inappropriate building codes have negative effects on the housing situation of the urban and rural poor. They have led to the low quality of building materials and construction techniques used in informal low-income settlements (Turner, 1976). Most existing codes favour import-based construction materials which, despite their high cost or scarcity, are often imposed as the only choice available to the low-income builder. Thus, attempts to introduce improved traditional building materials and to develop the backward linkages in the building-materials industry offered by residential development have been hampered (UNCHS, 1987).

Building codes forbidding the use of earth as a construction material have particularly limited the building of cheap shelter in urban low-income settlements. As a result there is usually an absence of codes and specifications designed to regulate the quality and use of earth and other traditional materials.[4] Consequently, tender and contracting procedures do not tend to promote the inclusion of traditional materials in low-cost construction projects carried out by governmental agencies. Resistance to the use of earth as a building material is widespread, but in developing countries, earth-based materials are not merely the only ones that are affordable by a large majority of the people, they are also perfectly adequate for most construction needs, provided they are used in appropriate ways.

As standards have concentrated on the best, they have, as Burns and Grebler (1977) point out, driven out the good. As Cotton and Franceys (1991) argue, small servicing improvements from a "zero baseline" of no services at all can result in substantial health benefits. The regulation of living environments occupied by the poor should, therefore, seek routes through which to make incremental improvements rather than holding up the finished masterpiece as the only acceptable standard.

---

3. The plight of the middle-aged mason resettled from a squatter settlement to a "good-quality" house, with the attendant loss of earnings from his wife's SSE and the new rent to pay, featured by Turner (1976), has been often quoted as an example of this.

4. As an example, there is currently no specification for pisé, although the United Kingdom's ODA is sponsoring the development of one.

In order to improve the housing situation of the urban and rural poor, reformed regulations aimed at encouraging affordable housing to be as safe and durable as possible within the socio-cultural values of low-income target groups may play a pivotal role. Possibilities for creating special codes and regulations for housing and infrastructure in low-income settlements, which can be upgraded over time, will need to be considered. These could include lower standards for very-low-income areas, even to where the only control may be that exercised by neighbours on each other, with the mediation of a local leader. As this is the level of control existing in many of those areas in the absence of their legal status, an absence of formal control may have little influence in "turning the place into a slum," which is a frequently voiced fear over reducing standards.

Informal contributions to the shelter sector that currently fall outside existing laws and regulations need to be recognized and gradually legitimized. In addition, policies should address existing procedures by which housing is provided, albeit illegally, and attempt to encourage these processes while controlling any harmful features.[5] In this way, all the agents, formal and informal, involved in shelter construction can be harnessed for the development process.

C.   The legal and financial context for HBEs

As Gilbert (1988) reflects in his review of HBEs, many SSEs are bound to be unsuccessful. However, others will survive and form the basis for larger, successful companies. Meanwhile, their cycle of founding and floundering or survival sustains a level of economic activity which is intrinsically valuable. He recommends that the best policy for government to adopt is tolerance and non-intervention. Within this, however, there are approaches which are likely to impose some control on the problems while allowing the potential to be developed. Gilbert's (1988) experience in low-income settlements in Colombia, Mexico and Venezuela, suggest that the establishment of neighbourhood councils, to act as development control agents and arbitrators in disputes, is likely to result in locally-sensitive judgements on the level and nature of economic activity in residential areas. He also proposes more tolerance of HBEs in government housing areas.

In the past, "top-down" housing solutions have typically incorporated small plots, in order to make the services provided affordable, and even smaller units in which there is no space to incorporate income-generating enterprises. Where plots are set aside for the development of commercial activities or the repair and manufacturing industry, these are often unsuitably located. Regulations governing the use of plots and the type of structures to be developed on them also have the effect of pushing out the low-income earners. Studies have found that the lack of adequate and suitable space can be as much an inhibiting factor as lack of credit in the development of income-generating opportunities.

---

5. For example, the propensity to build on sites liable to flooding, land-slip etc.

If the aim is to encourage the development of self-sustaining neighbourhoods with provision for all types of manufacturing, service industry and commerce to flourish, a range of plot sizes should be provided. The targeting of specific income groups should be substituted with an approach which recognizes that areas grow and change according to the income-earning capacity of the residents. Land should therefore be sub-divided and provided with minimal but upgradable services to enable developments by individuals in response to the requirements of their businesses and their ability to pay. These sites could be made available to those who are best able to exploit them for employment generation, which may involve very different land-allocation procedures than those currently in use. At the same time, as was argued in chapter VII, there should be few restrictions on the type of structures to be built on residential and small industrial or commercial plots; temporary structures should be allowed with renewable licences, if necessary.[6] It is assumed that successful entrepreneurs will improve their working conditions in line with their requirements and ability to afford the improvements (UNCHS, 1989b).

The promotion of home-based income generation, as suggested above, requires that housing units, provided either by the public or the private sector or built by self-help, should be designed in such a way as to be able to accommodate income-generating activities. This means that designs which allow for the multiple use of space and opportunities for occupiers to adapt and extend them should be provided and not discouraged by lease or tenancy agreements (UNCHS, 1989b). In addition, the current activity of altering and extending formal-sector (and often government-built) housing for not only additional residential accommodation but also income-generating activity, should be encouraged within "proscriptive" controls (Turner, 1976) to guard against serious problems (Tipple, 1991; 1992b).

Support from housing agencies tends not to include loans for small businesses. However, loans for home improvement meant for accommodating economic activities could be a part of their services. Since returns can be expected to be quite rapid, short-term loans may be appropriate (Nientied and others, 1987). In the context of Afghanistan, Bahawi (1992) proposes that credit opened to small-scale artisans and craftspeople would encourage increased production and improved quality of handicrafts, promote the training of skilled personnel, and improve work conditions.

It has been suggested that HBEs are so common and of such value to the economy, at household, neighbourhood and government levels, that housing should be treated as productive infrastructure and be eligible for loans on the same terms as factories (Fass, 1977). However, there seems to be little empirical work on

---

6. However, this may require changes in planning and licensing laws where, for example, trading licenses cannot be issued for activities carried out in temporary structures. This would reduce the disadvantages currently facing these doubly-illegal activities.

which the costs and benefits of HBEs can be assessed as a start to policy-making. If governments begin to value full employment, especially for the poor, with the vigour which the Employment Policy Convention, 1964 (No. 122) implies, it is likely that HBEs will be given a better deal.

D.   Scope for support by public sector agencies

1.   Use of labour-intensive methods, the informal sector, and SSEs

Governments are major employers in developing countries and also the instigators of a large proportion of all development. In African countries, public-sector activity in employment and investment as represented by government's share of expenditures on wages and salaries ranged from 8.7 per cent in Nigeria to 53.6 per cent in Burkina Faso (von Braun and others, 1991). Expenditure on wages and capital, when combined, tend to account for about 50 to 60 per cent of total government expenditure in 18 African countries. The capital share, alone, exceeds 30 per cent of the budget in six of these countries. Thus, if government policy led to even a marginal increase in the labour content of these capital expenditures, there could be a substantial difference in employment. Similarly, increasing the labour share in "goods and services" may provide for significant employment expansion.

Von Braun and others (1991) identify four broad trends currently influencing the environment for labour-intensive public works programmes in Africa — the first three work in favour of, the fourth against such programmes:

•   macro-economic incentives as increases in capital/labour price ratios are inducing investments to be more labour-intensive;

•   food insecurity is becoming increasingly a problem of labour-market-dependent people in rural and urban areas, which argues in favour of employment-focused interventions rather than non-sustainable food subsidy systems;

•   rapidly deteriorating infrastructure for which fiscal and foreign-exchange constraints inhibit maintenance and new construction by capital-intensive technology;

•   limited institutional capacities with which to design, supervise, and execute sound public-investment programmes. These have been generally eroded in the context of fiscal constraints and progressive dismantling of public institutions.

Through the GSS, Agenda 21 and the other initiatives reviewed in chapter VIII, governments are being encouraged to regard the creation of jobs for low-paid workers as a positive element in development. Governments should adopt lower technologies, lower-cost products and labour-based methods, so that significant increases in direct labour employment per unit of expenditure can be achieved.

Labour-based initiatives aimed at the poor can be successful in undercutting equipment-based operations because labour is so cheap. In line with the more general concept of sustainability, a major thesis of this publication is that people's time and energy is cheaper than fossil fuels and capital goods. Yet, care must be taken to guard against abusing the weak position of poor, un-unionized workers whose employment currently depends upon their low wages. A balance must be struck between a low wage which benefits labour-based works and allows most people to at least have some income,[7] and a situation of exploitation where unfairly low wages keep workers in poverty.

It can be argued that productivity is the key to increasing wages. It is, therefore, incumbent on public-sector developers to include on-the-job training as a right for workers so that supervisors and those capable of learning technical skills can be equipped for those important, productive and better-paid tasks. In addition, contractors who are encouraged in labour-based technologies should also be required to act similarly.

Current tendering procedures in public works, tend to favour large contractors being engaged to carry out large contracts in capital-intensive ways. However, some large local authorities, like RAJUK in Dhaka and the City of Soweto, have demonstrated that it is possible to favour labour-based contractors. It would be very fruitful for the purpose of increasing employment if government departments set up a network of contacts with smaller contractors so that the work could be granted to a large range of enterprises. This may require some modification to qualification criteria (e.g., in the scale of capital which a contractor has to have at his or her disposal), but it would be reasonably straightforward, given the political will. Maintenance work would be an obvious starting point.

Experience in Sri Lanka with engaging community contractors in relatively complex works, such as a sewerage system in an upgrading exercise, has met with sufficient success to encourage others to entrust similar contracts to groups of artisans operating in the informal sector. Even in countries where the level of sophistication in these matters has not reached that of Sri Lanka, it is possible to reduce extensive government contracts into smaller pieces and encourage SSEs or community contractors to bid for them. This requires a political will to devote the time and resources to ensuring that SSEs are equipped to cope with the tasks;[8] and there may be an increased risk of problems over completion of contracts by small companies. However, its pay-off in reduced cost (particularly foreign-exchange cost), increased employment and local income multipliers, and a sense of pride in the area and its infrastructure, may be very large.

Both the Sri Lankan experience with community contractors and the experience in Ghana and Kenya with SSEs in road construction, point to major possibilities for local authorities and central government to have contractual

---

7. But this may also be a form of underemployment according to Sabot (1979).

8. In terms of training, new forms of tendering, increased publicity of contracts requiring tenders, etc.

relationships with a greater variety of entities than currently. As van Dijk and Glissenaar (1987) conclude:

> the factors that seem important for maximum employment effects of urban projects are a positive attitude towards small enterprises and providing assistance to them. A positive attitude from the authorities is required to realize the employment potential...so much depends on the local situation and in particular the political support given to the programmes (quoted in UNCHS, 1989b, p. 36).

2.　Technical and financial assistance

Few informal-sector workers have access to formal training institutions although, in many countries, traditional apprenticeship systems have proved to be extraordinarily effective in the transmission of skills — in some cases fairly sophisticated skills. However, there is always a potential element of exploitation in informal apprenticeship systems — the tendency for apprentices, who normally receive little if any remuneration, to be regarded as a source of cheap labour.

The provision of training for the entrepreneurs in the informal sector in basic techniques of bookkeeping, marketing, production organization, costing, pricing etc. is thus particularly critical. Without such knowledge, they will remain at a great disadvantage in relation to formal-sector enterprises (ILO, 1991).

Training programmes, such as those instituted by the ILO for SSEs[9] will be needed for large-, medium- and small-scale builders and for community groups engaged in shelter production and upgrading, to train and give technical assistance in accounting, budgeting, inventory control and other basic skills. Such training and technical assistance could usefully be combined with lending programmes through trade associations. Training should also be extended to community groups so that they can play a role in designing and implementing shelter programmes (UNCHS, 1990). It is essential, however, that newly trained contractors receive contracts to carry out public works so that they can gain experience and an entry point to the world of contracting.[10] Thus, training should be part of an on-going commitment to sub-contracting public works functions in construction, maintenance and service provision.

Governments spend large amounts of money on job creation in urban areas. These grants or loans tend to be channelled towards the large- and medium-scale enterprises. If there are occasions when SSEs are assisted, they are almost always in the formal sector. The difficulties that informal-sector producers face in obtaining credit on the same terms as formal-sector enterprises are among the one of the main obstacles to their growth, since they have no formally recognized

---

9.　The "Improve Your Business" and "Improve Your Construction Business" projects.

10.　As in the Ghana Feeder Roads Improvement Programme (see chapter IV).

collateral to offer. They are thus obliged to resort to borrowing from money-lenders on highly unfavourable terms, or to informal sources of finance. The solution is not to be found in a few, preferentially structured loans, but in the opening of the financial market to borrowers with less conventional forms of collateral (such as jewellery, tools, vehicles, community guarantees, or informal-sector housing), over relatively short periods.

At the bottom of the scale of borrowing requirements, the UNDP's Micro-capital Grants programme recognizes that the poor also deserve an opportunity to enlarge their options (see chapter VIII). The requirements for building the capacity in the informal sector are typically very small amounts of capital in the form of materials, cash, or credit. At this level, it would seem reasonable that governments could follow UNDP's lead. Before investing in the capital-intensive import-substitution factory, they could consider making many tiny grants to reinforce productive capacity in a group of existing SSEs.

3.   Help for the poorest

Targeting the poorest groups is not easy, especially as, whenever goods in shortage are rationed in some way, those with power and money tend to displace the target group. Although income groups cannot be ring-fenced and other groups be prohibited from occupying this form of housing or that type of neighbourhood, there is evidence to suggest that residents of informal housing, densely-populated inner-city tenements, and peripheral squatter settlements are generally not as well-off as those in formal housing, detached suburban neighbourhoods, or government estates. Thus, policies which allow a more productive and less expensive life in the former should be favoured as poverty-alleviation measures against those which, currently, subsidize transport, access, waste collection, land ownership, and other functions which generally make life even more comfortable in the latter.

The only sure way of reaching most people with better housing and services is to have efficiently operating supply markets. It is likely, even then, that the lowest income group will benefit less than any other as the minimum price of even basically serviced accommodation may be too high for its members. Yet, it has been found in the past that subsidies directed to people are a more effective way of targeting the poor than interventions in the price of the goods (in this case housing) which they consume.

Some social groups are more likely to be poor than others. Women-headed households, households containing many dependents, the aged and the very young are likely to be among the poorest groups. In some places, other groups may be identifiable. Amole and others (1993) identify occupants of family houses as likely to be among the poorest people in West African cities. Particular occupations are also confined to the poorest: those who clear solid waste (conservancy workers, scavengers, sweepers etc.), day labourers, carriers and porters, rickshaw pullers, home-workers in South Asia; they vary in different places but are usually well-known locally or can be discerned. Policies targeted at these are more likely to succeed in reaching the poorest groups than those targeted through housing subsidies or procedures based on measures of income. Some sort of housing allowances of some sort (or simply welfare payments equal to the rent for a minimum housing unit) directed at the poorest groups are therefore preferable to subsidies offered on particular sorts of housing.[11]

Benefits (or at least opportunities — some of which may end in failure) can be concentrated on the working poor by supporting SSEs, encouraging government institutions to transfer many of their functions to small contractors, and by increasing the labour-intensive nature of direct works.[12] The group below the working poor in income and capability, who can neither earn a meagre living nor look after their own well-being, can only adequately be supported through some form of welfare benefits. However, the possibility of financing these will be greater if the economic benefits of assisting the informal sector are gained by society at large.

The most productive way to assist the working poor appears to be through creating opportunities for them to earn a living wage. It has been shown how labour-based public works programmes tend to employ the poorest workers. In addition, assistance to HBEs, in the form of small loans (without subsidy), encouragement of home-workers to form associations to lobby for their requirements, and minimum levels of servicing in residential areas are all likely to be helpful to the poor.

There are also positive measures which can be efficient in redistributing wealth from richer to poorer. When development is occurring, wealth is created. Through positive measures, such as cross-subsidies, this wealth can be redistributed in favour of the poor. The most obvious example of this, which has been successful in Thailand, is land-sharing in which profits made from redeveloping part of a site can subsidize poor people's purchase of small plots on the remainder of a site (Boonyabancha, 1990; UNCHS, 1991b). A simpler method is simply to create some plots for the poor and sell them at below cost. The remainder of the plots are priced at a slight premium with the profit covering the loss on the others. In this procedure, there are opportunities to use the intrinsic characteristics of the layout to generate potential for cross-subsidy. For example, corner plots where main routes meet can be particularly highly priced because, upon development, they would be well-suited to commercial activity. On the other hand, smaller plots deep within the residential area can be sold more cheaply to the poor and are less likely

---

11. This may not be a direct subsidy currently paid by government; rent controls constitute a subsidy paid by landlords to their tenants even though the latter may be no worse off than the former.

12. This is the group who, however long they may work, will not manage to earn more than a mere subsistence without encouragement and assistance, or at least the absence of harassment.

to filter upwards. Strict zoning laws and unimaginative planning tend to remove the possibility of using well-located sites for economic activity.

4.   Encouraging rental housing

As was argued in chapter VII, efforts should be made to stimulate the production of rental housing — including both informal housing, such as the rental of rooms in a house, and more formal rental units (such as apartments) — and to encourage relatively low-income households to add rooms for rent to their dwellings. Tax benefits on rental income would be helpful in places where landlords routinely pay tax,[13] especially in formal-sector houses or in areas where informal housing is being formalized. In Nigeria, where most urban residents live in rented accommodation, the Government has plans to reduce taxes on rents to below those on earned income. In Turkey, there is a grace period of five years between first occupation and when tax have to be paid (UNCHS, 1991b). Governments can also encourage banks to give loans for investment in housing and house extensions. Thailand has a "capital adequacy allowance" which can be applied to home-loan assets (UNCHS, 1991b).

As incentives such as those discussed above involve the expenditure of tax-payers' money, their destination with the middle- and upper-income groups is less than ideal. However, it can be argued that the simple availability of standard-interest loans to lower income groups (most of whom do not fulfill current qualification criteria) would be sufficient to induce increased expenditure on housing among them, with the consequent increase in rental rooms as a by-product of the owner-occupier dwelling. Korboe (1993) argues, however, that no incentives are required for his sample of occupants of traditional housing in Kumasi, Ghana. The monetary motive is so secondary to the achievement of security, that the availability of the inputs to housing (particularly land) is all that is required to boost housing starts. A similar argument is expressed by Kapoor and Maitra (1987) who hold that land and finance together should form the nexus for any major initiatives for tackling the housing deficits in India.

The efficiency of extensions made for renting out, in areas where services are already in place, deserves more attention. While extensions are discouraged by planning regulations on maximum use of plots or by estate owners, occupants of relatively well-built and well-located housing may be discouraged from supplying rooms for rent which they can well afford to build (Tipple, 1991; 1992b). The addition of rooms to an existing house is comparatively inexpensive — possibly as little as half the price of a new building as no new land is required (Hansen and Williams, 1987) and at least some of the structure is already in place. In addition,

---

13. It is not uncommon for rental income to be more heavily taxed than "earned" income. In Ghana, for example, theoretical tax levels are much greater on rents than on other income (Tipple, 1988).

extension work is labour-intensive, ideally suited to SSEs and has potentially large multipliers. In some cities where there is a hiatus on new building (for reasons of land supply, inadequate infrastructure, or topographical constraints), the supply of rooms through upward and outward extensions can make the difference between housing crisis and sufficiency.[14] It is also evident, from the work of Gilbert and Varley (1991) and Tipple and Willis (1991b), that owners of premises with rooms rented out tend to be less well-off than owners of accommodation which is exclusively for them. The reasoning behind this will include that prospective owners can take account of the likely rental income in their calculations of whether they can afford a house. Thus, policies which accept the need for increasing the supply of rental units by encouraging homeowners to rent out rooms and add rental units, may be the most efficient way to increase shelter in third world cities, and the prospects for cost recovery of infrastructure investment are greater than in less-dense, low-income communities (Hansen and Williams, 1987).

Among the policies appropriate to expanding the supply of rental housing are credit programmes targeted to owners who add on rental units and the inclusion of rental components within sites-and-services and upgrading projects. In addition, homeowners should be guided in the design of their houses so that rental units can be added on later as family income permits. Another way to stimulate rental-housing supply lies in the reform of rent-control policy. Many developing countries with rent controls have experienced little or no new construction and noticeable deterioration of existing stock. In addition, recent evidence suggests that tenants as well as landlords can lose from rent controls (Malpezzi and others, 1990; Malpezzi and Ball, 1991). Tenants in controlled units often suffer more than they gain because they may live in sub-optimum units in terms of space, quality, or location. Rent-control reforms vary by country, but the reforms most needed include exempting new units from controls, decontrolling units as they become vacant, and improving the enforcement of maintenance requirements (Hansen and Williams, 1987).

5. Infrastructure provision

Adequate investment in infrastructure networks are crucial to meeting the shelter needs. The artificial shortage of land which can be created by poor infrastructure provision could be overcome through a planned programme of investment in infrastructure (UNCHS, 1990, p. 26), and through ensuring that services are paid for in full through the tariff system. The practice by governments

---

14. According to Tipple and Willis (1992), growth in the number of rooms in Kumasi, Ghana, has kept pace with population growth (albeit at a high occupancy rate) since 1980 while the number of houses has fallen behind. Thus, most of the increase in housing during that period has been through additional rooms added onto houses, or rooms converted from kitchens, store-rooms etc.

of setting an uneconomic ceiling on charges and, at the same time, insisting that a utility undertaking breaks even, must be discontinued. However, at the same time, the per capita costs of infrastructure must be reduced to ensure adequate coverage. Costs may be reduced in many ways. Of these, the adoption of inexpensive and resource-conserving technologies and the use of locally-produced materials and components hold the greatest promise. The fact that such technologies are also (usually) labour-based is doubly helpful.

Improvements in infrastructure to a neighbourhood can provide the setting for better dwellings and more productive HBEs, which generate the income which promotes better conditions in the neighbourhood (Strassmann, 1986; Gilbert, 1988). Water, electricity and sanitation services can be as important for HBEs as for residential uses in general.

The frequency of HBEs in different neighbourhoods, and the proportion of various types of HBEs vary in relation to cost of space and access to markets — either allowing competition or giving protection against it. The predominance of retail stores for the immediate neighbours in squatter settlements and of prospering metal-products enterprises and furniture-making in older, more centrally-placed areas reflect these factors. They suggest that infrastructure, especially transport, can raise productivity and, at the same time, threaten the viability of the comparatively unproductive for whom competition will be unwelcome (Strassmann, 1986).

As was argued in chapter IV, the "ultimate level" concept provides a useful and adjustable threshold for utility agency to hand over control of servicing to private entrepreneurs or community organizations. The ultimate level may be the edge of the settlement, or the entrance to an alley, or any other place at which local control can conveniently be assumed. Activities of maintenance, improvement and service delivery for which the community takes control must be clear to the users, the community representatives, the operators appointed by the community, and the utility agency.

The public authority would be responsible for bulk supplies of water, or collection of wastes, at a few locations and at relatively low unit cost (analogous with a wholesaler). Distribution, maintenance and revenue-collection responsibilities (analogous with retailing) would then be locally-based and provide the level of service which the community members choose. There would, obviously, be scope for entrepreneurs to act for more than one community (analogous to having a chain of shops in different locations but all being supplied by a single wholesaler's truck calling at each location), or for an SSE to spring up locally to provide a single service in one location. The pricing of delivery at the ultimate level should be seen to be fair by all parties, involving both a reasonable revenue for the utility agency and an opportunity for adding to the unit cost to cover the community or entrepreneur's contribution to the service plus a profit to be used to improve the service.

In garbage disposal, the ultimate level could be a skip, a large dump into which a series of skips have been emptied, a dump only for materials which a particular community cannot recycle, or a number of delivery points for recycled products at particular levels of sorting, cleaning, baling etc. In such a case, the party taking over downstream from the ultimate level might also be in the private sector, and may be a single entrepreneur or a series of specialists. The current practice in which some people select which garbage to throw away and which to reuse in the household (e.g., through feeding clean organic waste to animals) is a reflection of different ultimate levels already in operation. In the optimum system, the local authority would be left with no garbage-disposal function at all as recyclers, farmers, biogas manufacturers and scrap dealers compete for the material available.

6. Local building materials

Special action is needed to support local production and use of indigenous materials. The GSS states that this may require policies to support governmental investment in surveying and assessment of raw-material resources and their use, feasibility studies for the exploitation of promising resources, testing and upgrading of indigenous materials and products,[15] promotion of products in the market place and acceptance and use of indigenous materials in government projects as an example to others. In addition, action is needed to promote local factors of production for construction — notably building materials, construction labour and basic tools.

A rapid expansion of the supply of basic building materials at low cost can be achieved by promoting the small-scale sector. By adopting recent technological innovations, it is possible to develop an entire building-materials industry exclusively based on small-scale production units. However, the small-scale sector is especially vulnerable because of the predominance of unskilled labour, a high rate of illiteracy, lack of access to credit (especially foreign exchange), lack of access to information on technological innovations and, most of all, lack of appropriate institutional support for technological choice. Thus, a strategy for the application of appropriate technology in the small-scale sector should address the following three areas, of which the first two issues (but particularly the first) should be given priority attention:

- the shortcomings in performance of technologies already established in production;
- the issue of new investments in technologies to overcome those limitations;

---

15. However, so much experimentation and improvement work has already been done that it is more a matter of using existing results and replicating lessons learned from pilot projects already completed than spending money on primary research into materials.

- the identification of innovations which are yet to be transferred either from local sources in laboratories and research institutions or from international sources (UNCHS, 1990).

E. Scope for strengthening the capacity of poor, unemployed residents and their community organizations

According to the GSS, the main objective of a national strategy should be to improve the shelter situation of those whose housing is below the national average. Because resources for improvement of shelter are scarce, it is important to concentrate the resources on improvement of the situation of the most needy. This applies particularly to public resources, but it should also be a guideline for how public authorities influence the use of private resources, or bring private resources under the influence or decision of public authorities (UNCHS, 1990).

The CBO appears to be the most useful vehicle for strengthening the technical and organizational capacity of the poor. The community contracts experience in Sri Lanka shows how this can be done through workshops and seminars targeted at the clientele, through diplomatically-assisted community elections so that true representatives of the people can emerge, and through building up trust between public authorities and CBOs. In doing this, the role of NGOs as intermediaries between the community and local government can be vital in successfully managing urban development. Experience has shown that, in order to get good results from community participation, the community and NGOs need to be involved in all stages of urban development: planning, programming, implementation, operation and maintenance, and not just in the last two stages as has often been the case. Their participation is required both in kind (through ideas at the planning stage and labour contributions during project implementation and later operation and maintenance) and financially (through faithfully paying fees and taxes, through their own investments, and through land contributions).

1. Technical assistance

From the Sri Lankan community contract experience (Yap, 1988), it is possible to gauge the importance and effectiveness of well-found technical assistance from local authorities, public bodies and NGOs, given within practical experience of planning and implementation. In Sri Lanka, very poor people were trained in simple skills like reading plans and filling in forms, so that they could go on to contribute to planning their own infrastructure and public facilities. At the implementation level, local artisans who were employed for their skills found that the responsibility they held in the small project, and the increasing complexity of projects which the community contracting entity could tackle, led to a gradual but noticeable improvement of skills. In tackling a sewerage system, artisans found themselves learning more about levelling and gradients than they had previously known. They learned partly by having to do the work, and partly through the technical assistance given by the NHDA technical staff assigned to oversee the project. These examples represent true technology transfer from the formal to the informal sector, enabling the poor to improve their conditions through increased productivity. Through pilot projects for housing and services, planned within local social, cultural and economic contexts, similar self-perpetuating processes should be sought and set in motion.

Technical assistance to the materials-supply industry has proved fairly straightforward. The Humama women's successful building-materials operation in Nairobi (see chapter V) shows how technical problems can be overcome given close cooperation between an NGO (in this case the AHF) and the enterprise. If the operators are well trained, they can make reasonable profits to pay back start-up capital and pay workers a living wage. However, they can only operate where markets exist for their products. Governments and international agencies can assist here by making a point of using products which result from such initiatives until commercial markets develop. Just as the road contractors in Ghana were assured future contracts (subject only to a satisfactory standard of work), building-materials producers should be assured markets for the early, vulnerable period of operation (subject only to the quality of the product). Both examples show the importance of a relationship between donors and the incipient enterprises which encompasses stages from planning the enterprise to becoming established with customers and contracts. Assistance should, therefore, concentrate on this longitudinal support rather than sowing seeds whose outcomes must survive in inhospitable environments.

2.   Organizational assistance

One of the most important outcomes of the community contract experience in Sri Lanka appears to be the increased confidence which the people have after tackling public works provision for themselves. Each form successfully filled in, each letter written, and each meeting held, constitute learning experiences for poor people. Not only does the fact of seeing a simple structure designed and built by themselves actually completed give poor people confidence for tackling more complex projects, the experience of entering the maze of bureaucracy and coming out the other end with what they wanted gives them a confidence which dispels hopelessness. Never again will members of a successful community development council be fobbed off by a petty bureaucrat without a good reason.

This situation then calls for a new attitude from the public authorities. Once they have empowered CBOs, they must be able to help in ways which are required and allowed free rein. The relationship established in Sri Lanka between the NHDA and the CBOs is referred to as a "Creative Praxis" which, according to Sirivardana (1986, pp. 96–97), is captured by the Million Houses Programme's slogan of "Minimal intervention, maximal support by the State: maximal involvement of the user families." Its underlying ethos of increasing user participation while giving support from the authorities in all stages of the shelter process is one which should be at the heart of future approaches towards increasing the ability of households to escape from poverty by the use of their resources in a creative partnership working towards a holistic approach to urbanization and development.

X. Conclusions and proposals for assisting employment generation in shelter, infrastructure and services provision

A. Conclusions

In the past, housing has all too often been regarded as a consumption good or a part of citizen welfare, not a part of the general productive development process. The argument was that it should be provided because people need it. Thus, in competition with other sectors of the economy, housing has not been allocated sufficient resources to keep pace with either need or demand in the current circumstances of continuous high rates of growth in both general populations and urban populations in developing countries. In the absence of formal-sector alternatives, increasing numbers of people have turned to informal-sector housing, either as squatters gathering around the periphery of existing cities, or as tenants of increasingly crowded inner city housing.

Recently (and notably in the GSS), it has been increasingly accepted that housing may also be a productive sector, capable of acting as the engine of an economy, providing both growth in the sectors responsible for all the parts needed in house and infrastructure construction and opportunities for economic activities within the residential environment. However, in the past there has been little concentrated research and analysis on the employment, and consequent economic benefits, inherent in housing. As Gilbert (1988) points out, this is probably because employment and housing belong to different strands of academic endeavour which rarely meet.

It is evident from this review that shelter in all its components holds enormous potential for increasing economic activity. Not only does the building of houses and provision of services already provide considerable numbers of jobs to all sectors of the populations, but they also generate backward linkages to other sectors of the economy, and forward linkages through the use of housing for income generation, with significant income multipliers accruing.

The cooperation between UNCHS (Habitat) and the ILO provides a potentially fertile ground for cooperation in increasing employment opportunities while addressing the shelter challenge of the next decade. This review has been conducted in the context that there should be a positive attitude towards employment creation; that the employment of more people should be an aim of shelter and public works programmes, and that their success should partly be judged on the criterion of how much employment results from their implementation and maintenance, and how much of that employment accrues to poorer members of the community.

The role of the informal sector in providing employment and housing opportunities is increasingly recognized as not only substantial in reality but also potentially beneficial to the development of a country's economy. Its tendency to use local materials and technology, and relatively unskilled labour recruited locally or even within the family, has been recognized as maximizing the potential for poverty alleviation. However, they have been particularly prone to low productivity in the past, partly because little encouragement has been directed towards them from official circles. Moreover, the informal sector harbours some of the most exploitative and dangerous employment practices, and many of its entrepreneurs display a disregard for taxation and formal accounting procedures which make it difficult for governments and formal-sector contractors to use its services in formal ways.

It is clear that large numbers of households (certainly in excess of 10 per cent and possibly 25 per cent) use their home for some economic activity. Although information about HBEs is less comprehensive than that on the informal sector in general, it is evident that they are an important element in the economies of households as well as of countries. In the past, official attitudes have tended to concentrate upon the problems with HBEs. Yet, the evidence reviewed here suggests that, on balance, HBEs are essential to the people who operate them and their benefits probably far outweigh their costs. In order to formulate enabling policies which maximize the benefits and minimize the costs, mixed residential and economic uses of housing should be encouraged through pilot projects carried out in parallel with further research on costs and benefits.

In the construction industry, the informal sector provides housing at prices which the formal sector cannot match and in places in which the formal sector does not operate. For a considerable proportion of the population, especially the poor, the informal sector presents the only housing supply system available. In the context of the GSS, it is recognized that there is a need to ensure that shelter policies are directed not only towards housing supply efficiency but also towards economic development, particularly as it affects the poor. Thus, the needs of women and other groups who have been disregarded in the past are to be taken into account. In this context, the informal sector is important and the deeply hostile attitude of many government and local authority officials towards informal-sector housing needs to be changed if all the actors in the housing process are to be effective in housing supply.

It has been shown that there is considerable potential to increase these positive economic effects of shelter provision by encouraging housing and services which use locally-produced raw materials put together through simple technologies. The cheaper the housing is, the more is spent on labour per unit of total expenditure. In addition, cheaper housing, especially if built in the informal sector, generates a greater proportion of its benefits to the working poor, not only because they might be able to afford the housing constructed but also because they become increasingly dominant in the labour force involved in its construction and the backward linkages. It is also evident that SSEs could be involved in all types of housing construction, from new-build, through sites-and-services and upgrading, to the maintenance of existing stock. While this is currently prevalent in the informal sector, a change in policy is required for the formal sector, particularly government departments, to involve SSEs in their operations. If this were to be implemented, the potential returns in increased efficiency, higher multipliers, and improved income redistribution could be significant.

It is also evident that provision and maintenance of infrastructure is capable of providing many opportunities for employment and for SSEs. Equipment-based methods of road building, drainage, and installation of water pipes and sewerage systems have been favoured in the past, not least by international donor agencies. However, the heavy use of foreign exchange and low employment creation characteristics of this type of construction have less positive effects on development than more labour-intensive approaches. Thus, it is proposed that, where public agencies continue to provide infrastructure, they do so using labour-intensive methods wherever possible.

It is self-evident that maintenance tasks are well suited to single artisans and small firms; the low technology and scattered location of operations tend to ensure this. However, successful projects by the ILO have shown that SSEs are capable of relatively large contracts in infrastructure provision. Examples in road building and water reticulation have proved the point. In addition, the community contracts system in Sri Lanka has demonstrated how local communities can organize themselves not only to carry out small infrastructure works in their own neighbourhoods but also to undertake contracts for more complex activities (e.g., sewerage reticulation) outside their areas.

While the provision of all services to each household is an ideal towards which most servicing authorities probably aim, the reality of current and foreseeable future provision falls very far short of this. The potential provided by transferring responsibility for operating and maintaining services to SSEs and community groups could bring higher quality services to more people than the sole efforts of service agencies.

Two conceptual tools are offered to assist in the decisions about where service agency responsibility for provision, maintenance and operation should end and local participation begin. The first recognizes the right of people to fair remuneration for work done except in activities which could fairly be regarded as benefiting only the local community. To this end, public works can be separated into "minor" (those which may be done through voluntary unpaid community work) and "major" (those for which paid labour is appropriate). The second considers the suitable threshold at which a service is relinquished by the agency and accepted as the consumers' responsibility. Determination of the location of this threshold, called the "ultimate level" in this publication, can provide various mixes of public and private or community responsibility and, if required, convert the agencies' role into that of wholesalers of services. Within this transfer of functions towards communities and SSEs, experience in Sri Lanka with community contracts provides useful lessons which, with modification for local circumstances, may be applicable elsewhere.

In the context of the need to maximize the use of existing resources, both for ecological reasons and to economize on foreign exchange, the potential of waste-recycling comes to the fore. There are many opportunities for employment in garbage collection and recycling; the task ahead is to maximize their potential and minimize their problems, particularly those concerned with the poverty currently experienced by most informal-sector garbage pickers and the very poor working and living conditions which they endure.

Current activities by international donors and NGOs demonstrate that new approaches, based on urban management and policy environments, have the potential for poverty alleviation in a more effective way than that achieved by shelter projects in the past. In their shelter sector activities, it is proposed that government, NGO, and international donor interventions should concentrate on the supply of housing and infrastructure, and do so at as low a point in the technological continuum as is possible in order to maximize employment and use of local resources. Efforts should concentrate upon the supply markets: land at affordable prices, local and inexpensive building materials and components, appropriate finance available as far down the income scale as possible and at market interest rates, and a suitable blend of skilled and unskilled labour. In addition, attention must be given to the regulatory framework in order that the supply process can function effectively to the benefit of the low-income majority. As public-sector and large formal suppliers cannot keep pace with demand, there is a need to increase the viability of enterprises of all scales, but particularly small-scale, in the construction sector, in the manufacture of building materials, and in recycling and other infrastructural and servicing functions. All should be encouraged to use labour-based technologies, even to the extent of its being a condition of tendering for public-sector contracts.

An efficient supply system confronts the twin horns of the shelter dilemma — shortage of housing and poverty of the unhoused — in parallel. Its effectiveness in alleviating the problem appears to increase in inverse proportion to the cost of the housing and infrastructure provided. Thus, international donor efforts should be concentrated on providing governments with the encouragement to furnish a hospitable and stimulating policy environment in which low-income housing can be provided through labour-based technologies, using local resources, by the private formal and informal sector. This implies active support for strategies linking the goals of shelter for all and employment for all as a common strategy for poverty reduction.

B. Specific project proposals for action by the international donor community (including NGOs)

Following from this review of the relationship between employment and shelter, and from a recent review of experience in enabling shelter strategies (UNCHS, 1991b), several specific actions for the short and medium term can be proposed.

1. Encouraging a healthy housing supply industry

In the GSS, emphasis is laid on the scaling-up of housing programmes which cannot be achieved by a traditional project approach alone. Sites-and-services schemes and settlement-upgrading have their place, and the latter can be important in neighbourhoods currently occupied by the poor. However, making them the corner-stones of housing strategy has diverted attention away from the need to encourage housing output for all consumers and involve all possible means of production.

While the self-help approach has its advantages, and many householders do in fact get their hands dirty building their houses, it is evident that efforts should be concentrated on professional builders. Householders need to be empowered to deal with professionals, to be able to judge whether work is done properly and at the right price; they need this more than to know how to build. This is the householder/contractor interface. In addition, and more importantly for scaling up supply, artisans and contractors need to be able to build. They need the inputs (land, materials, regulatory frameworks, finance, skilled and unskilled workers) to be available, advice on how to improve their efficiency, on new and traditional methods and materials, and the other issues which they may confront at the contractor/house interface.

Informal-sector enterprises should be able to compete on a fair basis. The currently advantageous position of some large-scale formal-sector contractors should thus be removed and a more hospitable political, economic and financial environment be created in which the informal sector can operate, particularly in the construction sector. This may involve controls on imported items which can be manufactured locally, especially those involving traditional crafts. Whatever assistance is available for industry should not be concentrated on the large equipment-intensive companies who tend to benefit currently, but instead be concentrated on those SSEs which show potential for survival and efficient production of shelter and infrastructure. Assistance should take technical and financial forms, focusing on appropriate technology development, product improvement and diversification, control over market networks, and strengthening local financing.

The establishment of a healthy housing supply industry, preferably based on labour-intensive methods, using local materials in locally acceptable and appropriate ways, is a paramount need in many developing countries. International donors should enable local developers and contractors (and would-be developers and contractors) to form the units of the supply industry through on-the-job training (by mounting pilot projects), through visits to countries where successful development methods are applied, and through the encouragement of local training institutions. Successful initiatives such as the Ghana Feeder Roads Improvement Programme, and the Sri Lanka community contracts, in both of which artisans are encouraged to join together to form legal entities capable of taking on larger contracts, should be replicated in other places within the local social, economic and political contexts.

2. Developing potential through pilot projects

Assistance in the form of finite projects should generally be limited to pilot projects whose purpose is to enable local people to become competent in development skills, to establish local solutions to supply-side issues, or to demonstrate appropriate development techniques. Donor agencies and national governments should direct their efforts into pilot projects which allow the principles and practices of a particular technique or project to be tried out relatively quickly and inexpensively. In so doing, experience is gained on costs, timing and phasing, skills and equipment required and their relationship, and the likely pitfalls in implementing a larger project. Lessons should be learned from the commercial world, where pilot projects are usually done from capital and represent speculative investment, they tend to be as small and as sharply focused as possible, commensurate with finding out the information required. The pilot project is intrinsically small and experimental. Its outputs (houses, permanent jobs, infrastructure etc.) are incidental and a form of bonus rather than being the aim of the project. The purpose is the test; the measure of success is whether and how far the technique tested is disseminated through initiatives arising from the pilot project.

The upgrading projects of the 1970s, where thousands of squatters on the site were assisted and their housing conditions have improved, might be regarded as successful and lessons have been learned from them. However, they took years to mount, further years to implement, and cost large amounts of money both from immediate government spending and in loan repayments over time. Thus, their opportunity cost was substantial. Although often intended to be models of how other areas could be treated, their effects have tended to stop at the project boundaries because of insufficient cost-recovery to continue elsewhere (or because of other problems). Thus, they could not be regarded as successful pilot projects. On the other hand, pilot projects can be mounted very quickly (three months is not an unusual lead time), can have a very brief implementation period (say six months) and, thus, demonstrate in a very finite and immediate way the costs and benefits of a particular approach. This immediacy has several advantages:

- it allows current issues to be addressed in the short term (rather than two or three years down the line);

- it assists donor agencies by minimising overhead costs;
- there is considerable reinforcement of initial enthusiasm when something concrete can be done relatively quickly.

Although the importance of the pilot project is in the learning experience, the output of some houses, a school, a drain, or a road, also has intrinsic worth which can be discounted against the cost of mounting the project. The small project for the paving of the market parking yard in Kampala (see chapter IV) was designed to test the technique of labour-intensive paving. However, the smooth parking yard which resulted is a welcome bonus.

In house construction, pilot projects can be used to teach labour-based techniques, their management, and all aspects of the developer's art. This will have costs — in terms of training materials, trainers' time, tools and equipment, and the materials used to construct houses used as training media — and benefits in terms of trained supervisors, managers, and developers who can then put their expertise to work in labour-based construction. However, the resulting houses are also likely to be worth quite a substantial sum at the end of the project. Their sale can provide funding for the next pilot project or for any other purpose.

Pilot projects in house-building or service provision are ideally suited to UNDP micro-capital grants and to the involvement of UNVs, both in-country and internationally. Their small-scale and rapid completion allows a complete pilot project to be carried out within a brief period and then the volunteer can go away and train others. In addition, NGOs and CBOs are likely to be able to tackle innovative pilot projects while they would lack the capacity to implement larger projects.

The encouragement of pilot projects must not be interpreted as recommendations that donors take a project-based approach to development. There is a need for all donors to realize that the project-based solutions of the past probably will not improve the housing and employment prospects of the poor as much as project promoters may hope. There is now a recognition that, for example, sites-and-services projects are too expensive to reach the poorest households. They, and similar projects, are typically too large-scale and require organizational, managerial and bureaucratic inputs beyond the scope of local resources and which raise the costs to project participants. Shelter costs per plot in World Bank sites-and-services projects, for instance, seldom fall under the $750 to $1,000 range and consequently rarely reach the lowest 20 per cent by income (Linn, 1983). Therefore, the poor who lack the resources for initial entry and the income stability to make a fixed housing investment do not have access to sites-and-services projects. Indeed, the mismatch between housing cost and incomes has often resulted in massive defaults on monthly payments, or the original poor project participants have sold off their participation to more well-off families. Consequently, the intended beneficiaries often do not ultimately participate in the project (Hansen and Williams, 1987).

3. Promotion of mixed uses

In contrast to existing planning control and some lease agreements, and as argued in chapter VII, the use of housing for HBEs should be recognized as a valid development strategy and promoted in some areas.

Housing as workplace as well as residence is a necessary reality for a considerable but unquantifiable number of households, most of whom are poor. Currently, in most developing countries, this activity is treated as illegal and undesirable. However, although there are a number of useful studies of aspects of HBEs in some cities, there is no overall picture available of their costs and benefits. The balance of the argument so far appears to be in favour of allowing HBEs. Whether the balance is well enough established to encourage them, not only to cease harassment but also to enable, is less easy to assert. Their presence argues a greater benefit than cost for those in whose home they occur; whether the benefits would be greater and costs less if they were separated from, but still close to, the home, is not known. What their effects are on neighbours (their externalities), and the balance of positives and negatives of particular uses, are also unknown.

Therefore, it is proposed that a series of pilot projects be carried out to examine the modalities of establishing mixed-use areas. These projects should test the logistics of integrating work-place and residential space in a variety of house types in differing cultures, examine the economic relationship between expected income and willingness to pay for housing and services, and determine whether residents without economic activities would choose to live in such areas (e.g., because they offered employment or services, or simply because they were unconcerned about the externalities).

C. Directions for future research

In recommending future research, it is desirable to indicate avenues through which knowledge can directly illuminate issues central to the theme of this review.

1. Analysis of costs and benefits in labour-based approaches

There is a need for empirical research on the scale of benefits likely to accrue from particular levels and types of employment generated by adopting labour-based methods for public works provision, and the likely number of jobs which will result from particular policy choices. Given that both employment creation and having people unemployed have costs, the research should assess real and marginal costs and benefits of employment creation within labour-based technologies in both the formal and informal sectors. Such research should be international in scope and comparative in nature, in order that the thin and impressionistic data reviewed in this publication can be supplemented with more weighty and reliable information. Issues which need to be examined include the effects on labour costs and efficiency of large-scale use of labour-based methods in public works provision; and ways in which the exploitative component of low wages can be minimized through bonuses, training etc.

Current research points to the effectiveness of low-technology shelter investment as a generator of multipliers and linkages. However, the extent of the differences between technologies and between shelter and other sectors has not been adequately quantified in the literature. Research efforts should be directed towards making informed decisions about encouraging shelter and infrastructure investments in competition with other sectors, the advisability of reducing capital costs in exchange for (or in order to achieve) labour inputs for maintenance, and other policy issues in the choice of labour-based technologies.

2. The implications of home-based economic activities on residential environments and income generation

The work done by Strassmann (1985b), Gilbert (1988) and others on HBEs began to ask questions about their effectiveness and implications for the housing stock. There is a need to supplement the proposed pilot projects of establishing some small areas of mixed uses with studies of other cities, to see how far Strassmann's and Gilbert's findings represent the picture elsewhere. This research would be aimed at the following:

* To establish values for some of the variables in the cost-benefit equations in mixed-use areas for particular uses and neighbourhood types both to the entrepreneur households and, through externalities, to the neighbours.

* To set out draft codes of conduct within which public authorities, community groups and individuals could settle issues arising from planned or existing HBEs. The codes should aim to be proscriptive in controls, only setting limits beyond which activities should be prevented from passing, e.g., uses which would be wholly unacceptable in houses, and promotional in interventions, e.g., alternatives for service provision with indications of proportional costs and benefits.

3. The implications of community control of local services: application of the "ultimate level" concept

Employment generation and the delegation of traditional tasks to SSEs in urban public works provide a valuable context in which the community control of services within the "ultimate level" threshold could be tested. It would be useful to select a city in which the records of pipework and other services are relatively complete. With reference to neighbourhood groups of appropriate size in the particular cultural milieu existing, the distribution network could be divided up at alternative notional ultimate level thresholds. In consultation with public authorities and community groups, the modalities of community control within ultimate level thresholds could be examined. In addition, issues could be modelled such as the feasibility of dividing the system into finite units and thereafter maintaining and extending them, the wholesaling of service by the public sector, the financial implications in terms of price of service and collection modalities etc. Using multivariate analysis of various types, including discriminant and contingent analysis techniques (see Tipple and Willis, 1991a), alternative scenarios can be tested for price, level of service, foreseeable problems and general feasibility. Ultimately, a pilot project to test different ultimate levels could provide experimental evidence to gauge the accuracy of the predictive models in order to assist in evaluating the process elsewhere.

4.   A healthy housing supply system

The housing supply industry should be developed in depth. There is little point in increasing the supply of bricks if there is a shortage of contractors willing or able to use them. Similarly, there is little point in encouraging efficient contracting methods to increase the construction capacity if there are too few materials or land to absorb the activity. However, surprisingly little is known about housing supply in developing countries. Thus, an analysis of action in countries should begin with an appraisal of the housing supply system in order to locate bottlenecks in the supply markets, examine the potential for alternative materials, assess the capacity of the construction industry, and recommend measures for improvement. The recent World Bank International Study of Rent Control (Malpezzi and Ball, 1991) provides a useful model for the scope of such a study.

The analysis should treat informal and formal sectors as part of the same overall system so that their linkages, and relative strengths, can be identified. From that, and within the local context, policy interventions designed to encourage appropriately sized and equipped enterprises could be drawn up, reducing the chance of the wasteful and morale-sapping failures which have dogged the encouragement of building-materials enterprises in the absence of developing markets.

5.   The dissemination of research on appropriate building materials and technologies

There is a large amount of useful research into the suitability of local building materials locked away in research institutes around the world, unused by the people who could benefit from them because they have not been tried out. There is a need for research on how dissemination can best be carried out and what would increase the chance of local, labour-intensive materials and technologies becoming socially acceptable. It must be said, however, that this is not a proposal for more research on the materials themselves. Impressionistic evidence from West Africa suggests that more than enough research has been done on improving the durability of local materials and establishing the case for using them from the standpoint of physical performance.

6.   Alternative financial institutions

In order for the working poor to help themselves, it is necessary to develop mechanisms whereby they can have access to credit. It is absurd to expect the poor to spend money on housing improvements if their own immediate concern is to pay back their debts for frequent personal emergencies or to raise money to set up a small income-generating enterprise. There is considerable scope for research into innovative financial mechanisms that can enable the poor to escape the evils of being constantly at the mercy of money-lenders. Such mechanisms might enable the poor to increase their income-generating potential. Only then can it be expected that the poor will give priority to improvements in housing stock.

D.   Future roles of the public sector, NGOs and international donors

This review indicates fairly well-defined roles for the public sector, NGOs and international donors, most of which are in the enabling and facilitating quadrant and very few in the implementing. Public authorities, increasingly bound by fiscal problems and exceptional demands for services, are increasingly unable to be providers and implementers. The enabling role outlined in this publication requires strong and cohesive government action to support community-level initiatives within a hospitable policy and financial environment.

Governments must ensure that the supply markets for shelter services are operating efficiently and encourage appropriately low-technology solutions to housing and infrastructure requirements. As providers of services, they may find the role of wholesaler to community organizations more tenable than their current retailing role. In addition, they must cultivate new skills to manage cities and towns whose services are being run cooperatively with many different entities and whose housing are being built by numerous SSEs.

NGOs will have an important role as encouragers and coordinators, standing between the public authorities and the various active community groups and associations of SSEs. Being closer to the people, they will be important in voicing concerns to the public authorities and bringing together disparate issues raised at the community level to be negotiated with the public authorities. They will also provide locally-relevant inputs to training of community groups in their roles as contractors for public works, honest brokers for financial matters, and retailer of infrastructural services. The role of NGOs as facilitators of international donor participation will also be vital if, for example, small capital grants and loans are to be distributed to where they are needed and will be effective. Thus, NGOs have a role as the eyes and ears of public authorities, and as the mouthpiece of the community groups.

International donors are influential in shaping governments' opinions towards policies in the shelter sector which will contribute to poverty alleviation. They should concentrate on enabling the enablers; on sponsoring pilot projects to try out innovative labour-based approaches, on training for community participation in planning, implementation, financing, and maintaining services and housing; and on research which will reduce the incidence of incongruous policies. By concentrating their project inputs on small pilot projects, they will encourage innovation without establishing a culture of dependence, and try out ideas in order that local enterprises and authorities can short-circuit the learning process.

If donors are serious about the GSS, they will press for labour-based approaches and local participation which can only effectively be implemented by locally-based and community-based organizations. If multi-million dollar housing projects are a thing of the past, which seems likely, the disbursement of funds will have to be decentralized. This calls for sensitivity to the issues of the community more than just as a facility of finance and economics. It will be a challenge.

Bibliography

Abrams, C. (1964). *Man's Struggle for Shelter in an Urbanizing World,* Cambridge, Massachusetts, MIT Press.

Afrane, S.K. (1987). "Job-creation in residential areas: A comparative study of public and private residential communities in Kumasi, Ghana", paper presented at the International Seminar on Income and Housing in Third World Urban Development, New Delhi, 30 November to 4 December.

———. (1990). "Job creation in residential areas: A comparative Study of Public and Private Residential Communities in Kumasi, Ghana", in Raj, M., and Nientied, P. (eds.), *Housing and Income in Third World Urban Development*, London, Aspect Publishing.

Ahsan, R.M., Haque, N.N., and Haque, A. (1992). "Collection, sorting and recycling of solid waste in Dhaka City, Bangladesh", paper presented to the UNDP/ILO Inter-regional Workshop on Employment Generation in Urban Works Programmes through Efficient Use of Local Resources, United Nations Centre, Nairobi, 6–10 April.

Akhtar, W., Ali, I., Ali, S.M., and Ali, S.A. (1992). "Solid waste management in a katchi abadi", paper presented to the 18th WEDC Conference, Kathmandu, Nepal, 30 August to 3 September.

Ameen, M.S. (1988). "Housing for low-income people in third world peri-urban areas: a case study of Dhaka, Bangladesh", unpublished PhD dissertation, School of Architecture, University of Newcastle-upon-Tyne, United Kingdom.

Amole, B., Korboe, D., and Tipple, A.G. (1993) "The family house in West Africa: A forgotten resource for policy makers?" *Third World Planning Review*, vol. 15, No. 4 (Nov).

Anand, S. (1977). "Aspects of poverty in Malaysia", *Review of Income and Wealth,* vol. 23, No. 1.

Angal, A. (1991). "The conflict between the built environment created by the recent housing schemes in Algiers and the expectations of those for whom they are designed", unpublished PhD dissertation, University of Newcastle-upon-Tyne, United Kingdom.

Aragon, M.A.M. (1988). "Building materials in Central America" (ID/WG.479/1), background paper for a Regional Expert Group Meeting, UNIDO.

Archer, R. (1992). "Guided Land Development (GLD) in Indonesia", *Trialog,* vol. 32, No. 1.

Aryee, G. (1981). "The informal manufacturing sector in Kumasi", in S. V. Sethuraman (ed.), *The Urban Informal Sector: Employment, Poverty and Environment*, Geneva, ILO.

Asiama, S.O. (1985). "The rich slum-dweller: a problem of unequal access", *International Labour Review,* vol. 124, No. 3, pp. 353–362.

Bahawi, M. (1992). "Employment prospects in urban activities (Afghanistan)", paper presented to the UNDP/ILO Inter-regional Workshop on Employment Generation in Urban Works Programmes through Efficient Use of Local Resources, United Nations Centre, Nairobi, 6–10 April.

Bahl, R., and Lin, J. (1987). "Intergovernmental fiscal relations in developing countries", in Tolley, G.S., and Thomas G. (eds.), *The Economics of Urbanization and Urban Policy in Developing Countries,* Washington, D.C., The World Bank.

Baily, M.A. (1981). "Brick manufacturing in Colombia: A case study of alternative technologies", *World Development,* vol. 9, pp. 201–213.

Bamberger, M., Sanyal, B., and Valverde, N. (1982). "Evaluation of sites and services projects: the experience from Lusaka, Zambia", World Bank Staff Working Papers No. 548, Washington, D.C., The World Bank.

Baross, P. (1983). "Four experiences with settlement improvement policies in Asia", in Skinner, R.J., and Rodell, M.J. (eds), *People, Poverty and Shelter: Problems of Self-help Housing in the Third World*, London, Methuen.

Barrett, D.E., and Shahidullah, M. (1992). "Public sector stimulus for private sector repair systems", paper presented to the 18th WEDC Conference, Kathmandu, 30 August to 3 September.

Bassir, I. B. (1991). "NGOs, women and community water", paper presented at the 17th WEDC Conference, Nairobi, 19–23 August.

Batarfie, A. (1987). "Higher living, higher income?", paper presented at the International Seminar on Income and Housing in Third World Urban Development, New Delhi.

Beier, G., Churchill, A., Cohen, M., and Renaud, B. (1976). "The task ahead for cities of developing countries", *World Development*, vol. 4, No. 5, pp. 363–409.

Benjamin, S.J. (1985). "India: formal v. informal", *Architectural Review*, No. 1062, pp. 32–36.

———. (1990). "Income and housing: Understanding household productivity within the framework of urban structuring", in Raj, M., and Nientied, P. (eds.), *Housing and Income in Third World Urban Development*, London, Aspect Publishing.

Bezboruah, R. (1985). "Annapurna-Mahila Mandal, Bombay", Geneva, ILO (CONDI/T) (unpublished country case study).

Bhatt, E. (1989). "Towards empowerment", *World Development*, vol. 17, No. 7, pp. 1059–1065.

Bhatt, V., Navarett, J., Casault, A., Zhang, J., Zhou, Q., Huang, Q., Fu, G.H., Yang, W., and Wu, X.Z. (1993). "Housing a billion: design ideas for rural China", Montreal, Minimum Cost Housing Group, McGill University.

Bhattacharjee, N., and Nientied, P. (1987). "Employment in World Bank urban development projects in West Africa", paper presented at the International Seminar on Income and Housing in Third World Urban Development, New Delhi, 30 November to 4 December.

Birkbeck, C. (1979). "Garbage, industry, and the 'vultures' of Cali, Colombia", in Bromley, R., and Gerry, C. (eds.), *Casual Work and Poverty in Third World Cities*, Chichester, Sussex, John Wiley.

Boonyabancha, S. (1990). *Evaluation of Experience with Initiating Enabling Shelter Strategies in Thailand*, Nairobi, UNCHS (Habitat).

Bose, M. (1990). "The urban informal sector revisited: Some lessons from the field", Discussion Paper 276, Institute of Development Studies, Falmer, Sussex, University of Sussex, July.

Briscoe, J., and de Ferranti, D. (1988). *Water for Rural Communities — Helping People to Help Themselves*, Washington, DC., The World Bank.

Bromley, R., and Gerry, C. (1979). "Who are the casual poor?", in Bromley, R., and Gerry, C. (eds.), *Casual Work and Poverty in Third World Cities*, Chichester, United Kingdom, John Wiley.

Buckley, R., and Mayo, S. (1988). "Housing policy in developing economies: Evaluating the macro-economic impacts", Infrastructure and Urban Development Department Discussion Paper INU 19, Washington, D.C., The World Bank.

——, ——. (1989). "Housing policy in developing economies: evaluating the macro-economic impacts", *Review of Urban and Regional Development Studies*, vol. 2, pp. 27–46.

Bulmer-Thomas, V. (ed.) (1982). *Input-Output Analysis in Developing Countries*, Chichester, United Kingdom, John Wiley.

Burgess, R. (1982). "Self-help housing advocacy: A curious form of radicalism. A critique of the work of John F. C. Turner", in Ward, P.M. (ed.), *Self-help Housing: a Critique*, London, Mansell.

——. (1985). "The limits of self-help housing", *Development and Change*, vol. 16, No. 2, pp. 271–312.

Burns, L.S., and Ferguson, B. (1987). "Criteria for future shelter and settlement policies in developing countries", in Rodwin, L. (ed.), *Shelter, Settlement and Development,* Boston, Massachusetts, George Allen and Unwin.

Burns, L.S., and Grebler, L. (1977). *The Housing of Nations,* London and Basingstoke, Macmillan.

Burns, L.S., Healy, R.G., McAllister, D.M., and Tjioe, B.K. (1970). "Housing: symbol and shelter", International Housing and Productivity Study, University of California, Los Angeles, California.

Burra, N. (1989). "Out of sight, out of mind: Working girls in India", *International Labour Review,* vol. 128, No. 5, pp. 651–660.

Bushra, M. (1992). "Recycling as a necessary part of solid waste", paper presented to the UNDP/ILO Inter-regional Workshop on Employment Generation in Urban Works Programmes through Efficient Use of Local Resources, United Nations Centre, Nairobi, 6–10 April.

Centre for Development Studies. (1975). *Poverty, Unemployment and Development Policy.* Trivandrum, Kerala, Centre for Development Studies.

Chana, T.S. (1984). "Nairobi: Dandora and other projects", in Payne, G.K. (ed.), *Low-income Housing in the Developing World,* New York, John Wiley, pp. 17–36.

Chatterjee, L. (1981). "Housing development in Nigeria", United States Agency for International Development, Office of Housing, Occasional Paper Series, Winter 1981.

Christie, C., and Harris, C. (1992). *Kumasi Waste Disposal Social Survey Report,* Epsom, United Kingdom, W. S. Atkins.

City of Soweto. (1992). "Contractor development in labour-based construction", Soweto, South Africa, City Engineer's Department.

CNC (Centro Nacional de la Construcción). (1976). "Diagnosis of the economic and technological state of the Colombian brickmaking industry", Doc. No. CEN 10-76, Santafé de Bogotá.

Cohen, M.A. (1981). "Urban sector strategies for Africa: The next twenty years", World Bank Draft Paper, 22 January.

Cotton, A., and Franceys, R. (1991). *Services for Shelter: Infrastructure for Urban Low Income Housing,* Liverpool, United Kingdom, Liverpool University Press.

Dasgupta, A.S. (1987). "Spatial planning and home based economic activities: design considerations", paper presented at the International Seminar on

Income and Housing in Third World Urban Development, New Delhi, December 1987.

———. (1990). "Negotiating for growth and change: A study of user initiated transformation of formal housing", *Open House International*, vol. 15, No. 4.

David, J. (1983). *Low Income Housing and Employment for the Poor: First Look,* Geneva, ILO.

Davidson, F. (1984). "Ismailia: combined upgrading and site and services projects in Egypt", in Payne, G.K., (ed.), *Low-Income Housing in the Developing World*, New York, John Wiley, pp. 125–148.

de Soto, H. (1986). *El otro sendero*. Lima, Editorial el Barranaco.

Diop, O.E. (1992). "Employment creation and solid waste management: some case studies", paper presented to the UNDP/ILO Inter-regional Workshop on Employment Generation in Urban Works Programmes through Efficient Use of Local Resources, United Nations Centre, Nairobi, 6–10 April.

Doebele, W.A. (1977). "The private market and low income urbanization: The pirate subdivisions of Bogotá", *American Journal of Comparative Law*, vol. 25, No. 3, pp. 531–564.

Dowall, D.E. (1989). "Bangkok: A profile of an efficiently performing housing market", *Urban Studies*, vol. 26, pp. 327–339.

Drewnowski, J. (1974). "On measuring and planning the quality of life", The Hague, Institute of Social Studies.

Edmonds, G.A., and Miles, D.W.J. (1984). *Foundations for Change: Aspects of the Construction Industry in Developing Countries*. London, Intermediate Technology Publications.

Edwards, M. (1990). "Rental housing and the urban poor: Africa and Latin America compared", in Amis, P., and Lloyd, P. (eds.), *Housing Africa's Urban Poor,* Manchester, United Kingdom, Manchester University Press for the International African Institute.

Environmental Quality International (1991). "Recycling solid waste in Kampala: A feasibility study", paper presented to the UNDP/ILO Inter-regional Workshop on Employment Generation in Urban Works Programmes through Efficient Use of Local Resources, United Nations Centre, Nairobi, 6–10 April.

Epstein, D. G. (1973). *Brasilia, Plan and Reality: A Study of Planned and Spontaneous Urban Development,* Berkeley, University of California Press.

Farbman, M. (ed.) (1981). "The Pisces Studies: Assisting the smallest economic activities of the urban poor", Washington, D.C., US Agency for International Development.

Fass, S.M. (1977). *Families in Port au Prince: A study in the economics of survival,* Washington, D.C., US Agency for International Development.

———. (1980). "The economics of survival: A study of poverty and planning in Haiti", 3178534-6, Office of Urban Development, Bureau for Development Support, Washington, D.C., US Agency for International Development — International Development Cooperation Agency.

Frankenhoff, C.A. (1970). "The economic potential of a slum community in a developing economy", paper presented at the United Nations Interregional Seminar on Improvement of Slums and Uncontrolled Settlements, Medellín, Colombia.

Galukande, J. (1991). "Local views and attitudes on maintenance of infrastructure, solid waste recycling and other income generating activities", Kampala, Uganda, UNDP/ILO.

Ganesan, S. (1975). "Employment generation through investments in housing and construction", PhD thesis, London, University College London.

Germidis, D.A. (1974). *Labour Conditions and Industrial Relations in the Building Industry in Mexico*, Paris, Organisation for Economic Cooperation and Development Centre, Employment Series No. 11.

Ghana, Government of. (1987). *1984 Population Census of Ghana: Demographic and Economic Characteristics, Total Country*, Accra, Ghana Statistical Service.

Gilbert, A.G. (1983). "The tenants of self-help housing: Choice and constraint in the housing markets of less developed countries", *Development and Change,* vol. 14, No. 3, July.

———. (1988). "Home enterprises in poor urban settlements: constraints, potentials, and policy options", *Regional Development Dialogue*, vol. 9, No. 4 (Winter), pp. 21–37.

———. (1993). *In Search of a Home*, London, University College London Press.

———, and Gugler, J. (1981). *Cities, Poverty and Development: Urbanisation in the Third World*, Oxford, United Kingdom, Oxford University Press.

Gilbert, A.G., and Varley, A. (1990). "Renting a home in a third world city: Choice or constraint?", *International Journal of Urban and Regional Research,* vol. 14, No. 1, pp. 89–108.

———, ———. (1991). *Landlord and Tenant: Housing the Urban Poor in Urban Mexico*, London, Routledge.

Glewwe, P., and Van der Gaag, J. (1990). "Identifying the poor in developing countries: Do different definitions matter?", *World Development*, vol. 18, No. 6, pp. 803–814.

Gokhale, V. (1992). "Eating on the run", *IDRC Reports*, vol. 20, No. 2.

Gracey, M., Stone, D.E., Sutoto, S., and Sutejo, S. (1976). "Environmental pollution and diarrhoeal disease in Jakarta, Indonesia", *Journal of Tropical Pediatrics*, vol. 22, pp. 18–23.

Grimes, O.F. (1976). *Housing for Low-income Urban Families*, Washington, D.C., The World Bank.

Hake, A. (1977). *African Metropolis, Nairobi's Self-help City*, New York, St. Martin's Press.

Hansen, E., and Williams, J. (1987). "Economic issues and the progressive housing development model", in Patton, C.V. (ed.), *Spontaneous Shelter*, Philadelphia, Pennsylvania, Temple University Press.

Haque, M.A. (1987). "Rawsan Benarasee Saree Estate — housing and home based enterprises, Mirpur Dhaka", paper presented at the International Seminar on Income and Housing in Third World Development, New Delhi, 30 November to 4 December.

Harberger, A.C. (1971). "On measuring the social opportunity cost of labour", *International Labour Review*, No. 103 (June)

Hardoy, J. E., and Satterthwaite, D. (1981). *Shelter: Need and Response*, Chichester, United Kingdom, John Wiley.

Harpham, T., Lusty, T., and Vaughan, V. (1988). *In the Shadow of the City: Community Health and the Urban Poor*, Oxford, United Kingdom, Oxford University Press.

Harris, N. (1989). "Aid and urbanisation: an overview", *Cities*, August, pp. 174–185.

Hasan, A. (1990). "The Orangi Pilot Project", in Cadman, D. and Payne, G. (eds.), *The Living City: Towards a Sustainable Future*, London, Routledge.

Hellen, J.A., and Tipple, A.G., with Prince, M.A. (1991). "Environmental risk assessment in a tropical city: An application of housing and household data from Kumasi, Ghana", in Hinz, E. (ed.), *Geomedizinische und biogeograpische Aspekte der Krankheitsverbreitung und Gesundheits- versorgung in Industrie — und Entwicklungsländern*, Frankfurt, Peter Lang.

Hughes, G. (1976). "Low-income housing: a Kenyan case study", in Little, I.M.F., and Scott, M.F.G. (eds.), *Using Shadow Prices*, London, Heinemann, pp. 73–85.

————. (1991). "Cost-benefit analysis: Housing and squatter upgrading in East Africa", in Tipple, A.G. and, Willis, K.G. (eds.), *Housing the Poor in the Developing World; Methods of Analysis, Case Studies and Policy*, London and New York, Routledge.

Hughes, R.B. (1976). "Interregional income differences: Self-perpetuation", *Southern Economic Journal*, 28.

Hussmanns, R., Mehran, F., and Verma, V. (1990). *Surveys of Economically Active Population, Employment, Unemployment and Underemployment. A Manual on Concepts and Methods*, Geneva, ILO.

ILO (International Labour Office). (1976). *Employment, Growth, and Basic Needs*, Tripartite World Conference on Employment, Income Distribution and Social Progress and the International Division of Labour, Geneva.

————. (1984). *Small-scale Brickmaking*, Technical Memoranda, Technology Series No. 6, Geneva.

————. (1987a). *Employment Policy and Job Creation in and through the Construction Industry*, Geneva.

————. (1987b). *Guidelines for the Development of Small-scale Construction Enterprises*, Geneva.

————. (1990). "Informal sector and urban employment; A review of activities on the urban informal sector", World Employment Programme, Technology and Employment Branch, Geneva.

————. (1991). *The Dilemma of the Informal Sector*, Report of the Director-General, International Labour Conference, 78th Session, Geneva, 1991.

ILO/UNDP. (1992). "Labour-intensive paving of Namuwongo Market parking yard — a small-scale experiment with cement paving blocks in Kampala, Uganda", INT/89/021, Employment generation in urban works programmes through the efficient use of local resources, Geneva, ILO.

Ismael, A., and Marulanda S., L. (1992). "Urban development through 'co-development': A development consultant's view", *Trialog*, vol. 32, No. 1.

Jagannathan, N.V., and Halder, A. (1987). "Income-housing linkages: A case study of pavement dwellers in Calcutta", paper presented at the International Seminar on Income and Housing in Third World Urban Development, New Delhi, 30 November to 4 December.

————, ————. (1990). "Income, housing linkages: A case study of pavement dwellers in Calcutta", in Raj, M., and Nientied, P. (eds.), *Housing and income in Third World Urban Development*, London, Aspect Publishing, pp. 141–148.

Jere, H. (1989). "Housing and employment — an example of the work of the Human Settlements of Zambia", paper presented at the Sixth SINA Regional Workshop on Housing, Construction and Building Materials Co-operatives, May.

Jiménez, E. (1983). "The Magnitude and Determinants of Home Improvements in Self-help Housing: Manila's Tondo Project", *Land Economics*, vol 59, No. 1, pp. 70–83.

Joshi, J. (1992). "Infrastructure provision in housing", paper presented to the 18th WEDC Conference, Kathmandu, 30 August to 3 September.

JUNIC (Joint United Nations Information Committee). (1987). *Women and Shelter,* Resource kit prepared by the JUNIC/NGO Programme Group on Women, New York.

Kaboré, A.Y. (1991). "Study on local building materials in Burkina Faso", paper presented to the UNDP/ILO Inter-regional Workshop on Employment Generation in Urban Works Programmes through Efficient Use of Local Resources, United Nations Centre, Nairobi, 6–10 April.

Kaplinsky, R. (1990). *The Economies of Small: Appropriate Technology in a Changing World*, London, IT Publications.

Kapoor, R.M., and Maitra, M.S. (1987). "The marginal land owners in low income housing settlements", paper presented at the International Seminar on Income and Housing in Third World Urban Development, New Delhi, 30 November to 4 December.

Kardash, H. S. (1990). "The transformation process of government housing in Cairo: The case of Helwan, El Tebbeen and Imbaba", unpublished working paper in preparation of PhD dissertation, Centre for Architectural Research and Development Overseas, University of Newcastle-upon-Tyne, United Kingdom.

Kasongo, B.A., and Tipple, A.G. (1990). "An analysis of policy towards squatters in Kitwe, Zambia", *Third World Planning Review,* vol. 12, No. 2, May.

Katumba, R. (1990). "Mathare Valley group finds that success follows good planning", *African Housing Fund*, August.

Keare, D.H. (1983). "Assessing project impacts", in Yeung, Y.M. (ed.), *A Place to Live: More Effective Low-cost Housing in Asia*, Ottawa, IDRC.

——, and Parris, S. (1982). *Evaluation of Shelter Programs for the Urban Poor; Principal Findings*, World Bank Staff Working Paper No. 547, Washington, D.C., The World Bank.

Keddie, J., and Cleghorn, W. (1978). "Least-cost brickmaking", *Appropriate Technology*, vol. 5, No. 3.

Kirke, J. (1991). "Appropriate planning, affordable standards — the Madras experience from an engineering/planning view" in Meikle, S., and Mumtaz, B. (eds.), *Successful Shelter Strategies,* Proceedings of the ODA Shelter Seminar, World Habitat Day, London, University College, London, Development Planning Unit.

Kitwe City Council (1976). *Low Cost Housing in Kitwe; Its Characteristics and Implications on Housing Policy,* Kitwe, Zambia, City Engineer's Department.

Klaassen, L.H., and Burns, L.S. (1963). "The position of housing in national economic and social planning", in Harris, W.D., and Gillies, J. (eds.), *Capital Formation for Housing in Latin America,* Washington, D.C., Pan-American Union, pp. 108–119.

Klaassen, L.H., Hoogland, J.G.D. and Van Pelt, M.J. (1987). "Economic impact and implications of shelter investments", in Rodwin, L. (ed.), *Shelter, Settlement and Development,* Boston, Massachusetts, Allen and Unwin.

Kombe, W.J. (1992). "Lessons of experience from informal housing settlements in Chang'ombe and Chamwino, Tanzania", paper presented to the UNDP/ILO Inter-regional Workshop on Employment Generation in Urban Works Programmes through Efficient Use of Local Resources, United Nations Centre, Nairobi, 6–10 April.

Korboe, D. T. (1993). "The low-income housing system in Kumasi: an empirical examination of two neighbourhoods", unpublished PhD dissertation, University of Newcastle-upon-Tyne, United Kingdom.

Lalkaka, D. (1984). "Urban housing in China", *Habitat International,* vol. 8, No. 1, pp. 63–73.

Laquian, A.A. (1983a). *Basic Housing: Policies for Urban Sites, Services and Shelter in Developing Countries,* Ottawa, International Development Research Centre.

———. (1983b). "Sites, services and shelter — an evaluation", *Habitat International,* vol. 7, No. 5/6.

Lee-Smith, D. (1989). "Urban management in Nairobi: A case study of the matatu mode of public transport", in Stren, R.E., and White, R.R. (eds.), *African Cities in Crisis; Managing Rapid Urban Growth,* African Modernization and Development Series, Boulder, Colorado, Westview Press.

Lewin, A.C. (1976). *Self-Help Housing Through Cooperatives: Prospects and Problems for Urban Africa,* Cologne.

Lewis, W.A. (1954). "Economic development with unlimited supplies of labor", *Manchester School* 22 (May), pp. 54–114.

Leynes, A.F. (1987). "Impact of the slum upgrading program in Metropolitan Manila, housing-based income generation activities", paper presented at the International Seminar on Income and Housing in Third World Urban Development, New Delhi, 30 November to 4 December.

———. (1990). "Impact of the slum upgrading program in Metropolitan Manila on the housing-based income generation activities", in Raj, M., and Nientied, P. (eds.), *Housing and income in Third World Urban Development*, London, Aspect Publishing.

LHPET (Lusaka Housing Project). (1978). *Draft Report on Observation of Mutual Help Block-making in Garden Overspill*, Lusaka, Zambia, April.

Linn, J. (1983). *Cities in the Developing World: Policies for Their Equitable and Efficient Growth*, New York, Oxford University Press.

Lipton, M. (1980). "Family, fungibility and formality: Rural advantages of informal non-farm enterprise versus the urban-formal state", in Amin, S. (ed.), *Human Resources, Employment, and Development*, vol. 5, *Developing Countries*, Proceedings of the Sixth World Congress of the International Economic Association, Mexico City, (London, Macmillan).

Ljung, P., and Farvacque, L. (1988). *Addressing the Urban Challenge,* Report INU 13, Washington, D.C., The World Bank.

Lobo, S. (1982). *A House of My Own: Social Organization in the Squatter Settlements of Lima, Peru,* Tucson, University of Arizona Press.

Louw, A., and Holiday, J. (1992). "Choosing an appropriate sanitation system", paper presented to the 18th WEDC Conference, Kathmandu, 30 August to 3 September.

Lyby, E. (1992). "Background paper", paper presented to the UNDP/ILO Inter-regional Workshop on Employment Generation in Urban Works Programmes through Efficient Use of Local Resources, United Nations Centre, Nairobi, 6–10 April.

———, Connolly, J., Mukunya, C., Higobero, S. and Ocaya, V. (1992) "Employment generation in urban works programmes in Uganda", UNDP/ILO INT/89/021, Geneva, ILO.

———, Tournée, J., and Nnkya, T. (1991). "Employment generation in urban works programmes in Tanzania, vol. I", paper presented to the UNDP/ILO Inter-regional Workshop on Employment Generation in Urban Works Programmes through Efficient Use of Local Resources, United Nations Centre, Nairobi, 6–10 April.

Mabogunje, A.L., Hardoy, J.E. and Misra, R.P. (1970). *Shelter Provision in Developing Countries.* New York, John Wiley.

Maldonado, C. (1986). "Mobilisation et maitrise des capacités propres aux petits producteurs urbains. Evaluation et leçons d'une expérience participative en cours au Mali, Togo et Rwanda", Geneva (unpublished).

———. and others (1988). *Petits producteurs urbains d'Afrique francophone — Analyse et politiques d'appui*, Geneva, ILO.

Malpezzi, S. (1990). "Urban housing and financial markets: Some international comparisons", *Urban Studies,* vol. 27, No. 6.

———, and Ball, G. (1991). "Rent control in developing countries", World Bank Discussion Paper No. 129, Washington, D.C., The World Bank.

———, Tipple, A. G., and Willis, K. G. (1990) "Costs and benefits of rent control: A case study of Kumasi, Ghana", World Bank Discussion Papers No. 74, Washington D.C., The World Bank.

Marris, P. (1962). *Family and Social Change in an African City: A Study of Rehousing in Lagos,* Chicago, Illinois, Northwestern University Press.

Martin, R. (1976). "Upgrading", in Simons, H.J. and others (eds.), *Slum or Self-Reliance: Urban Growth in Zambia,* Lusaka, University of Zambia, Institute of African Studies Communication, No. 12.

———. (1983). "Upgrading", in Skinner, R.J., and Rodell, M.J. (eds.), *People, Poverty and Shelter: Problems of Self-help Housing in the Third World,* London, Methuen.

Mawhood, E. (1983). *Local Government in the Third World: The Experience of Tropical Africa,* Chichester, United Kingdom, John Wiley.

Mayer, J. (1989). "International labour standards and technical co-operation: The case of special public works programmes", *International Labour Review,* vol. 128, No. 2, pp. 155-175.

———. (1991). "The employment policy convention: Scope, assessment and prospects", *International Labour Review,* vol. 130, No. 3, pp. 339-358.

Mazumdar, D. (1976). "The urban informal sector", *World Development,* vol. 4, No. 8, pp. 655-679.

McAuslan, P. (1985). *Urban Land and Shelter for the Poor,* London, Earthscan.

McCutcheon, R. (1985). "The use of donkey-drawn carts in labour-intensive road construction in Botswana", CTP 42, Geneva, ILO.

———. (1988). "The District Roads Programme in Botswana", *Habitat International,* vol. 12, No. 1.

McGee, T.G. (1976). "The persistence of the proto-proletariat: Occupational structures and planning of the future of third world cities", *Progress in Human Geography,* vol. 9, No. 1.

————. (1979). "Conservation and dissolution in the third world city: the shanty town as an element of conservation", *Development and Change*, vol. 10, No. 1, pp. 1–22.

Mehta M., and Mehta, D. (1990). "Home upgradation and income generation from housing", in Raj, M., and Nientied, P. (eds.), *Housing and Income in Third World Urban Development*, London, Aspect Publishing.

Meier, G. (1976). "The informal sector in Kenya" in Meir, G., *Leading Issues in Economic Development*, New York, Oxford University Press.

Mesa, N.E. (1987). "Economic use of housing 'pirata' and invasion 'barrios', Medellín", paper presented at the International Seminar on Income and Housing in Third World Urban Development, New Delhi, 30 November to 4 December.

————. (1990). "Economic use of housing 'pirata' and invasion 'barrios', Medellin", Raj M., and Nientied P. (eds.), *Housing and Income in Third World Urban Development*, London, Aspect Publishing.

Mhenni, S.B. (1987). "The impact of improvement of housing conditions on the incomes and on the expenditures of low income groups — a Tunisian case study", paper presented at the International Seminar on Income and Housing in Third World Urban Development, New Delhi, 30 November to 4 December.

Mies, M. (1982). *The Lacemakers of Narsapur: Indian Housewives Produce for the World Market,* London, Zed Press.

Miles, D., and Andersson, C.-A. (n.d.). "IYCB: Genesis of a sectoral business development programme", Geneva, ILO internal paper.

Mirikau, A. (1992). "UNICEF Urban Basic Services Project in Kenya", paper presented to the UNDP/ILO Inter-regional Workshop on Employment Generation in Urban Works Programmes through Efficient Use of Local Resources, United Nations Centre, Nairobi, 6–10 April.

Moavenzadeh, F. (1987). "The construction industry", in Rodwin, L. (ed.), *Shelter, Settlement and Development*, Boston, Massachusetts, Allen and Unwin.

————, and Hagopian, F. (1983). *The Construction and Building Materials Industries in Developing Countries,* TAP Report 83-19, Technology Adaptation Program, Cambridge, Massachusetts, MIT.

Monahan, J.P. (1980). "The economic realities of sites-and-services schemes. Two case studies: Malawi and Seychelles", *Habitat International*, vol. 4, No. 3.

Moser, C. (1989). "Gender planning in the third world: Meeting practical and strategic gender needs", *World Development*, vol. 17, No. 11, pp. 1799–1825.

——, and Peake, L. (1987). *Women, Human Settlements and Housing*, London, Tavistock.

Mosse, J.C. (1993). *Half the World, Half the Chance: An Introduction to Gender and Development*. Oxford, United Kingdom, Oxfam.

Msukwa, L., and Kandole, B. (1981). *Water by the People: An Evaluation of the Rural Water Supply Programme in Zomba District*, Zomba, Malawi, Centre for Social Research.

Muchene, R. (1992). "Undugu's experience (a case study)", paper presented to the UNDP/ILO Inter-regional Workshop on Employment Generation in Urban Works Programmes through Efficient Use of Local Resources, United Nations Centre, Nairobi, 6–10 April.

Mukunya, C.H. (1992). "The use of local resources in building sector — labour intensive technology", paper presented to the UNDP/ILO Inter-regional Workshop on Employment Generation in Urban Works Programmes through Efficient Use of Local Resources, United Nations Centre, Nairobi, 6–10 April.

Nangia, S. (1987). "Spatial reorganisation of low income urban communities and its impact on the quality of housing and income (a case of Metropolitan Delhi)", paper presented at the International Seminar on Income and Housing in Third World Urban Development, New Delhi, 30 November to 4 December.

NBO. (1990). *Handbook of Housing Statistics*, New Delhi, Government of India.

Nha, N.T.T. (1987). "Income-generating and housing. A new approach in the Vietnamese housing policy.", paper presented at the International Seminar on Income and Housing in Third World Urban Development, New Delhi, 30 November to 4 December.

Nientied, P., Bhattacharjee, N., and Bharati, M.B. (1987). "Housing for income, practice and policy relevance", paper presented at the International Seminar on Income and Housing in Third World Urban Development, New Delhi, 30 November to 4 December.

Niyom, P., Boonyabancha, S., and Chauayklieng, S. (1990). *Ruamjai Samakki Resettlement Project*, Bangkok, Human Settlements Foundation.

Obudho, R.A., and Mhlanga, C.C. (eds.) (1988). *Slum and Squatter Settlements in Sub-Saharan Africa; Towards a Planning Strategy*, New York, Praeger.

Okpala, D.C.I. (1989). "Received concepts and theories in African urbanisation studies and urban management strategies: A critique", *Urban Studies*, vol. 24, pp. 137–150.

Ouedraogo, J.B. (1992). "A comparative study of two neighbourhoods in Ouagadougou: Ouayalgue and Bendogo", paper presented to the UNDP/ILO Inter-regional Workshop on Employment Generation in Urban Works Programmes through Efficient Use of Local Resources, United Nations Centre, Nairobi, 6–10 April.

Parry, J.P.M. (1983). "Technical options in brick and tile production", paper presented to an Intermediate Technology Workshop, Birmingham, United Kingdom.

Pasteur, D. (1979). *The Management of Squatter Upgrading*, Farnborough, United Kingdom, Gower.

Payne, G. (1989). *Informal Housing and Land Subdivisions in Third World Cities: A Review of the Literature*, London, ODA.

Peattie, L.R. (1981). "What is to be done with the informal sector? A case study of shoe manufacturing in Colombia", in Safa, I. (ed.) *Towards a Political Economy of Urbanisation*, New Delhi, Oxford University Press.

——. (1987). "Shelter, development and the poor", in Rodwin, L. (ed.), *Shelter, Settlement and Development*, Boston, Massachusetts, Allen and Unwin.

——. (1990). "Participation: A case study of how invaders organize, negotiate and interact with government in Lima, Peru", *Environment and Urbanization*, vol. 2, No. 1, pp. 19–30.

Peil, M. (1976). "African squatter settlements: A comparative study", *Urban Studies*, vol. 13, pp. 155–166.

——, and Sada, P.O. (1984). *African Urban Society*, Chichester, United Kingdom, John Wiley.

Plant, R. (1983). *A Short Guide to the ILO World Employment Programme*, Geneva, ILO.

Raj, M., and Mitra, B. (1990). "Households, housing and home based economic activities in low income settlements", in Raj, M., and Nientied, P. (eds.), *Housing and Income in Third World Urban Development*, London, Aspect Publishing.

Ravallion, M., Datt, G., and van de Walle, D. (1991). "Quantifying absolute poverty in the developing world", *Review of Income and Wealth*, vol. 37, No. 4.

Redd Barna. (1992). "Urban upgrading and employment — Ethiopia's experience", paper presented to the UNDP/ILO Inter-regional Workshop on Employment Generation in Urban Works Programmes through Efficient Use of Local Resources, United Nations Centre, Nairobi, 6–10 April.

Reidel, J., and Schultz, S. (1978). *Bauwirtschaft und Baustoffindustrie in Entwicklungsländern,* Munich, Weltforum Verlag.

Rodell, M.J. (1983). "Site and services and low income housing", in Skinner, R.J., and Rodell, M.J. (eds.), *People, Poverty and Shelter: Problems of Self-help Housing in the Third World,* London, Methuen.

——, and Skinner, R.J. (1983). "Introduction: Contemporary self-help programmes" in Skinner, R.J., and Rodell, M.J. (eds.), *People, Poverty and Shelter: Problems of Self-help Housing in the Third World,* London, Methuen.

Rodwin, L., and Sanyal, B. (1987). "Shelter, settlement, and development: An overview", in Rodwin, L. (ed.), *Shelter, Settlement & Development,* Boston, Massachusetts, Allen and Unwin.

Rondinelli, D. A. and Cheema, G.S. (1985). "Urban service policies in Metropolitan Areas: Meeting the needs of the urban poor in Asia", *Regional Development Dialogue,* vol. 6, No. 2 (Autumn), pp. 170–190.

Royat, S. (1992). "Dynamic urban spatial planning: Towards a new perception for urban development planning and management", *Trialog,* vol. 32, No. 1.

Sabot, R. H. (1979). *Economic Development and Urban Migration: Tanzania 1900–1971,* Oxford, Clarendon Press.

Sarin, M. (1982). *Urban Planning in the Third World: The Chandigarh Experience,* Oxford, Mansell.

Sawyer, M.C. (1975). "Policy in some developed countries", paper presented at 14th General Conference of IARIW, Aulanko, Finland, August.

Schlyter, A. (1987). "Commercialisation of housing in upgraded squatter areas: The case of George, Lusaka, Zambia", *African Urban Quarterly,* vol. 2, No. 3 (August), pp. 287–297.

Schneider de Villegas, G. (1990). "Homework: A case for social protection", *International Labour Review,* vol. 129, No. 4, pp. 423–439.

Seshachalam, P., and Rao, P. V. (1987). "Housing and development policy perspectives for urban informal sector, a case study of Greater Hyderabad", paper presented at the International Seminar on Income and Housing in Third World Urban Development, New Delhi, 30 November to 4 December.

Sethuraman, S.V. (1981). "The urban informal sector in developing countries: Employment, poverty and environment" Geneva, ILO.

——. (1985). "Basic needs and the informal sector; the case of low-income housing in developing countries", *Habitat International*, vol. 9, No. 3, p. 4.

——. (ed.) (1991). *The Urban Informal Sector in Developing Countries: Employment, Poverty and Environment*, Geneva, ILO.

Sirivardana, S. (1986). "Reflections on the implementation of the Million Houses Programme", *Habitat International*, vol. 10, No. 3, pp. 91–108.

SKAT (Swiss Centre for Development Cooperation in Technology and Management). (1991). *Building Materials in Bangladesh*, Geneva.

Spence, R. and Cook, D.J. (1983). *Building Materials in Developing Countries*, Chichester, United Kingdom, John Wiley.

——, Wells, J., and Dudley, E. (1993). *Jobs from Housing: Employment, Building Materials, and Enabling Strategies for Urban Development*. London, Intermediate Technology Publications.

Strassmann, W.P. (1970). "Construction productivity and employment in developing countries", *International Labour Review*, vol. 101, No. 5, May, pp. 503-518.

——. (1976). "Measuring the employment effects of housing policies in developing countries", *Economic Development and Cultural Change*, pp. 623–632.

——. (1977). "Housing priorities in developing countries: A planning model", *Land Economics*, vol. 53, No. 3, pp. 310–326.

——. (1980). "Housing improvement in an opportune setting: Cartagena, Colombia", *Land Economics*, vol. 56, No. 2, May.

——. (1985a). "Employment in construction: Multicountry estimates of costs and substitution elasticities for small dwellings", *Economic Development and Cultural Change*, vol. 33, No. 2, pp. 396–414.

——. (1985b). "Home-based restaurants, snack bars, and retail stores: Their contribution to income and employment in Lima, Peru", Working Paper No. 86. East Lansing, Michigan, Women in International Development, Michigan State University, May.

——. (1986). "Types of neighbourhood and home-based enterprises: Evidence from Lima, Peru", *Urban Studies*, vol. 23, pp. 485–500.

——. (1987). "Home-based enterprises in cities of developing countries". *Economic Development and Cultural Change*, vol. 36, No. 1, pp. 121.

Stren, R.E. (1989). "The administration of urban services", in Stren, R.E., and White, R.R. (eds.), *African Cities in Crisis, Managing Rapid Urban*

Growth, African Modernization and Development Series, Boulder, Colorado, Westview Press.

Stretton, A. (1979). "Instability of employment among building industry labourers in Manila", in Bromley, R., and Gerry, C. (eds.), *Casual Work and Poverty in Third World Cities*, Chichester, United Kingdom, John Wiley.

Struyk, R. (1990). "Early experiences with enabling national housing strategies", *Cities*, November, pp. 315–322.

Sulabh International (n.d.). "Sulabh International marches from urban to rural areas", New Delhi.

Summers, R., and Heston, A. (1988). "A new set of international comparisons of real product and price levels estimates for 130 countries, 1950–1985", *Review of Income and Wealth*, vol. 34, pp. 1–26.

Sundaram, P.S.A. (1990). "Evaluation of experience with initiating enabling shelter strategies in India", Nairobi, UNCHS (Habitat).

Syagga, P.M. (1989). "Technical recommendations on standards and specifications for the use of soil blocks in Kenya", UNCHS (Habitat)/ CSC Workshop on Kenya Standards and Specifications for Soil Blocks, Nairobi, 26–30 May.

——. (1992). "Natural resources and development", paper presented to the UNDP/ILO Inter-regional Workshop on Employment Generation in Urban Works Programmes through Efficient Use of Local Resources, United Nations Centre, Nairobi, 6–10 April.

——, Kamau, R.G., and Ondiege, P. (1989). *Access by Women and Urban Poor to Urban land and Credit: A Socio-Economic Evaluation of the Third Urban Project in Kenya*, Nairobi, University of Nairobi, HRDU.

Sylos-Labini, P. (1964). "Precarious employment in Sicily", *International Labour Review*, vol. 89, No. 3, pp. 268-85.

Szal, R.J. (1977). "Poverty: measurement and analysis", Income Distribution and Employment Programme, World Employment Research Working Paper, Geneva, ILO.

Szelenyi, I. (1983). *Urban Inequalities under State Socialism*, Oxford, United Kingdom, Oxford University Press.

Tipple, A.G. (1988). "Upgrading and culture in Kumasi: Problems and possibilities", in Obudho, R.A., and Mhlanga, C.C. (eds.), *Slum and Squatter Settlements in Sub-Saharan Africa: Towards a Planning Strategy*, New York, Praeger, pp. 71–88.

————. (1991). *Self Help Transformations of Low Cost Housing: An Introductory Study*, Newcastle-Upon-Tyne, United Kingdom, Urban International Press, for the Overseas Development Administration, London.

————. (1992a). "Employment-rich house-building: A sustainable approach", paper presented to the UNDP/ILO Inter-regional Workshop on Employment Generation in Urban Works Programmes through Efficient Use of Local Resources, United Nations Centre, Nairobi, 6–10 April.

————. (1992b). "Self help transformations to low-cost housing: initial impressions of cause, context and value", *Third World Planning Review*, vol. 14, No. 2, pp. 167–192.

————. (1993). "The pisé building method in low cost housing provision", paper presented to the XXIst IAHS World Housing Congress, Cape Town, South Africa, 10–14 May.

————, and Willis, K.G. (eds.) (1991a). *Housing the Poor in the Developing World; Methods of Analysis, Case Studies and Policy*, London and New York, Routledge.

————, ————. (1991b) "Tenure choice in Kumasi, Ghana", *Third World Planning Review*, vol. 13, No. 1, pp. 27–45.

————, ————. (1992a). "Who rents, who owns: Tenure choice in a West African City", in Kilmartin, L., and Singh, H. (eds.), *Housing in the Third World: Analysis and Solutions,* New Delhi, Concept Publishing Co.

————, ————. (1992b). "Why should Ghanaians build houses in urban areas?" *Cities,* February, pp. 60–74.

Todd, D. (1991). "Social issues in the Kumasi Waste Disposal Project", report to Messrs Mott Macdonald Environmental, Croydon, United Kingdom, (mimeo.).

Treiger, B., and Faerstein, E. (1987). "The effects of an upgrading project on income-generating activities in a Brazilian squatter settlement — the case of Pavao-Pavaozinho", paper presented at the International Seminar on Income and Housing in Third World Urban Development, New Delhi, 30 November to 4 December.

Turner, J.F.C. (1967) "Barriers and channels for housing development in modernizing countries", *Journal of the American Institute of Planners,* May, pp. 167–181.

————. (1972). "Housing issues and the standards problems", *Ekistics*, vol. 196, pp. 152–158.

————. (1976). *Housing by People; Towards Autonomy in Building Environments*, London, Ideas in Progress, Marion Boyars.

————, and Fichter, R. (eds.) (1972). *Freedom to Build,* London, Macmillan.

United Nations. (1962). *Report of the Ad-hoc Group of Experts on Housing and Urban Development,* New York.

——. (1970). "Investment and development policies for improvement of slums and uncontrolled settlements", in *Improvement of Slums and Uncontrolled Settlements,* Sales No. E.71.IV. 6, New York.

——. (1978). *Non-conventional Financing of Housing for Low-income Households,* New York, Department of International and Social Affairs.

——. (1993). *World Urbanization Prospects. The 1992 Revision,* New York.

UNCED (United Nations Conference on Environment and Development). (1992). Agenda 21, Chapter 7: Promoting sustainable human settlement development. Rio de Janeiro, 14 June.

UNCHS (United Nations Centre for Human Settlements) (Habitat). (1978). Final Report of an Ad Hoc Expert Group Meeting on Criteria for the Selection of Appropriate Building Technologies, Amman, Jordan, December 1977, Nairobi.

——. (1982). *Development of the Indigenous Construction Sector,* Nairobi.

——. (1984). *Community Participation in Squatter Settlement Upgrading,* Nairobi.

——. (1985a). *Rehabilitation of Inner-city Areas: Feasible Strategies,* Nairobi.

——. (1985b). "Rethinking the third world city", report of the Round-table Meeting in Stockholm, Sweden, May.

——. (1985c). *The Role of Women in the Execution of Low-income Housing Projects,* Nairobi.

——. (1987). *Global Report on Human Settlements 1986,* Oxford, United Kingdom, Oxford University Press for UNCHS (Habitat).

——. (1988). *Community Leadership and Low-income Housing,* Nairobi.

——. (1989a). *Community Credit Mechanisms,* Nairobi.

——. (1989b). *Improving Income and Housing: Employment Generation in Low-income Settlements,* Nairobi.

——. (1989c). *Strategies for Low-income Shelter and Services Development: The Rental-Housing Option,* Nairobi.

——. (1990). *The Global Strategy for Shelter to the Year 2000,* Nairobi.

——. (1991a). *Assessment of Experience with the Project Approach to Shelter Delivery for the Poor,* Nairobi.

——. (1991b). *Evaluation of Experience with Initiating Enabling Shelter Strategies,* Nairobi.

———. (1991c). "Human and institutional resources and employment: The Sri Lanka experience" (mimeo.), Nairobi.

———. (1991d). *Human Settlements Development through Community Participation*, Nairobi.

———. (1992). *Community Participation in Zambia. The DANIDA/UNCHS Training Programme*, Nairobi.

———. (1993a). "Building materials for housing", Report of the Executive Director to the fourteenth session of the Commission on Human Settlements, Nairobi.

———. (1993b). *Community Participation in Bolivia. The DANIDA/UNCHS Training Programme*, Nairobi.

———. (1993c). *Public/Private Partnerships in Enabling Shelter Strategies*, Nairobi.

———. (1993d). "The relationship between underemployment and unemployment and shelter provision", Report of the Executive Director to the fourteenth session of the Commission on Human Settlements, Nairobi.

———. (1993e). *The Urban Poor as Agents of Development: Community Action Planning in Sri Lanka*, Nairobi.

———. (1994a). *National Experiences with Shelter Delivery for the Poorest Groups*, Nairobi.

———. (1994b). *National Trends in Housing-production Practices. Volume 1: India*, Nairobi.

———. (1994c). *National Trends in Housing-production Practices. Volume 2: Indonesia*, Nairobi.

———. (1994d). *National Trends in Housing-production Practices. Volume 3: Mexico*, Nairobi.

———. (1994e). *National Trends in Housing-production Practices. Volume 4: Nigeria*, Nairobi.

———. (1994f). *The Community Construction Contract System in Sri Lanka*, Nairobi.

UNDP (United Nations Development Programme). (1994). *Human Development Report*, New York.

———. (n.d.). "Governing Council paper on Micro-Capital Grants", New York (draft) (mimeo.).

UNDP/ILO/World Bank/Government of Ghana. (n.d.). *Feeder Roads Improvement in Ghana: Contractors Use Labour-based Technology*, Accra.

UNIDO (United Nations Industrial Development Organization). (1969). *Construction Industry*, UNIDO Monographs on Industrial Development, No. 2, New York.

———. (1985). *The Building Materials Industry in Developing Countries*, Sectoral Studies Series No. 6, Vienna.

Urban Edge. (1979). "The garbage war: Need for defence", vol. 3, No. 8.

———. (1988a). "Housing, macro policies: Tracing the links", vol. 12, No. 3.

———. (1988b). "Making development work for urban women", vol. 12, No. 1.

Useche de Brill, I. (1990). "Evaluation of experience with initiating enabling shelter strategies in Colombia", Nairobi, UNCHS (Habitat).

Vaidya, C., and Mukundan, K. (1987). "Role of rental housing in slum upgradation programme — some issues", paper presented at the International Seminar on Income and Housing in Third World Urban Development, New Delhi, 30 November to 4 December.

van Dijk M.P., and Glissenaar, M. (1987). "Employment in World Bank urban development projects in West Africa", paper presented at the International Seminar on Income and Housing in Third World Urban Development, New Delhi, 30 November to 4 December.

von Braun, J., Teklu, T., and Webb, P. (1991). "Labour-intensive public works for food security: Experience in Africa", Working Papers on Food Subsidies, No. 6, Washington, D.C., International Food Policy Research Institute.

Water and Sanitation for Health (WASH). (1988). *Water Vending and Development: Lessons from Two Countries*, WASH Technical Report No. 45, May, Arlington, U.S.A.

Watermeyer, R.B. (1993). "Community-based construction: Mobilising communities to construct their own infrastructure", paper presented at the 21st IAHS World Housing Congress, Cape Town, South Africa, May.

Wegelin, E.A. (1978). "Urban low income housing and development", Leiden and Boston, Martinus Nijhoff.

Wells, J. (1985). "Construction investment and economic growth", *Habitat International*, vol. 9, No. 1.

Wheeler, D. (1982) "Major relationships between construction and national economic development", Cambridge, Massachusetts, Center for Construction Research and Education, Massachusetts Institute of Technology.

Whittington, D., Smith, V.K., Okarafor, A., Okore, A., Liu, J.L., Ruiz, L.K., and McPhail, A. (1990). "Giving respondents time to think in contingent valuation studies", Washington, D.C., The World Bank.

WHO (World Health Organization). (1992). *Our Planet, Our Health. Report of the Commission on Health and Environment*, Geneva.

Woodfield, A. (1989). *Housing and Economic Adjustment*, London, Taylor and Francis, for and on behalf of the United Nations.

World Bank. (1980). *Shelter*, Poverty and Basic Needs Series, Urban Projects Department, Washington, D.C.

——. (1991). *Urban Policy and Economic Development: An Agenda for the 1990s*, Washington, D.C.

——. (1993). *Housing: Enabling Markets to Work*. Washington, D.C.

World Bank/UNCHS/UNDP. (1991). *Revised Prospectus: Capacity Building for Urban Management in the 1990s*, Washington, D.C., Nairobi, New York, Urban Management Programme.

Yap, K. S. (1988). "The construction and management of infrastructure in low-income urban settlements through community participation: An example from Sri Lanka", HSD Working Paper No. 26, Bangkok, Asian Institute of Technology, Human Settlements Division.

Yingfan, W. (1987). "On reform of urban housing system in China", paper presented at the International Seminar on Income and Housing in Third World Urban Development, New Delhi, 30 November to 4 December.

Young, K. (1981). "Domestic outwork and the decentralisation of production: A new stage in capitalist development?", paper presented at the ILO Regional Meeting on Women and Rural Development, Mexico, August 24–28.

Zambia, Department of Town and Country Planning. (1972). *Low-cost Residential Development in Lusaka*. Lusaka, Development Planning and Research Unit.

Ziss, R., and Schiller, G. (1982). "Employment and income effects of housing construction in Ghana", paper presented at an International Seminar on Housing and Employment as a Decision-making Nexus in Urban Development, Berlin (West), November.

Subject index

Geographical index

Author index